I greatly welcome this publication as do
have struggled with the vexed question of de
function and an appropriate translation of the ραιυιες ιοου and ἴδε
(traditionally 'lo'/'behold') so frequently occurring in New Testament
texts. Approaching the question within a coherent linguistic framework
(Construction Grammar), Dr. Bailey offers a detailed analysis of every
New Testament occurrence of these particles, carefully categorizing
their uses. For each of these he not only indicates their distinctive formal
features but also the specific semantic-communicational contributions
they are expected to make and how they may best be translated.

Heinrich von Siebenthal, PhD
Giessen School of Theology (Freie Theologische Hochschule Giessen)
Author of Ancient Greek Grammar for the Study of the New Testament
(Oxford: Peter Lang, 2019)

The words ἰδού and ἴδε 'behold' cause problems for many exegetes
and translators of the New Testament. On the one hand, grammars and
commentaries often just apply one vague, unifying label to these words
such as 'attention getter', 'thetic element' or 'presentational device'.
On the other hand, translators feel that these words do a number of
different things. But which things precisely? And how to distinguish
them in clear and convincing ways? This book provides translators and
exegetes a principled basis to distinguish the meanings and functions
ἰδού and ἴδε in the different constructions that they form part of, by
a brilliant application of the best tools that linguistics has to offer to
all occurrences of these words in the Greek New Testament, and by
comparing biblical usage to the ways ἰδού and ἴδε are used in extra-
biblical Koine Greek.

Prof. dr. Lourens J. de Vries
Professor of Bible Translation and General Linguistics
Vrije Universiteit Amsterdam

This is an exemplary study of Ancient Greek discourse. In his convincing
analysis of ἰδού and ἴδε, Nicholas Bailey successfully combines
linguistic theory, more specifically Construction Grammar, with a great
interpretative acumen. His study demonstrates to what important
insights this powerful combination may lead.

Rutger J. Allan, PhD, LLM
Lecturer of Ancient Greek Language and Literature
Vrije Universiteit Amsterdam

Bailey's work provides a much-needed bridge for translators and exegetes over the confluence of semantic streams contributing to the varied uses of ἰδού and ἴδε that have defied elegant description. His adoption of Construction Grammar enables him to correlate the five proposed uses in Koine Greek with the syntactic and deictic factors motivating each construction. His typological stance facilitates the mapping of these uses in other languages, illustrating from modern European languages how mismatches can be overcome in translation. This volume not only offers readers an elegant description of these particles, but also offers a heuristic model for description of comparably complex forms.

Steven E. Runge, DLitt
University of Stellenbosch, South Africa
Research Associate, JW Wevers Institute for Septuagint Study
Scholar-in-Residence at Faithlife Corporation

Why did Jesus go around using words like "Behold" and "Lo," which sound archaic and unnatural to modern ears? He did not, of course, as those are English words—a traditional rendering of the pair of [Koine] words ἰδού/ἴδε as recorded in the Greek New Testament. In order to properly render these Greek words into Modern English or any other language, one has to know the meaning, and to understand the meaning, one must understand the function or functions of words in context. Bailey's comprehensive analysis of ἰδού/ἴδε in the Greek New Testament, the Septuagint, and other Koine Greek writings clearly enumerates a set of related but distinguishable functions of these words as they function in various contexts. They may be translated as an imperative form of a verb of visual perception such as "Look!" or some other verb of perception such as "Listen!" or a phrase like "Pay attention!" or some other syntactic means, depending both on contextual usage and the natural lexico-syntactic resources—called here "constructions"—of the receptor language.

David B. Frank, PhD
Senior Consultant in Linguistics and Translation, SIL International

Nicholas Bailey's examination of ἰδού and ἴδε brings new insights into our understanding of how these two particles function. He has made a valuable contribution both to our understanding of Greek information structure and to Bible translation generally.

Michael G. Aubrey, MA
Linguist & Bible Researcher, SIL International
Senior editor at Koine-Greek.com

The Meaning and Translation of
ἰδού and ἴδε 'behold'

SIL International®

Publications in Translation and Textlinguistics 11

Publications in Translation and Textlinguistics is a series publication of SIL International®. The series is a venue for works covering a broad range of topics in translation and textlinguistics. While most volumes are authored by members of SIL, suitable works by others will also form part of the series.

Image of Vincent van Gogh's *The Sower*, used with permission, Kröller-Müller Museum, Otterlo, The Netherlands.

Series Editor
Susan McQuay

Managing Editor
Eugene C. Burnham

Editorial Staff
Eleanor McAlpine, Proofreader

Production Staff
Priscilla Higby, Production Manager
Judy Benjamin, Compositor
Barbara Alber, Graphic Designer and Cover Designer

The Meaning and Translation of ἰδού and ἴδε 'behold'

A Construction Grammar Analysis

Nicholas A. Bailey

Foreword by Richard A. Rhodes

SIL International®
Dallas, Texas

Library of Congress Control Number: 2023940980

ISBN: 978-1-55671-450-4 (pbk)
ISBN: 978-1-55671-476-4 (Epub)
ISSN: 1550-588X

Copies of this and other publications of SIL International® may be obtained through distributors such as Amazon, Barnes & Noble, other worldwide distributors and, for select volumes, publications.sil.org:

SIL International Publications
7500 W. Camp Wisdom Road
Dallas, TX 75236-5629 USA

General inquiry: publications_intl@sil.org

Pending order inquiry: sales@sil.org

To Nadirê Efo and Sûrênê Şirîn,
their dear families,
and their community

Ἀκούετε. ἰδοὺ ἐξῆλθεν ὁ σπείρων σπεῖραι.

Καὶ ἤκουσα φωνῆς μεγάλης
ἐκ τοῦ θρόνου λεγούσης·
ἰδοὺ ἡ σκηνὴ τοῦ θεοῦ μετὰ τῶν ἀνθρώπων,
καὶ σκηνώσει μετ᾽ αὐτῶν.

Contents

Figures and Tables

Figures

Tables

Foreword

It might at first seem odd that a scholar with an international reputation for work on Native American languages would be the person to introduce a book on an innovative approach to a knotty problem in Koine grammar —except if that person had a life-long interest in Bible translation and Biblical languages. Barely out of my teens, and just starting to study linguistics, I attended the Summer Institute of Linguistics (SIL) summer program in Norman, Oklahoma. Throughout the 1970s and into the 1980s I taught at SIL's North Dakota summer program, and later, in 2000, at the program in Oregon. And in 2006 my longtime SIL friend—and fellow Algonquianist—Wayne Leman invited me to become a regular contributor to the Better Bibles Blog, applying my linguistic expertise to public debates on the translation of Koine, which in turn led directly to my joining the Society for Biblical Literature, and beginning serious research on Koine.

It was through SIL connections that I first met Nick Bailey.

In the early 1980s I connected with an SIL translator and student of Kurdish languages, Terry Todd, at the University of Michigan. In the summer of 1989, on my way from Berlin to a conference in Giessen, I made a short detour to visit Terry in the small Hessian town of Merkenbach, where he was studying the language of Kurdish guest workers. There he introduced me to Nick, who was also working on Kurdish with SIL. Nick is a Cal graduate, and I had just recently moved to UC Berkeley from the University of Michigan. It turned out that Nick and I knew many of the same people—including a number from the Jesus People movement in Berkeley at the time of the Free Speech Movement. But it was a decade later, in the summer of 2000, that I really got to know Nick well. At the end of a sabbatical in Austria, I was recruited to go back one more time and teach at the SIL summer program in Eugene, Oregon. There Nick and I started deeper conversations about the theoretical concepts that underlie his dissertation. That connection led to an invitation to be the external member at Nick's dissertation defense at the Vrije Universiteit in Amsterdam. One chapter from that dissertation is the source of this book.

The issue addressed in this book concerns a puzzle about a pervasive Koine usage: what does the word ἰδού (and its variant ἴδέ) mean? The authoritative sources on Greek—Liddell, Scott, and Jones and Bauer, Danker, Arndt, and Gingrich—leave much to be desired. LSJ simply glosses ἰδού as "lo, behold" and gives citations to examples. BDAG is more insightful in pointing out that ἰδού is used to direct attention and/or to introduce something new. But absent a framework for understanding what it means to "direct attention", or "introduce something new", any attempt to apply the BDAG characterization to any particular translation task falters badly, as can be seen in the often awkward phrasings of many contemporary English translations.

What Dr. Bailey brings to the table in this book is a way to understand what it means to introduce an entity into a discourse and to direct attention in a text. Bringing together insights from the fields of discourse analysis with insights from cognitive linguistics, Dr. Bailey teases apart ἰδού constructions in a way that is readily understandable to anyone conversant in basic linguistics, clearly explaining the communicative functions of each construction. He presents the distinctions by construction type: ἰδού + NP (There's some water. Here's the bridegroom.), ἰδού + locative (There's the log in your eye. There are two swords here.), ἰδού + clause (Two more horrors come right after that.) and so on. He also draws on wider Greek literature to illustrate these uses with particularly clear examples. He goes on to show how ἰδού constructions are extended to uses in narrative where they sometimes function as de facto miratives. (I looked and a white horse appeared. Jesus was speaking and all at once a crowd showed up.)

Because the older English translations that we have heard since childhood have glossed ἰδού stiltedly as 'Lo!' or 'Behold!', we are dulled to the sense of how ordinary ἰδού constructions were in the tongue of the original writers. Understanding the various senses in context is invaluable to the translator, who might otherwise miss what the writer of Scripture is actually communicating.

Even newer English translations' use of thetic and mirative expressions don't always land right, sometimes missing the clear communicative force of particular ἰδού constructions. Dr. Bailey's array of distinctions provides a platform for arguing for contextually natural renderings, which, for translators struggling to find natural phrasings, provides an invaluable contribution to clarity in the target language. It was exactly the demands created by distinctions in Kurdish thetics that brought Dr. Bailey to this topic in the first place.

Readers will find in this book, not only distinctions in ἰδού constructions, but creative ways of thinking about the text more generally. These will pay off richly. That's why I'm delighted to have the opportunity to recommend this book to you, gentle reader, so you can see things in the structure and meaning of the languages you work with and share some of the thrill of discovery doing the work of translation brings. You couldn't ask for a better guide than Dr. Bailey.

Richard A. Rhodes
Professor emeritus of Linguistics, Thomas Garden Barnes Chair of Canadian Studies
Interim Director of Canadian Studies
University of California, Berkeley

Preface

Translators are often puzzled by the Koine particles ἰδού and ἴδε, and the translation of these particles in the New Testament and other works is often mechanical and unidiomatic (e.g., *behold*). In this study, a systematic analysis of these particles is presented that posits (at least) five different uses—that is, they are used in five different 'grammatical constructions'. Each of the five uses are illustrated, and idiomatic translations in English and other languages are suggested. Although all five uses are cognitively related to each other, they nevertheless differ significantly in function and syntax such that no one use can be entirely predicted from the others. The differences in the five uses are reflected most clearly in their functional differences in information structure and deixis. This analysis serves as a major refinement of the entries of these particles in the standard lexicon, BDAG.

This study is based on chapter 6 of my dissertation (Bailey 2009), and it includes some corrections, modifications, and additional data. For the original chapter, I am grateful for ideas and feedback from Lourens de Vries, Rutger Allan, Richard A. Rhodes, and Heinrich von Siebenthal. It was in fact Lourens de Vries who encouraged me to include in my dissertation an exhaustive study of ἰδού and ἴδε from the New Testament. Heinrich von Siebenthal kindly discussed many passages with me by email, which was very beneficial to me. I was also greatly encouraged by Stephen Levinsohn who interacted with me after I gave a summary presentation on the topic at the Eurasia Area Linguistics Forum in 2009.

For the current version of this study, I am especially thankful to Tony Pope for many helpful comments and ideas, for encouraging me to study the use of ἰδού in Chariton and *Joseph and Aseneth*, and for discussing with me some of the textual variants in the New Testament and *Joseph and Aseneth*. This current version also benefited from feedback and discussion with Jim Watters, especially on the topic of Construction Grammar(s). I am also grateful to Bob Dooley, especially for feedback on the glossary at the end of the book.

I am also very grateful for the discussions I had with the speakers of certain European languages; each of them graciously shared their thoughts and native intuitions about the data and translations in their respective languages. For Italian, I thank Marco Librè; for French, Paul Solomiac; and for Russian, Tatiana Mayskaya, Alexey Somov, and Vitaly Voinov.

I also benefited from feedback given when I presented summaries of this study to several groups: (i) Eurasia Area Linguistics Forum 2009, Horsleys Green, High Wycombe, UK; (ii) CanIL Linguistics Colloquium Series 2010, Canada Institute of Linguistics, Trinity Western University, Langley, British Columbia, Canada; (iii) the Bible Translation 2015 conference, Dallas, TX, USA. Special thanks are due to Michael Aubrey for feedback and for kindly presenting a similar summary on my behalf at the Society of Biblical Literature Annual Meeting in 2010, in Atlanta, GA.

Others to whom I am indebted must also be mentioned. SeungJung Kim kindly procured permission for the use of the line drawing of the Swallow Vase by H. Anh Thu Nguyen, which appears in Kim 2017. Concerning permission for the use of other images, I am grateful to those who assisted me at The State Hermitage Museum (St. Petersburg), The British Library, and the Kröller-Müller Museum (Otterlo).

Most recently, in the final stage of preparing the manuscript for publication, I have been blessed to have input and support from the editing team of SIL International Global Publishing Services, including (alphabetically) Gene Burnham, George Huttar, Eric Kindberg, Sue McQuay, and Gayle Sheehan.

Finally, I wish to thank Denise Bailey, who has encouraged and assisted me in countless ways during all the phases of this project.

While many coworkers, colleagues, and scholars have inspired and assisted me along the way, either directly or through their writings, I am responsible for any shortcomings in this work. My greatest hope is that this study will be an aid to translators who are attempting to understand the meaning of these elusive particles in their different contexts and thereby gain deeper insight into the language of the New Testament and the hope offered by that Book to the world.

Conventions

Typographical conventions

In this study, **bold type** highlights terms being introduced or reintroduced in a section.

For language data from English and other languages (including English translations), *italics* are used in my prose but not in the numbered examples. *Italics* are also used to indicate emotive emphasis as well as to bring attention to certain technical terms and phrases. (Italics are not used for Greek, Hebrew, or Russian.)

Words in CAPITAL letters indicate primary sentence stress.

Quote marks '...' are used in most of the conventional ways: e.g., to mark a quoted element, such as a technical term or sentence (but not for vernacular translations). Quote marks are also used to set off English glosses in my prose. In addition, they are used to mark propositions and parts of propositions that underlie utterances. In this way, propositions and their parts are graphically distinguished from the actual words used to express them. For example, in the prose, a sentence like *He entered it* could be cited, where the underlying proposition was 'Paul entered the synagogue'. The clause in italics represents the actual spoken or written words. As a part of the sentence, I could refer to the subject phrase *he*, which refers to the entity 'Paul'.

Bible book abbreviations and passage lists

For ease of searching this document electronically, three-letter abbreviations (as used in Paratext and BART) have been used for every citation from a Bible book. For multiple citations from the same book, the book abbreviation is repeated (e.g., Mat 1:1; Mat 2:2). These abbreviations can be found in the index.

The symbol → has been used to flag the primary list of passages under discussion in each section.

Conventions for quoting vernacular translations

[...]   Brackets in the vernacular translations indicate my
            editorial comments or additions.

<u>English</u> <u>Underlining</u> is used in the longer examples of vernacular
            translations to highlight the construction being
            illustrated in the Greek.

italics   Italics are in the original.

¶   This symbol indicates a paragraph break in a text.

|| This indicates a parallel passage, e.g., where the same
            saying or episode occurs in another Gospel.

Conventions for Greek examples

[...]   Brackets in the Greek examples set off words that are
            textually disputed.

–   is used to gloss discourse particles (e.g., δέ) and articles
            (e.g., ὁ 'the') that can be ignored.

*   is sometimes used in place of a gloss for a difficult word
            under discussion (e.g., ἰδού).

<u>αβγ</u>/**αβγ** <u>Underlining</u> and **bold** indicate Greek words under
            discussion.

J&A   *Joseph and Asenath*

Grammatical information in the glossing of the Greek (and other
languages) is only provided where it is deemed crucial for the argument
at hand. The glossing typically follows *The New Greek-English Interlinear
New Testament* (1990, electronic version 2003, from BART). Number and
person on verbs is always indicated (e.g., 'I', '3s'=third person singular;
see below), but other verb morphology is usually only implied in the
glosses (e.g., an English simple past usually represents a Greek aorist, an
English imperfect with '-ing' represents a Greek imperfect, etc.).

Greek morphological glossing

Nominals, Adjectives, Participles

Slot 1: Case: N=nominative, G=genitive, A=accusative, D=dative

Slot 2: Number: s=singular, p=plural

Slot 3: Gender: m=masculine, f=feminine, n=neuter

Examples with nouns: ὄχλου 'crowd.G.s.m'; τινος 'of.a.certain.G.s'; υἱοί 'sons.N'

Examples with a participle: ὄντος 'being.G.s.m'

Examples with adjective (=Adj): ὑγιεῖς 'healthy.Adj.A.p.m'

Verbs including Infinitives and (again) Participles

Tense-aspect-mood is indicated only if relevant.

Aor=aorist, Impf=imperfect, Pres=present, Prf=perfect, PluPrf=pluperfect, Inf=infinitive, Prt=participle

act=active, ps=passive, '!'=imperative

3s=third person singular, 3p=third person plural

'you'= singular or plural, 2s=second person singular

'I'=first person singular, 'we'=first person plural

Examples with verbs: ἤκουεν '3s.was.listening.Impf' (=imperfect)

Examples with participles: καθήμενον 'sitting.Pres.A' (present accusative; I ignore here that it is singular and masculine); παρακαθεσθεῖσα 'having.sat.beside.Aor.N.s.f' (=aorist, nominative, singular, feminine)

Examples with (tense)-aspect: καταλελειμμένος 'left.behind.Prf.ps' (=perfect, passive)

Abbreviations

A	accusative	N	nominative
act	active	nab	N. A. Bailey
Aor	aorist	NP	noun phrase
C1 … C5	ἰδού/ἴδε constructions	NT	New Testament
C2c-NP	C2c construction with a NP	OT	Old Testament
CF	constituent-focus	p	plural
D	dative	Pres	present
f	feminine	Prf	perfect
G	genitive	Prt	participle
Impf	imperfect	ps	passive
Inf	infinitive	s	singular
LXX	Septuagint Greek translation of OT	v	verse
m	masculine	vv	verses
n	neuter		

1

Introduction

Exegetes and lexicographers are often at a loss about what to do with the Koine Greek 'particles' ἰδού and ἴδε,[1] and the confusion about their meaning and function is often reflected in unidiomatic and/or unsystematic renderings in translation. Some translations mechanically use modern renderings (e.g., *see* or *look*) or even outdated ones (e.g., *behold* or *lo*) in most contexts, while other translations use greater variety, although not necessarily in a systematic way.[2]

A major conclusion I draw from my study of these particles is that such variety in translation is justified, and it is in fact to be expected for most, if not all, languages. This expectation follows from the fact that these particles have different uses (senses) that are based on different syntax and on different functions, details that are extensively illustrated in the pages that follow. In other words, it would be inaccurate to claim that these particles occur in only one syntactic structure, and it would be misleading to claim that their uses could be reduced to a single

---

[1] I use 'particle' as an overarching neutral label along with more specific grammatical descriptions for certain individual uses. BDAG also calls them 'particles' (ἰδού is called a 'demonstrative or presentative particle', and ἴδε is 'stereotyped as a particle'), and LSJ calls ἰδού an 'adverb'. BDF (§ 101, ὁρᾶν), Robertson (1934:302, 1193), and Moulton (1908:11) call ἰδού an 'interjection'. Wallace (1996:60) calls ἰδού and ἴδε 'interjections', which can coincide with a 'nominative of exclamation'. The term ('particle of') 'exclamation' is also occasionally used (Robertson 1934:231, 302; Turner 1963:231). See footnote 119 in ch. 4 for why I avoid 'interjection'.

[2] Common English renderings include *behold, here, there, now, then, look, see, consider, hereby,* as well as Ø. We also often find 'double translations', where a translator has used more than one word (e.g., for Act 10:19, ἰδού ἄνδρες τρεῖς ζητοῦντές σε, GNB renders ἰδού by *listen ... here: Listen! Three men are here looking for you.* Although 'double translations' may be used on purpose and often justified, I believe that they often indicate a translator's indecision or confusion.

pragmatic function such as to 'highlight' or 'emphasize' something in the discourse or to indicate 'vividness'.

Translations that employ a single word for most uses typically obscure different senses. This was certainly the case for the King James Version in the early 1600s that used *behold* for both words nearly 200 times (and *lo* about 30 times). More problematic are modern translations, such as the ESV, that perpetuate the use of *behold*. Although *behold* may have been idiomatic 400 years ago, today it is not idiomatic, and though it is well known to educated readers of English, using it today as a highlighting particle suggests an archaic or affected register. Such a rendering is especially incongruent when ἰδού and ἴδε occur in a colloquial register or in emotional speech.

Thus, to be true to the meaning and function of the Greek particles in the various discourse contexts where they occur, translators will likely find they will need several renderings in their receptor languages, which will in turn require a clear understanding of the linguistic resources in the receptor languages that have comparable ranges of functions.

That these particles have different uses (senses) is already suggested in the entries of the standard lexicon BDAG, which lists several subdefinitions for both. Having said that, the subdefinitions offered by BDAG overlap to varying degrees in unnecessary and confusing ways, thus making it difficult for exegetes to know which definition should apply when (see section § 3.1 below for more detail on the BDAG entries). The analysis that I present here largely substantiates the categories and uses offered by BDAG, but my analysis attempts to identify more precisely the different uses and to give reasonable grounds for the linguistic motivation of these different uses.

From my analysis I conclude that these particles can be employed in at least five different uses—or 'grammatical constructions' in the terminology of 'Construction Grammar'. Although each of the five uses is cognitively related to the others, they all significantly differ from each other functionally and/or syntactically such that no single use can be entirely predicted from the others. The differences in the five uses are reflected most clearly in their functional differences in **information structure** and **deixis**. **Emotive emphasis** (indicating e.g., surprise, akin to a common use of exclamative constructions)[3] also plays a conventionalized role in the meaning of a few of the uses, but for most uses it is not part of the meaning, even though it may be often suggested by the discourse context.

---

[3] There is thus a conceptual overlap between the term "emotive emphasis" as I use it and that of "mirativity", which refers to the grammatical marking of surprise, unexpectedness, the unprepared mind, etc., on the part of the speaker or hearer.

In this study, I treat all instances of ἰδού and ἴδε in the text of the twenty-eighth edition of Nestle-Aland[4] (200 instances of ἰδού and 29 of ἴδε). I also refer occasionally to instances in variant readings, as well as to many instances in the LXX (Rahlfs-Hanhart 2006 edition, unless stated otherwise) and several non-biblical passages (from *Joseph and Aseneth*, Chariton, several papyri, Aristophanes, Epictetus, and an Attic vase).

At the end of the introductory chapters (chapters 1 through 3), I present in section § 3.2 a summary with an example of each of the five major uses. Then, in chapter 4, a detailed discussion is offered of all instances of ἰδού and ἴδε in the New Testament. Chapter 4 also includes discussion of many translations (in English, French, Italian, German, and Russian). Difficult tokens are also noted, including ones that could reasonably have more than one interpretation. To aid translators, summary lists of all instances for each sub-use are provided (flagged by →). There is also an index to help the reader locate where each token is discussed or listed.

---

[4] The NT text of the twenty-eighth edition of Nestle-Aland is equal to that of the fifth edition of the UBS Greek NT.

2

Theoretical Background

This chapter provides some necessary theoretical background to my analysis. The first section (§ 2.1) offers a definition of the grammatical construction; this definition is illustrated by examples from English. The second section (§ 2.2) illustrates deictic constructions from the English family of *there/here* constructions (following George Lakoff's analysis, 1987), including how different constructions involve different types of deixis. These deictic *there/here* constructions are also contrasted with non-deictic *there* constructions (also known as 'existential *there*' sentences). The third section (§ 2.3) offers a short introduction to major information structure categories (based on Lambrecht 1994).

2.1 The 'grammatical construction' in Construction Grammar

There are a handful of approaches to grammar that have been called Construction Grammar, several of which are closely tied to the Cognitive Linguistics movement. One important point of similarity between all construction grammarians is that they 'emphasize the importance of "starting big", i.e., allowing units larger than the word as the building blocks of syntactic analysis' (Sag et al. 2012:19), that is, such constructions, or 'building blocks', are grammatical entities and not epiphenomenal.[1] Another important point is that 'the distinction between lexical and grammatical entities is blurry, motivating a uniform conception of lexical and constructional constraints' (Sag et al. 2012:5). In other words, there is a similarity between the lexicon and constructions, and so the idea of a grammatical construction (to be defined immediately

---

[1] Chomsky, in contrast, views constructions as grammatically epiphenomenal and irrelevant (Chomsky 1981:121, 1993:4 cited in Croft and Cruse 2004:228–9; see also Lakoff 1987:467–8, Goldberg 1995:1, Goldberg and Casenhiser 2006, and Michaelis 2006:73).

below) can be considered the basic unit in language, as it can cover everything from the morpheme up to multi-sentence phenomena (see examples below). Finally, this approach is compatible with the idea that grammar (syntax) is *not* autonomous from semantics and pragmatics, an assumption shared by typological approaches to language.[2]

So, what is the definition of a 'grammatical construction'? The basic idea of the grammatical construction that I will assume here should not strike those used to reading traditional grammars as anything foreign or obscure. Lakoff, as one of the original promoters of one version of Construction Grammar, has in fact described the grammatical construction as 'a somewhat enriched version of its traditional sense' (1987:467).

More specifically, a grammatical construction is defined as a 'conventionalized form-function unit': it has a form—its phonological and morphosyntactic structure, and it has a function—its meaning and use conditions (compare again Lakoff 1987:467).

Goldberg (1995:4) offers the following somewhat more technical definition:

> According to Construction Grammar, a distinct construction is defined to exist if one or more of its properties are not strictly predictable from knowledge of other constructions existing in the grammar: C is a construction iff$_{def}$ C is a form-meaning pair <F_i, S_i> such that some aspect of F_i or some aspect of S_i is not strictly predictable from C's component parts or from other previously established constructions [...] A construction is posited in the grammar if it can be shown that its meaning and/or its form is not compositionally derived from other constructions existing in the language.[3]

Nevertheless, distinct constructions can be related to each other to the degree they resemble each other in form or function (by means of what are called 'inheritance' links).

---

[2]The primary sources on the theory of Construction Grammar used in my dissertation (Bailey 2009)--including for my analysis of ἰδού and ἴδε in chapter 6--were Fillmore et al. 1988; Lakoff 1987; Goldberg 1995, 2006, 2009; Lambrecht 1994, 2000; and Croft and Cruse 2004. Recent developments can be found in the journal *Cognitive Linguistics*, and there is a nice summary in Sag, Boas, and Kay (2012) of different approaches to Construction Grammar.

[3]In a subsequent discussion, Goldberg qualifies this definition by adding 'In addition, patterns are stored as constructions even if they are fully predictable as long as they occur with sufficient frequency' (2006:5).

Consider the following examples of a selection of English constructions. I begin small, illustrating the smallest type of construction —individual morphemes and lexical items—and then progress to larger types of constructions, including syntactic constructions that are schematic, like the Noun Phrase as well as larger, more complex constructions.

The word *the* is a construction. It has a **form** (which includes not only its phonological shape, but also the position it requires in a noun phrase, etc.) which is paired with a particular **meaning** (it indicates, roughly, that a noun phrase is 'definite' or 'identifiable'). Children (and other language learners) have to learn this association between the sound of the word and its meaning and use.

Similarly, the word *dog* is another construction, which, at some risk of oversimplification, is used in its most basic sense as a noun to refer to any instance of *Canis familiaris*. Like the word *the*, a child cannot predict that the sounds of the word *dog* should mean what they do.

But *dog* has other conventionalized meanings that instantiate related but distinct constructions. For example, according to Merriam-Webster's dictionary, *dog* also has the sense of 'a worthless or contemptible person'. A child or foreigner has to learn this as a separate form-function association since its semantics are not entirely predictable from the basic sense. Although some dogs may be considered worthless or contemptible, there is in fact no reason why calling a person a *dog* could not have a very different conventionalized meaning, such as the opposite meaning, 'a good and faithful person' (as suggested by the proverb, 'a dog is a man's best friend').

Certain other constructions involving *dog* are distinguished by their distinct syntax, such as when it is used as a verb to mean 'to chase or pursue' (analogous to 'to hound'), or when used as a past participle in the colloquial idiom *you were dogged*, meaning 'you were unfairly treated', or when used adjectivally in phrases like *dogged determination* to refer to a determination that does not give up.

Each of the different uses mentioned here of the noun *dog* as well as the syntactically derived forms (verb, past participle, etc.) instantiate distinct (though related) constructions, and in a dictionary, it would be justified to list each as a subentry or a separate entry.

Many constructions are composed of smaller constructions. An English noun phrase can be composed of a definite article, like *the*, followed by a noun, like *dog* (together with certain optional modifiers in certain positions), to form *the dog*. The order of elements in a noun phrase is another thing that a language learner must learn. And so the noun phrase is another kind of construction—a template or schematic construction.

Grammatical constructions also come in much larger sizes. For example, English has templates like *The X-er, the Y-er*, as illustrated by the proverb *The bigger they are, the harder they fall* as well as by sentences like *The more your dog growls, the more nervous I get*. There are several things about this construction that are not predictable, and so it is another construction that a language learner has to learn. For one, the word *the* is used in a very unpredictable way (due to the history of this form; it derives from the Old English instrumental demonstrative *þy* [Croft and Cruse 2004:235]).

We shall see below that ἰδού and ἴδε have multiple uses where each particle actually involves a family of related but distinct constructions, and therefore neither can be reduced in all its uses to a single meaning. Moreover, most uses involve schematic constructions.

2.2   Lakoff's 'family' of English deictic *there/here* constructions

My study of ἰδού and ἴδε found inspiration in George Lakoff's discussion of the 'family' of English deictic *there/here* constructions (1987:462–585, embedded in his chapter entitled '*There*-Constructions'). Lakoff's study of deictic *there/here* constructions is instructive, because the function and meaning of these English grammatical constructions overlap somewhat with the function and meaning of ἰδού and ἴδε constructions. Lakoff showed that English has not one, but several deictic *there/here* constructions. They count as distinct constructions because they are not entirely predictable from each other.

The following two sentences illustrate what Lakoff called the '**central construction**':

(1)   Here comes Harry.
(2)   Here comes Harry with our pizza.

Lakoff considered the 'central construction' to be the most **basic** subtype in the family of constructions. It is what children presumably learn first. It concerns the **here-and-now**, and so it is only used in the present tense; it involves real physical space, and simultaneous pointing is possible. The basic function of the construction is to intentionally (and not incidentally) point out to the hearer an entity or state of affairs that can be presently viewed, and which is necessarily positive and certain. For this reason, it follows that the construction is incompatible with negation and questions, as illustrated by the infelicity of:

(3)   *Here's not Harry!
(4)   *Here's Harry?

It is also infelicitous with the generic or habitual present, as well as with statements that involve uncertain or irrealis states of affairs:

(5)   *Here comes Harry from time to time.

(6)   *Here might come Harry.[4]

In addition to the central construction, or 'prototype', Lakoff argued for the existence of several other closely related constructions that diverge from the prototype in non-predictable ways—that is they have distinct syntax, meaning, and/or constraints on use—while nevertheless still resembling the prototype in many ways. These constructions are compared and summarized in the following table (based on Lakoff's discussion, especially pages 482–485, 489–491, and 508–537):

Table 1. The family of English deictic *there/here* constructions	
Central Construction (the prototype): Only present tense, involves real physical space, simultaneous pointing is possible.	There's Harry (with the red jacket on). Here comes Harry (with our pizza).
Perceptual: Non-visual perceptual space and motion are metaphorically understood as physical space and motion.[5] *Go* and *there* refer to the present or recent past, *come* and *here* to the immediate future.	There goes (the pain in) my knee. Here comes the beep.
Discourse: *here* and *there* refer to something in the discourse. Discourse space is metaphorically understood as physical space. **Go* is not allowed, *come* refers to future.	There's a nice point to bring up in class. Here comes the best part.

---

[4]This example is my own, which, like all of these infelicitous sentences, contrasts with an acceptable counterpart with non-inverted order (*Harry might come here, Harry comes here from time to time, Is Harry here? Harry is not here.*). Lakoff does not explicitly discuss the notion of 'certainty'. To be sure, it is possible to say things like *Here's a possible candidate*, which might appear to suggest something that is uncertain, but I assume this is a shorthand for *Here's a person (who is certainly there) who might run for office*, or the like.

[5]The conceptual relationship between the Central Construction and the Perceptual Deictic is described as involving 'a metaphorical mapping of physical space into perceptual space' (Lakoff 1987:509). Crucially, there are also syntactic differences between the two constructions (for details, see pp. 509–514).

Table 1 (*continued*)

Existence: Existence is metaphorically understood as location here, nonexistence as location away from here.	There goes our last hope. Here comes another outburst.
Activity Start: Activities are metaphorically understood in terms of motion along a path, and the locative adverb as the beginning. *Go* is allowed, but not **come.*	There goes Harry, meditating again.
Delivery: Used when something is being brought to the hearer or is in a nearby location ready to be received. **Go* is not allowed. Allows exaggerated vowel length in *here* and *there*.	He(eee)re's your pizza, piping hot. The(eee)re's your car, all washed and waxed.
Paragon: Involves special intonation and stress. Used to express awe about an exceptionally good specimen in a class.	Now THERE was a real ballplayer! Now HERE is a great cup of coffee!
Exasperation: Involves special intonation (e.g., sigh, throat constriction, nasalization, etc.). Used to express exasperation. Coincides with Activity Start and its constraints.	There goes Harry again making a fool of himself.
New Enterprise (Enthusiastic Beginning): Involves special rising intonation. Coincides with Activity Start and its constraints.	Here we go, off to Africa.
Narrative Focus: Functions to create a vivid picture of an imagined scene. *Here* and *there* refer to locations in the imagined scene. Allows both past and present tense.	*Past tense narrative:* There I was in the middle of the jungle ... There came the bus at last —and just as you might expect, it was full. *Present tense narrative:* Here come the killer bees, blackening the sky ...

Table 1 (*continued*)

Presentational Deictic: Syntactically marked: allows a locative or other element before verb; *there/here* is optional if another locative (designating a location relative to the speaker) occurs preverbally; the verb can contain a full auxiliary; permissible verbs allow a locative. Uses: in *narrative*, it indicates discovery, (re)introducing a significant entity into discourse; in *announcements*, it indicates something significant.	*Narrative:* (There) in the alley had gathered a large crowd of roughnecks. *Announcement:* (Here) on this hill will be built by the alumni ... a ping pong facility second to none.

What is especially worth noting is that many of the subconstructions involve various types of **metaphorical extensions** where the deictic adverbs *here* and *there* refer to something that is not visually present in the here-and-now physical world. For example, in the 'Perceptual' construction, *here* and *there* are extended to include non-visual perceptual space and motion (i.e., non-visual perceptual space and motion are metaphorically understood as physical space and motion), and in the 'Discourse' construction, these deictic adverbs point to something in the discourse (i.e., discourse space is metaphorically understood as physical space).

A metaphorical extension is also involved in the 'Narrative Focus' construction and in some uses of the 'Presentational Deictic' (i.e., in the final two construction types in the table, in bold), where *here* and *there* point to locations in an imagined scene in the discourse world. These constructions are normally used to create a vivid picture in the imagined narrative world. Later we will see that ἰδού is often used in narrative in a very similar way (see especially under 'Translation issues' in § 4.2.4).

Now, it is important to distinguish such deictic *there/here* constructions from **non-deictic *there* constructions**, as illustrated by:

(7)   There's a masked man outside.
(8)   There's no lid to this jar.

These sentences are not examples of deictic *there/here* constructions but of **non**-deictic *there* constructions (also known as 'existential *there*' sentences). There is a clear historical relationship between non-deictic *there* and the deictic one, and it may be easy at first to confuse the two and the constructions they occur in. But despite the same spelling, non-deictic *there* is pronounced and used differently.[6] It is unaccented and designates a 'mental space' (an abstract area of consciousness) where a conceptual entity is to be located.[7] Furthermore, in contrast to the deictic constructions, the non-deictic *there* construction is indeed compatible with negation and questions.

There are also special subtypes of non-deictic *there* constructions. For example, although the basic use requires that the subject entity be 'hearer-new' (i.e., 'indefinite' or new to the hearer; e.g., *a masked man*), nevertheless the entity can under certain conditions be 'hearer-old' (i.e., 'definite').[8] One special use is when the construction functions as a '**reminder**', that is, for example, when the speaker wishes to remind the hearer about something he might have forgotten.[9] For example, if two people needed to fetch something from the yard of a neighbor who was away, and one remembered that the neighbor had a dog (which both had previously known), he might say to the other: *But there's the DOG!* On a few occasions, ἰδού is also used with such reminders.

Another subtype is what Lakoff calls the 'Presentational Existential'. This construction will occasionally feature in my suggested renderings of ἰδού when used in narrative. The Presentational Existential both sets up a scene in a narrative world and introduces an entity into it. Like the Narrative Focus and Presentational Deictic constructions (with deictic *here/there*), the Presentational Existential (with non-deictic *there*) can also be used to add vividness to a narrative. Examples of the Presentational Existential are illustrated in the final row of the following table, which presents Lakoff's different proposed (sub)constructions based on existential *there* (the examples are from Lakoff 1987:558–574, especially p. 562):

Table 2. The family of English existential *there* constructions

Central Construction: *there* designates a mental space; +/- negation, +/- question, takes many but not all tenses. When the noun phrase is 'hearer-old' (definite), it can be used as a 'reminder' or 'list'.	There's a masked man outside. There's no lid to this jar. Reminder: But there's the dog!

---

[6] On the different *there's*, see the discussion and literature cited in Bailey (2009:71–72 and 77–82).

[7] On 'mental space', see Lakoff (1987:542–543), Croft and Cruse (2004:32–39), and especially Fauconnier (2007).

[8] The distinction between 'hearer-old' and 'hearer-new' is discussed further in § 2.3.

[9] On the use of existential *there* clauses with definite subjects as 'reminders', see Lakoff (1987:561–562) and the longer discussion and references in Bailey (2009:74–76).

Table 2 (*continued*)

Strange: there's = there has. Introduces an especially 'strange' event. [This subtype is not in my idiolect, nab]	There's a man been shot. There's a man been shot, hasn't there?
Ontological: Asserts whether or not an entity exists; the verb may be 'be' or 'exist'; the verb, or part of it, is stressed; the NP, even a proper name, can take the indefinite article.	There IS a Santa Claus. There EXISTS a Santa Claus living quietly at the North Pole.
Infinitival: Has a gapped infinitival clause.	There's food to eat. There's making dinner to start thinking about.
Presentational Existential: It both sets up a scene in a narrative world and introduces an entity into it. Allows intransitive verbs and auxiliaries; most negation and embedding are not allowed. For some speakers, 'the verb phrase cannot be much longer (or have much more informational content) than the noun phrase' (p. 571).	From an asylum near Paris, there recently disappeared an exceedingly singular person. There arose a commotion. Suddenly there burst into the room an SS officer holding a machine gun.

2.3   Some basic information structure categories

BDAG's entry for ἰδού begins by describing it as a 'demonstrative or presentative particle that draws attention to what follows'.[10] I assume that what is meant by 'presentative' here resembles what some linguists have defined more specifically as a type of **'thetic'** construction. According to Lambrecht's definitions (1994:144), a thetic construction *functions to introduce ('present') an entity or event into a discourse* (more on this below, including the special function of the subject constituent in such sentences). Many ἰδού and ἴδε clauses do in fact have this function, as illustrated by **Mat 25:6**, which introduces an entity, 'the bridegroom', and by **Jhn 12:15**, which introduces an entity, 'your king' by means of an event of arrival:

---

[10] To my knowledge the term 'presentative' was not used in earlier editions of the lexicon. The respective entries in Bauer (1958) and Gingrich and Danker (BAGD 1979) begin by describing the particle as only 'demonstrative'. So, 'presentative' was apparently added in the latest revision by Danker (BDAG 2000).

Mat 25:6 μέσης δὲ νυκτὸς κραυγὴ γέγονεν·   ἰδοὺ ὁ
mid- - night shout 3s.happened *   the.N
νυμφίος,   ἐξέρχεσθε εἰς ἀπάντησιν [αὐτοῦ].
bridegroom.N come.out! to meeting   him
nab: But at midnight there was a shout, 'Here's the
bridegroom! Come out to meet him.'

Jhn 12:15 ἰδοὺ ὁ   βασιλεύς σου   ἔρχεται, καθήμενος ἐπὶ
*   the.N king.N   of.you 3s.comes sitting   on
πῶλον ὄνου.
foal   of.donkey
GNB: Here comes your king, riding on a young donkey.

In Lambrecht's framework, a **thetic** construction is a type of
information structure.[11] The above two examples in fact conform to
Lambrecht's definition of a thetic construction, given that in both
(besides other reasons) what is introduced into the discourse is expressed
either partially or entirely by the **subject constituent** (ὁ νυμφίος and ὁ
βασιλεύς σου). Such sentences are also commonly called 'presentative'
or 'presentational'.

Now, when I first began studying ἰδού and ἴδε constructions, it was
within the context of studying a large variety of thetic constructions
in the NT, and so my goal was to discover to what degree ἰδού and
ἴδε interacted with theticity. A quick perusal of the data revealed that,
while many of their uses were indeed thetic, many were not and
in fact involved clause structures (i.e., syntax) that differed from the
above examples. It then became clear to me that analyzing the tokens
according to their different information structures would be helpful in
identifying their uses.

At this point, to aid the reader, we must further define what a thetic
construction is, and we will do this by first illustrating what a thetic
construction is not.

Imagine someone asks another person: *What happened to your car?*
This question primes the hearer to say something about his car. The
hearer might give one of the following answers:

---

[11] Not all linguists have defined thetic constructions in terms of information
structure. See Bailey (2009:43–75) and the references to Lambrecht and
Sasse below. For other recent discussions on theticity, including different
applications of the term 'thetic', see Abraham et al. (2020). For a recent
general introduction to information structure categories from different
theoretical perspectives, see Matić (2015). See also Dooley (2017) for a
practical introduction that treats a broad range of information structure
phenomena.

(9)   [My car]~Topic~ [broke DOWN.]~Focus Domain~

(10)   [It]~Topic~ [broke DOWN.]~Focus Domain~

In these answers, the subject constituent, which refers to the common ground between the speaker and hearer, expresses the topic (i.e., what the sentence is 'about'). The **predicate** *broke DOWN*, in turn, expresses that part of the sentence which is unpredictable. Thus, in the terminology of Lambrecht (1994), the predicate comprises the 'focus domain'.[12] Notice also that the word *DOWN*, which is part of the focus domain, takes the primary sentence stress (indicated by capital letters). This is the structural clue that the predicate comprises the focus (in English at least). Lambrecht calls this a **predicate-focus construction**. Predicate-focus constructions most typically have '**topic-comment**' function; the predicate makes a comment (says something unpredictable or newsworthy) about an entity that is expressed by the subject. The subject in turn may be expressed by a **noun phrase** (e.g., *my car* in [9]) or a **minimal form**, such as by a pronoun (e.g., *it* in [10]) or by Ø, which is normal in English with conjoined clauses (e.g., *It broke down and Ø wouldn't move*) and even more common in languages like Greek where the subject is often just indicated by verb morphology. Such minimal forms are typical when the entity referred to is judged by the speaker to be '**activated**', that is, 'in the hearer's short-term memory at the time of an utterance' (Lambrecht 2000:613).

Now imagine a different situation, where someone said *I heard your motorcycle broke down* and where you answered:

(11)   [My CAR]~Focus Domain~ [broke down.]~Open Proposition~

Here, it is the **subject** constituent that is accented and expresses the unpredictable element, and so it comprises the focus domain. The predicate in turn refers to something that is part of the common ground

---

[12]Different linguists use different terms to refer to 'focus'. Lambrecht distinguishes the **focus domain**, which in his theory is a grammatical category, from the **focus (of assertion)**, which refers to the (notional) proposition that is evoked by an utterance (see chapter 2 in Bailey 2009, especially pp. 8–11). I am describing the latter loosely as the 'unpredictable' element, and others have called it the 'new' element. But such labels should be viewed as imprecise shorthands, since, following Lambrecht, the 'new' idea in a sentence actually involves a **relationship** between the topic and focus, and it is that relationship that makes an utterance **informative**. For example, in the present example, the predicate *broke DOWN* by itself in this sentence does not inform; it is instead the predicate *broke DOWN* together with the topical subject that form a meaningful utterance. (See Lambrecht 1994:46–49.)

between the speaker and hearer,[13] which is the idea that *something broke down*. This type of sentence is called a **constituent-focus construction** because a single constituent, in this case the subject, is focal. (This structure is also called 'argument-focus' by Lambrecht and 'narrow focus' by others.) In constituent-focus constructions, the common ground is often described as an 'open proposition', which in this example would be 'the speaker's X broke down', where 'X' indicates the 'open' or missing element; the focal constituent (e.g., *my CAR*) then serves to identify the missing element in the open proposition. Constituent-focus sentences thus serve to answer an implicit or explicit content question (e.g., *What broke down?*).[14]

Neither of these last two constructions is thetic.

Now let's imagine a third situation where someone asked *Why are you late for work? What happened?* and you responded:

(12)   [My CAR broke down.]$_{\text{Focus Domain}}$

Here the speaker cannot assume that the hearer is thinking about either *his car* or that *something broke down*, so neither the subject nor the predicate expresses anything in the common ground. Instead, both the subject and the predicate, that is, *the entire sentence*, comprise the focus domain. This construction is called a **sentence-focus construction** or, alternatively, a **thetic construction**.[15] It functions to introduce a

---

[13]Lambrecht (1994) restricts the term 'topic' to 'discourse referents' and considers a discourse referent something that can only be expressed by a sentence argument (1994:74–77, 155). Therefore, it follows that open propositions and phrases serving as predicates cannot be topic expressions ('Predicates by definition do not denote discourse referents but attributes of, or relations between arguments', 1994:75). Nevertheless, Lambrecht (1994:222, 228) does assume that, like topics, open propositions are, 'in the presupposition' (what I am calling here the 'common ground') and that they can involve a topicality presupposition ('a center of current interest'; 2001a:476–477). See Lambrecht (2000:613) on four types of 'presupposition' relevant to information structure.

[14]The current example of constituent-focus involves strong contrast and an implied correction, that it was the speaker's car and not his motorcycle that broke down. But constituent-focus need not involve such obvious elements of contrast or correction. For example, this sentence would also be an appropriate response to *Was it your car or your motorcycle that broke down?* where the answer would not at all be corrective and the contrastive feeling would be typically diminished. And it would also be an appropriate response to *I heard you had something that was broken*, where the response would be neither contrastive nor corrective.

[15]I am using 'thetic construction' to refer to a form (a 'sentence-focus' struc-ture) with a function ('to introduce an entity or event'). But it is important to recognize that, depending on the language, a sentence can have **thetic**

new element into the discourse, in this example, an entire state of affairs—that the speaker's car broke down, which is an event that involves an entity, the speaker's car. Crucially, the subject constituent of a prototypical thetic construction is, by definition, not a topic expression.[16] In this example, the non-topical status of the subject *My CAR* is indicated by it being the sole accented element. In some English thetic constructions, the non-topical status of the subject is also reflected by its position after the verb. This marked order, also known as an 'inverted' order or 'inversion'[17] occurs in the above illustrated deictic *there/here* constructions (e.g., above in (1), *Here comes Harry*, where *Harry* is the grammatical subject but in the atypical position after the verb).[18]

---

function without having a sentence-focus *form*. As Lambrecht (2000:619) notes, 'All [sentence-focus] constructions express thetic propositions, but not all thetic propositions are expressed in special [sentence-focus] constructions.' (Compare Sasse's conclusions: 1996:50–52.) This fact may be illustrated by the English 'atmospheric' sentence *It's RAINING*, which is often cited in the literature as a sentence expressing a thetic proposition (Lambrecht 1987:368–369, 2000:619; Sasse 1987:512, 567). Given that the predicate is prosodically marked as focal, this English sentence has predicate-focus structure. But the Russian counterpart uses a dedicated sentence-focus structure: *DOSHT idyot* (ДОЖДЬ идёт) [RAIN goes]. Given the sole prosodic stress on the subject noun *dosht* 'rain', this has sentence-focus structure.

[16] In Lambrecht's framework, the distinction between the predicate-focus construction and the sentence-focus construction (that is, between topic-comment and thetic sentences) is such that the two constructions comprise a paradigm of functionally motivated contrasting sentence types (Lambrecht 2000:611, 642; see also 1994:6, 35, 120, 145 on 'allosentences', which are 'semantically equivalent but formally and pragmatically divergent sentence pairs', p. 6). Thus, Lambrecht (1994:145) writes: 'What counts for the definition of the formal category "thetic sentence" is that the constituent which would appear as the subject (or distinguished argument) NP in a corresponding categorical allosentence [i.e., in a predicate-focus sentence with topic-comment function, nab] gets formally marked as a NON-TOPIC, resulting in a departure from the unmarked pragmatic articulation in which the subject is the topic and the predicate the comment.'

[17] While thetics in English often involve 'inversion', not all inverted constructions are thetic, and, as illustrated by *My CAR broke down*, not all thetics involve inverted constituent order. See Bailey (2009:56–57) for more examples of thetics involving inversion.

[18] Lambrecht (2000) describes such atypical features of thetic subjects in terms of them 'behaving like objects'. He provides evidence showing that languages typically have systematic ways of distinguishing subjects as topic expressions (i.e., used in their cross-linguistically prototypical function) from subjects of thetic (alias sentence-focus) constructions where the subject behaves like a focal object.

There are many other types of English thetic constructions (for much more detail, see Bailey 2009, which builds especially on the work of Lambrecht 1987, 1994, 2000 and Sasse 1987, 1995a, 1995b, 1996). The next three examples illustrate some common types, all involving inverted orders and accented subjects. Each is composed of a single clause, and each introduces something into the discourse. Example (13) is of the deictic type, and (14) and (15) are of the non-deictic type. The latter two would typically be used to introduce an entity into a narrative.

(13)   THERE's HARRY.
(14)   Once there was a BOY ...
(15)   ... then in walked a BOY/HARRY ...

Notice also that (i) the indefinite phrase *a BOY* in (14) and (15) would normally be used to introduce an entity that would be unknown to the hearer (or reader, for a written text); but (ii) *HARRY* in (13) and (15) would normally be used to introduce someone that the hearer already knew (or knew of). Using terminology in Prince (1992), I shall refer to (i) as '**hearer-new**' and (ii) as '**hearer-old**'. In addition to the hearer-new/hearer-old distinction, Prince distinguishes between '**discourse-new**' and '**discourse-old**'. For example, if Harry is known to the hearer (i.e., hearer-old), he could also be discourse-old if two people were already talking about him when one of the speakers pointed out his arrival and uttered *THERE's HARRY*; but if nobody had already mentioned him, his introduction in this sentence would be counted as discourse-new.[19] Notice also that, depending on the context, the appearance of

---

[19] On my preference for 'hearer-old/new' and '(un)identifiable' over the terms 'definite/indefinite', see Bailey (2009:20–22), which builds on Chafe (1976, 1994), Prince (1981, 1992), and Lambrecht (1994). The chart below compares the terminology of Lambrecht, which is more refined, to that of Prince, which is easier to apply to written texts:

	Lambrecht (1994:109)	example	Prince (1992)
unidentifiable	unidentifiable (brand-new unanchored)	'a boy'	hearer-new, discourse-new
	unidentifiable anchored (brand-new anchored)	'a boy in my class'	" " (anchored to a hearer-old entity)
identifiable	inactive (unused)	'John'	hearer-old, discourse-new
	textually accessible	'John'	" discourse-old
	situationally accessible	'that boy over there'	[? *treated as* hearer-old, discourse-old]
	inferentially accessible	'my friend'	[? *treated as* hearer-old, discourse-old]
	active (given)	'he' or Ø	hearer-old, discourse-<u>old</u>

Harry in either (13) and (15) could entail a degree of surprise from the speaker's perspective (*Oh! THERE's HARRY!*) or from the hearer's perspective (*... then, suddenly, in walked HARRY!*). In our discussion of the different uses of ἰδού and ἴδε, we will often refer to the 'hearer-new/ hearer-old' distinction as well as note when an element of surprise (or other emotion) seems present and whether or not surprise should be viewed as part of the meaning of the construction or as simply implied by the context (i.e., a conversational implicature).

Both Lambrecht and Sasse have underscored the distinction between (a) thetic constructions that introduce an **entity**, as illustrated by *Once there was a BOY*, and (b) thetic constructions that introduce an **event** (which may involve an entity), as illustrated by *The CAR broke down*. For example, Lambrecht (2000:623) writes the following about the function of "SF" (=sentence-focus) constructions:[20]

> Concerning the [...] discourse function of SF constructions, I have argued elsewhere (Lambrecht 1987a, 1988a) that the overriding function of the SF category is presentational: SF constructions serve either to introduce a DISCOURSE-NEW REFERENT or to introduce an EVENT which involves a referent which is discourse-new or contextually construed as such. The two subtypes are aptly designated by Sasse (1987) with the terms ENTITY-CENTRAL and EVENT-CENTRAL thetic sentence.[21]

Equivalents for situationally accessible and inferentially accessible in Prince's system are not obvious. But Prince (1992:305) suggests (and Birner [1994:248–251] supplies supporting evidence for the claim) that 'inferrable [inferable]' entities (i.e., Lambrecht's inferentially accessible entities) are treated in language as hearer-old/discourse-old. This is because their identity depends on another entity, which is discourse-old. (Perhaps the same is true of situationally accessible entities.)

[20] In this quote (2000:623), Lambrecht uses 'presentational' as a cover term to describe the function of both entity-central and event-central thetics, which reflects how he used the term 'presentational' in his earlier works (e.g. 1987). However, elsewhere (e.g., 1994:144), he uses 'thetic' as the cover term, reserving 'presentational' for entity-central thetics and 'event-reporting' for event-central (or 'eventive') thetics.

[21] As argued elsewhere (Bailey 2009:46–52), the binary distinction between entity-central versus event-central thetics can occasionally require further nuancing. For example, depending on the resources of a language, the subject NP in a thetic can itself refer to a concrete entity (a 'first order entity' e.g., *a boy*), an event (a 'second order entity', e.g., *an earthquake*), or something propositional (a 'third order entity', e.g., *an idea*).

Lambrecht and Sasse have also underscored the point that thetics serve different functions in a discourse. Moreover, 'entity-central' and 'event-central' thetics tend to function differently in a discourse.[22] In (12) above, *My CAR broke down* was used to give a reason for a tardy appearance at work. If the boss had been satisfied with this answer, the worker might not have said anything else about his car. Furthermore, in narrative, event-central thetics often report events that are integrated into the narrative event line, and the introduced entity often does not persist.[23] But thetics that introduce a concrete entity are typically used in anticipation of saying something more about that entity, that is, the entity persists. For example, (14) *Once there was a BOY* would normally be followed by more statements about the boy, for example, *who lived in an old castle* … In other words, the thetic clause serves to introduce a new entity into the discourse, which will then become a topic in the next clause where the speaker says something informative about that new topic, that is, the speaker 'predicates' something about the new topic. I call such a clause a '**subsequent predication**'.[24] Subsequent predications also often occur after deictic thetics, as illustrated by the next two examples (where the symbol | separates the clauses).

(16)   THERE's a BOY | sitting on your DOORSTEP.

(17)   HERE's a BOY. | Maybe HE can help us.

---

[22] See Bailey (2009:61–65) for some of the common functions of thetics in discourse. There I summarize observations from Sasse (1995a:13–19, 1995b:163–168, 1996:30–43) and Lambrecht (1994, 2000).

[23] Event-central thetics occurring on the event line in the middle of a narrative typically have a surprising and interruptive effect on the story. Concerning such 'interruptive' thetics, Sasse (1995b:165) has observed that they 'may disturb the flow of topical continuity without opening a new topic chain.' We shall later see that many ἰδού thetics in narrative introduce a surprising element into the story, either (a) by introducing a new entity onto the discourse stage or (b) by reporting a surprising event that occurs on the event line. In the New Testament data, when an ἰδού thetic introduces (a) an entity into a speech, the entity usually persists, and when it introduces an entity into a narrative, it always persists. When the ἰδού thetic introduces (b) an event, the event always involves an entity, and such entities usually have some persistence in the discourse (see, e.g., Mat 17:5 'bright cloud'). For examples involving no persistence, see Mat 27:51 ('curtain', 'earth', 'rocks'); for an example involving implicit persistence, see Mat 8:24 (where 'a storm' on the lake persists implicitly since 'waves' and 'wind' belong to its semantic frame). On different types of persistence following introductions made by thetics, see Bailey (2009:65–69 and 146–156).

[24] For more on 'subsequent predications' including the many varieties that exist, see Bailey (2009:65–69). Compare Dooley's (2017:18–19) discussion of 'assertional detached elements'.

Some subsequent predications are syntactically and intonationally integrated (forming a tight-knit bi-clausal structure), as illustrated by (16), where *sitting on your doorstep* is grammatically subordinate to the thetic clause. But other subsequent predications may be expressed by an independent clause, as illustrated in (17) by *Maybe HE can help us.*

When we survey the different sets of ἰδού and ἴδε constructions, we will see that some introduce entities and others introduce events (which usually also involve an entity). Moreover, some of them function as deictic thetics. We will also occasionally need to mention the structure of subsequent predications that follow them.

3

A New Analysis of ἰδού and ἴδε

In the first section of this chapter, § 3.1, I summarize some important background about the linguistic forms ἰδού and ἴδε and offer a short survey of some relevant literature. This section also highlights the vagueness in previous analyses as well as the lack of consensus among analysts, thereby establishing the need for a more plausible categorization of the different uses. The first section ends with a list of research questions I kept in mind while studying the data.

Then, in section § 3.2, I present a summary of the five sets of uses that I propose, where each use is briefly illustrated. The detailed discussion of the different uses is not taken up until chapter 4.

3.1 Etymological notes, literature survey, and research questions

Historically, the particles ἰδού and ἴδε derive from, and are in fact identical to, imperative forms of a Greek verb that means 'see'. But because of their special functions and uses, grammarians (quite correctly) do not categorize them as imperatives.[1]

---

[1] One bit of evidence that these are not true imperatives is that, although based on singular forms, they are compatible with a plural addressee (BDF § 144; BDAG ἴδε; Schwyzer 1950:583–584). Consider, for example, Mat 26:65 where the addressee is 'you.plural' but ἴδε is still used (ἴδε ... ἠκούσατε 'behold ... you.plural.have.heard'). Besides that, many of their uses are simply incompatible with an imperative rendering of *See!* or *Look!* (even though these are good renderings in other contexts). For example, when used as (what I will describe as) a focus particle, an imperative rendering is not relevant (e.g., Luk 13:16 'This daughter of Abraham has been bound by Satan ἰδού EIGHTEEN YEARS'). An imperative rendering is also awkward for many thetic uses, for example, when something cannot be seen (e.g., Mat 3:17 'See [ἰδού] a voice said from heaven'), or when the speaker is

More specifically, ἰδού is equivalent to the second person singular aorist **middle** imperative ἰδοῦ of εἶδον 'see', except that the particle is written with ύ (or ὺ, depending on the environment) rather than ῦ; ἴδε is identical in form to the second person singular aorist **active** imperative of the same verb. It seems significant that ἰδού, which is based on the middle form and which is the more common of the two forms, often entails an emotive element (e.g., surprise, amazement, as well as other emotions) and frequently introduces something of providential or supernatural import (and thus can also involve an emotive element). If we consider the history of these particles, it seems possible that ἰδού, as the middle imperative, would become the more specialized of the two and for the active forms (singular ἴδε and plural ἴδετε) to continue their primary jobs as normal aorist imperatives. First of all, the middle imperative was the more **expressive** of the two (i.e., emotive) and therefore better suited for certain specialized functions. Allan (2006) and others have argued that in Classical Greek (e.g., in Sophocles and Homer) one of the uses of middle forms of certain verbs, including 'see' (ὁράομαι/εἰδόμην), was to indicate (in Allan's words) 'wonder or distress' or a related 'emotional overtone', in contrast to the active forms, which were unmarked for this meaning.[2] Another factor favoring the middle for certain specialized functions was that during the Classical and Koine periods middle forms of many verbs were losing ground (Robertson 1934:813–814, 332–333), including middle forms of 'see'. Thus, this development would have allowed an increasingly unemployed form, ἰδοῦ, to develop specialized functions.[3]

---

pointing out his own presence (e.g., in Act 9:10, Ἰδοὺ ἐγώ must be rendered as 'Here I am' rather than 'See I' or 'See me').

[2] In the case of ὁράομαι/εἰδόμην 'see', the viewer is affected (impressed, moved, frightened, etc.) by what he or she sees.

[3] According to BART (which uses the fourth edition UBS Greek NT), there is only one occurrence of a true (functional) middle form of the verb 'see'. This middle form, ὄψησθε, occurs in Luk 13:28 (it is an aorist subjunctive, but as a textual variant, there is also the future ὄψεσθε, which though middle in form is active in meaning). This middle form (with the nuance of 'wonder or distress') makes good sense here since the viewers see something that should horrify them (NRS: ... *when you see Abraham and Isaac and Jacob and all the prophets in the kingdom of God, and you yourselves thrown out.*). Note: The Koine paradigm for the verb 'see' with active meaning is an alliance of at least three stems: present ὁράω, aorist εἶδον, and future ὄψομαι. The future is middle in form but active in meaning. Other verbs have a role in the paradigm even if listed as separate entries in lexicons. For example, in the NT, the present subjunctive of ὁράω never occurs; βλέπω seems to serve this function. Conversely, there is no aorist subjunctive of βλέπω; forms of εἶδον seem to take on that role. Nor are there any imperfect forms of ὁράω;

Nevertheless, in studying all instances of these two particles in the New Testament (henceforth NT), I have found that, although ἰδού often clearly has an emotive element, it would be false to claim that this is always so (for more discussion, see especially § 4.1 and § 4.2.4.1 below, and Bailey 2009:325, 321, 315–318). Moreover, ἴδε may also occasionally involve an emotional overtone.

Grammarians and commentators of the LXX and NT have noted certain differences in the uses of the particles ἰδού and ἴδε, including the fact that ἰδού is much more common. For the LXX, this means that the translators chose ἰδού as the most frequent rendering of הִנֵּה (hinnēh and related forms), in fact some 900 out of some 1160 times, compared to ἴδε, which is used *only twice* for הִנֵּה (Gen 27:6; Jdg 19:24; see Andersen [2003:28–30] who lists other renderings for הִנֵּה).[4] (But it should be noted that ἰδού translates several other words, at least according to the Masoretic Text.)

For the Greek NT,[5] which is our primary concern, ἰδού occurs 200 times and ἴδε 29 times (these figures are from BART, which match Fiedler's [1969:13]). Given the greater number of ἰδού tokens, my discussion will tend to focus on it. Still, it must be noted that, in certain books, ἴδε is more frequent: namely in Mark (ἴδε 9x, ἰδού 7x) and John (ἴδε 15x, ἰδού 4x) (contrast Luke's writings, ἴδε Øx, ἰδού 80x; and Matthew, ἴδε 4x, ἰδού 62x).[6] ἼΔε is also more restricted in that it only occurs in 'speech', what Fiedler calls 'Rede' (i.e., mostly in speeches embedded in narrative, but

---

the synonyms βλέπω, θεωρέω, and maybe other verbs fill that role (compare BDF § 101).

[4] These counts for הִנֵּה are for the Masoretic Text, and following Andersen (pp. 26–27), it is reasonable to assume that the LXX was a relatively 'competent translation of a Hebrew text that was probably not much different from the MT we now have.' (But see Tov [2001, chapter 7] on some of the more significant differences between the Masoretic Text and the LXX that exist in certain books.)

[5] As mentioned in the introduction, my primary corpus is the twenty-eighth edition of Nestle-Aland Greek NT, which is equal to the fifth edition of the UBS Greek NT. I will only mention in passing some of the alternate readings noted in the critical apparatus of Nestle-Aland or in the text edited by Robinson & Pierpont. For example, the latter includes at least three variants (e.g., καὶ ἰδού instead of καί in both Mrk 5:22 and Luk 2:9; ἴδε instead of εἰ δέ in Jas 3:3) and at least three instances of variation between the two particles (ἴδε instead of ἰδού in Jhn 19:5; ἰδού instead of ἴδε in Jhn 19:26 and Jhn 19:27).

[6] Paul's epistles use ἰδού sparingly, 9x (and ἴδε, 1x), something Moulton (1908:11) considered to reflect purer Greek style compared to its frequent use in the narrative books, which he described as Semitic and 'quite un-Attic'.

also in one or two epistles, i.e., Gal 5:2 and possibly Jas 3:3;[7] we will also see that ἴδε is used in fewer ways than ἰδού). Ἰδού, on the other hand, often occurs in narrative ('Erzählung'), something underscored by Johannessohn (1942), Fiedler (1969), and others. Matthew uses ἰδού the most in narrative, then Luke (Luke-Acts).[8] In contrast, Mark and John, according to Fiedler, never use ἰδού in narrative (1969:21–22, 38).[9]

From Matthew and Luke's exuberant use of (καὶ) ἰδού in especially narrative, Fiedler (pp. 25, 29, 35, 38, etc.), Johannessohn (1942:30, 44, etc.), and Pryke (1968:420) concluded that Matthew and Luke were imitating LXX style. Fiedler in fact argued that ἰδού[10] was so used to grant the narrative a religious 'sound' (due to association with the LXX) and thereby lend religious authority to their accounts (1969:81–82, 46), which might suggest that the use of ἰδού is like an affected embellishment; in particular, it is the phrase καὶ ἰδού that is said to imitate LXX style, a combination Fiedler (pp. 21, 25) claimed he never found in any secular Greek text (Classical or Koine). But in contrast to Fiedler, Johannessohn (1942:34–35, 47–48) clearly underscored that Matthew and Luke most typically used (καὶ) ἰδού to highlight elements that are important to the flow of the narrative, namely (i) extraordinary and miraculous events, (ii) the introduction of individuals who come into contact with Jesus and typically experience something miraculous, and (iii) occasionally to highlight what someone says, which is important for the flow of the narrative (e.g., Mat 8:29, Mat 9:3). Thus, ἰδού is often associated with God's direction in the unfolding narrative. Below we shall return to the point that many uses in Matthew and Luke underscore providential[11] or supernatural introductions.

What is more relevant to our immediate interest is the variety of uses that have been identified by Fiedler and others (even if the different uses are not typically analyzed systematically). There is agreement that

---

[7] For Jas 3:3, this would require following texts that have ἴδε instead of εἰ δέ (as in the Nestle-Aland text). Varner (2014) gives a recent treatment of this issue.

[8] For ἰδού, Fiedler (1969:13–14) gives these counts for narrative/speech/LXX quote: Matthew 33/25/4; Luke 16/40/1; Acts 5/18/∅; Revelation 10/16/∅. As Johannessohn noted (1942:45), most narrative tokens in Luke's Gospel occur in the first fourteen chapters, and in Acts none occur after Act 16:1. See also the similar counts in Moulton (1908:11).

[9] The only possible exception to this generalization that Fiedler considers (1969:22) is Mrk 4:3, which begins a narrative within a reported speech (Jesus' parable of the sower). See § 4.5.5 where I discuss this passage.

[10] Fiedler (1969:81) includes ἴδε, but this seems inaccurate since ἴδε is hardly ever so used in the LXX.

[11] See also Moulton (1908:11) quoting Hort who uses 'providential' to describe some introductions in the Gospels.

ἰδού may function to introduce entities and events as well as (in some sense) to 'emphasize' statements. It has also been noted by many that in the Bible ἰδού may precede either just a nominative case noun phrase (a so-called nominal clause or verbless clause) or a more complex clause with a finite verb (where the subject, object or verb follows ἰδού).

For secular texts, both Classical and Koine, Fiedler notes (1969:17–21) especially ἰδού+*NP* (NP=noun phrase) and ἰδού+*finite verb* clause types, where in the latter the verb may be an imperative that is 'strengthened by ἰδού' (e.g., Fiedler p. 17). Two uses with a strong **emotive** element stand out: (i) where a speaker mockingly repeats a word that another just said, preceding it by ἰδού (Schwyzer 1950:584; LSJ § ἰδού.4 'quota!'; Fiedler p. 18); and (ii) where ἰδού precedes a time phrase (in the nominative!) in order to emphasize it, typically with a clear emotional overtone. The latter is illustrated by several tokens from Koine papyri (Fiedler pp. 19–20; Zilliacus 1943:38; Moulton and Milligan 1930:299; BDF § 144; BDAG ἰδού.1.b.ε). In subsequent sections, where relevant, I will illustrate non-biblical examples of some of the above-mentioned uses.

While the above uses in both non-biblical and biblical texts are well documented for ἰδού, one still finds that these grammarians struggle with how to categorize and differentiate many instances. One sees this, for example, in how the NT standard lexicon, BDAG, suggests several categories that are by no means mutually exclusive, and so it is often hard to know when a category really applies.[12] I summarize here BDAG's entries for both ἰδού and ἴδε. Note that, although the lexicon's treatment reflects an implicit awareness of theticity, it also obscures it. The two entries also betray an unnecessary disharmony, thereby blurring some similarity between ἰδού and ἴδε.

BDAG's entry for **ἰδού** begins by calling ἰδού a 'demonstrative or presentative particle that draws attention to what follows'; its use of 'demonstrative' is probably equivalent to my use of 'deictic' and, as already suggested earlier, 'presentative' may roughly equal 'thetic' in my terms. The entry then divides into two sections: In section (1), passages are listed where ἰδού is used as a 'prompter of attention'; it 'serves to enliven a narrative'. Several subtypes are listed, under which are cited both thetic and non-thetic tokens, as well as (1.b.ε) instances 'w[ith] emphasis on the size or importance of someth[ing]'

---

[12] A similar blurring of categories appears in Doudna's (1961:65) comment that ἴδε 'tends in Mark [e.g., Mrk 3:34] to retain its imperatival force, even where it has something of the quality of an interjection'. Doudna's statement, which is unfortunately echoed by Pryke (1968:419), Fiedler (1969:22), and Kilpatrick (1967:426), should not be taken as a solution to the problem but as fence-straddling. Presumably, ἴδε could have either function, one at a time, but not simultaneously.

(including 'times', as noted above). In section (2), ἰδού is designated a 'marker of strong emphasis'. Given the paraphrases offered ('see!' 'what do you know!' 'of all things!' 'wonder of wonders!'), I assume we are to understand 'emphasis' as implying surprise or amazement. But, interestingly, (we are told that) only passages are listed where ἰδού is 'used w[ith] a noun without a finite verb' and that ἰδού can be rendered as *here* or *there is (are), here or there was (were)* or *there comes (came)*. Thus, the uses proposed in sections (1) and (2) overlap in that both may involve thetic utterances and many may involve (in some sense of the word) 'emphasis'.

BDAG's entry for ἴδε divides into four sections, which, compared to the two for ἰδού, are more clearly distinguished: (1) 'to point out someth[ing] to which the speaker wishes to draw attention, *look! see!*'; (2) 'to introduce someth[ing] unexpected, *take notice*'; (3) 'to indicate a place or individual, *here is (are)* (like French *voici*)'; and (4) 'w[ith] obvious loss of its fundamental m[eani]ng as in our colloquial speech, *see! pay attention!* or '*here*'. In this entry, section (3) alone correlates with straightforward thetics. Deixis is a factor in at least (1) and (3).

To summarize, there are important similarities between all of the reviewed analyses that touch implicitly on theticity, deixis, attention, prominence, and emotive emphasis. But there is no clear consensus on how many different uses exist or on the syntactic role the particles have in each use. My goal therefore has been to outline the different uses while noting how they resemble each other in terms of form and function. My aim has been to offer a more plausible categorization. It will be argued that ἰδού and ἴδε can have more than one syntactic function, and so it is misleading for grammarians to seek a single tag for all uses (e.g., 'interjection', a tag favored by some traditional grammarians; or 'presentative particle'; or to consider all uses as 'discourse highlighters' or markers of 'vividness'). It will also be shown that the emotive element is consistently present in some but not all uses.

Therefore, in my analysis of each instance of ἰδού and ἴδε in the NT, I have kept in mind the following **research questions**:

- What kind of deictic function does the particle have in the sentence in which it occurs?
- Is there an obvious emotive element conveyed by the sentence (e.g., surprise or amazement)?
- What is the sentence's information structure?
- What syntactic relation holds between the particle and its sentence or its parts? Do different uses involve different types of relationships between the particle and its sentence or some constituent within the sentence?
- In what way do the different constructions conceptually and

syntactically resemble each other? (i.e., in Construction Grammar terms, what 'inheritance links' exist between them?)

- Which construction(s) seem(s) to be more basic or 'central' within the system (i.e., in the network of constructions)?

As a result of this study, I propose that the different uses of ἰδού and ἴδε can be categorized in (at least) five distinct sets. Each of the uses— or 'constructions'—pairs form and syntax with meaning and discourse-pragmatic conditions. I call these 'sets' because some of the five involve subtypes. This approach contrasts with that of a reductionist, who would ignore non-predictable differences in an attempt to reduce multiple uses to a lowest common denominator.

3.2 A summary of the five sets of uses

In this section, the five sets of uses of ἰδού and ἴδε are each briefly illustrated. The two particles, ἰδού and ἴδε, share several, but not all, uses. (Counts of possible NT tokens are indicated in parentheses; 'C' stands for 'construction'.)

C1 (ἰδού 11x; ἴδε 8x) [ἰδού/ἴδε + NP$_{NOM}$, here-and-now deictic thetic]: In this use, ἰδού and ἴδε function as **deictic thetic** particles (this terminology is reminiscent of BDAG's description of ἰδού as a 'demonstrative or presentative particle'). The particle followed by a nominative case NP forms a simple predication: ἰδού/ἴδε–NP$_{NOM}$ where NP$_{NOM}$ is the subject. The construction is prototypically used to point out to the hearer the presence of a visible entity in a here-and-now situation (special idiomatic and rhetorical uses of C1 are discussed later). The most plausible syntactic analysis of ἰδού and ἴδε is that they are **morphologically invariable verbs**, analogous to Italian *ecco* and French *voilà*. E.g., Mat 25:6 ἰδού ὁ νυμφίος, *Here's the bridegroom!* It may be that for some writers and some periods an emotive element was part of the conventional meaning of C1 (especially with ἰδού), but this is not clear for the NT; so an emotive element with both ἰδού and ἴδε in C1 is optional (thus any feelings of surprise, unexpectedness or other emotion are conversational implicatures).

C2 (ἰδού about 85x; ἴδε at most 1x): C2 covers various **deictic thetic** or **semi-deictic thetic** constructions that syntactically or conceptually diverge from C1.

Of the different subtypes, **C2a** most closely resembles C1. It is both thetic and (here-and-now) deictic; but, unlike C1, it involves a typical predicator, e.g., a finite verb or (verbless) locative predicate **[ἰδού + Clause, here-and-now deictic thetic]**. E.g., Jhn 12:15 ἰδού ὁ βασιλεύς σου ἔρχεται, *Here comes your king.*

C2b [ἰδού + Clause, 'spatially or temporally near' deictic thetic]
introduces something that is not quite here-and-now, but either (i)
spatially near (Mat 12:47 ἰδοὺ ἡ μήτηρ σου καὶ οἱ ἀδελφοί σου ἔξω
ἑστήκασιν *Hey, your mother and your brothers are standing outside*) or (ii)
temporally near (Rev 9:12 Ἡ οὐαὶ ἡ μία ἀπῆλθεν· ἰδοὺ ἔρχεται ἔτι δύο οὐαὶ
μετὰ ταῦτα *The first horror is past; two more horrors are right behind!*).

C2c [ἰδού + NP$_{NOM}$ or ἰδού + Clause, 'narrative' deictic thetic]: The
'narrative deictic thetic' is the most frequent subtype of C2 in the NT.
(There are two common subtypes of C2c: (i) *ἰδού–NP$_{NOM}$* (C2c-NP), which
is often followed by a participial subsequent predication (C2c-NP+Prt),
and (ii) ἰδού with a finite verb clause, C2c-FiniteV.) C2c adds immediacy
and vividness to the introduction of a new entity or state of affairs in a
narrative (in BDAG's terms, the particle 'serves to enliven a narrative'),
something that is often of providential or supernatural import. They are
'imagined' deictic thetics in the sense that they function to introduce a
state of affairs *not* into the *real* here-and-now world (like C1) but into the
here-and-now world that is to be visualized in an imagined scene of the
narrative. The introduction may be from the perspective of a character
on stage or from a more omniscient point of view. Luk 22:47 introduces
'a crowd' from the perspective of Jesus: Ἔτι αὐτοῦ λαλοῦντος ἰδοὺ
ὄχλος ... 'As he was still speaking, (look!) here (is) a crowd...' or more
idiomatically: *While he was still speaking, there in front of him appeared
a crowd*. Mat 27:51–52 introduces several (providential) events from an
omniscient point of view (on the larger stage of Jerusalem, just as Jesus
died): Καὶ ἰδοὺ τὸ καταπέτασμα τοῦ ναοῦ ἐσχίσθη ἀπ' ἄνωθεν ἕως κάτω
εἰς δύο καὶ ἡ γῆ ἐσείσθη ... *And down came the veil of the Sanctuary splitting
in two from top to bottom, the ground shook ...!*
There are also a few other types of C2 thetic or semi-thetic
constructions (**C2d, C2e**). C2c-NP and C2e are syntactically simple
like C1.

**C3 (ἰδού up to 5x; ἴδε 6x) [ἰδού/ἴδε + Clause, here-and-now
deictic]:** Ἰδού and especially ἴδε are used deictically as in C1 (i.e., the
speaker can simultaneously point to something in the real world), but
the clause's subject is topical, and so the clause is not thetic (i.e., it does
not have sentence-focus structure). Syntactically, the particles always
occur at the beginning of a sentence that involves a typical predicator
(verb or locative predicate), and so it appears that they come in a frozen
clause-initial position that mimics the position their ancestors would
have normally taken as imperatives of 'see'. This use is most likely the
oldest one, since the function of the particles is essentially that of the
literal meaning of the old imperatives (basically equivalent to 'Look!' at
something in one's field of perception). E.g., Mat 25:20 ἴδε ἄλλα πέντε

τάλαντα ἐκέρδησα. *Here/Look, I have gained five more talents*; Mat 25:25 ἴδε ἔχεις τὸ σόν. *There, you have what is yours.*

C4 (ἰδού up to 15x; ἴδε up to 7x) [ἰδού/ἴδε + Constituent-Focus Phrase, emotively emphatic]: The particle precedes a constituent-focus phrase that is **emotively** emphatic. As in C1, the particle forms a syntactic unit with a focused constituent, which in the case of C4 is a constituent-focus phrase (e.g., a noun phrase or adverb phrase), and so, for this use, ἰδού and ἴδε can be called '**emphatic focus markers**'.

In **C4a**, the focused constituent indicates a time duration and is presumably always nominative. E.g., BGU 948.6 ἡ μήτηρ σου Κοφαήνα ἀσθενεῖ ἰδοὺ δέκα τρεῖς μῆνες *Your mother Kofaina has been sick for THIRTEEN MONTHS!* Luk 15:29 ἰδοὺ τοσαῦτα ἔτη δουλεύω σοι *ALL THESE YEARS I've worked for you!* (Thus, C4a resembles C1 syntactically in that both are structurally ἰδού+NP$_{NOM}$.)

In **C4b**, the focused constituent may be of any other type: subject (nominative), object (accusative), adjective, or verb. Conceptually, the clearest instances of C4b emphasize an **extreme degree or measure** (and thus resemble exclamative constructions). E.g., Luk 23:15 ἰδοὺ οὐδὲν ἄξιον θανάτου ἐστὶν πεπραγμένον αὐτῷ· ... *absolutely nothing worthy of death has been done by him!* Perhaps things other than extreme degrees or measures may be emotively emphasized by C4. (There is also the use of οὐκ/χ ἰδού as a so-called rhetorical question marker, e.g., in Act 2:7 and often the LXX.)

C5 (ἰδού up to 86x; ἴδε up to 9x) [ἰδού/ἴδε + Clause, 'pay mental attention']: C5 resembles C3 and C1 in certain ways, while differing in others. C5 begins one or more sentences that report something the speaker wishes the hearer to pay special attention to. While C3 (and C1) instructs the hearer to pay *visual* attention to a state of affairs, C5, as a metaphorical extension of C3, instructs the hearer to pay *mental* attention. Thus, the particle in C5 is an 'attention pointer' or 'highlighter'. C5 diverges from C3 and C1 in that the particle is never used deictically to point to an entity in the here-and-now real world, and so it can be characterized as 'non-deictic'. Syntactically, much as in C3, the C5 particle always occurs at the beginning of a sentence that involves a typical predicator (verb or locative predicate), and so it appears that it comes in the same frozen clause-initial position as in C3. Depending on the context, C5 may be accompanied by special implicatures, including surprise. There is little constraint on the type of information structure the clause may have. Many cases have topic-comment function (e.g., in Mat 20:18 'we', marked alone on the verb, is the clause topic: ἰδοὺ ἀναβαίνομεν εἰς Ἱεροσόλυμα, καὶ ὁ υἱὸς τοῦ ἀνθρώπου παραδοθήσεται τοῖς ἀρχιερεῦσιν *Listen, we are going up to Jerusalem, and the Son of Man will be handed over to the chief priests ...*); others have constituent-focus function (where the focused constituent usually does not immediately follow the particle); and occasionally it coincides with (non-deictic) thetic function. Good translations include *pay attention, take note, listen, notice, remember (don't forget)*, metaphorical uses of *look, here,* and *there;* colloquial *hey!* is also possible; occasionally *certainly (indeed, yes),* and on rare occasion *hereby* (or *now*) are also appropriate.

Figure 1 below gives an overview of the five sets of uses, the basic split being between deictic/semi-deictic and what I am characterizing as 'non-deictic' uses.[13]

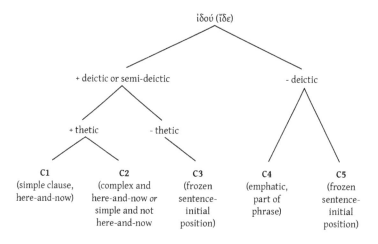

ἰδού (ἴδε)

+ deictic or semi-deictic   - deictic

+ thetic   - thetic

C1	C2	C3	C4	C5
(simple clause, here-and-now)	(complex and here-and-now *or* simple and not here-and-now	(frozen sentence-initial position)	(emphatic, part of phrase)	(frozen sentence-initial position)

Figure 1. The five sets of uses.

With C1, the speaker can physically point to the entity the speaker is bringing to the hearer's attention (there are no instances of C1 being used with 'hearing' or 'feeling' in the NT). Thus, C1 is only used in here-and-now situations. Similarly, C2a and C3 are only compatible with here-and-now situations. Other constructions, in contrast, are compatible with situations that are in one way or another removed from the here-and-now.

Some constructions resemble C1 in that they form a simple clause (ἰδού/ἴδε+NP$_{NOM}$) or a syntactic phrase (ἰδού/ἴδε+Phrase) with a focal constituent, whether it has thetic function (C2c-NP and C2e) or constituent-focus function (C4). In other thetics (C2a, C2b, C2d, and C2c), as well as in C3 and C5, there is a typical predicator (verb or locative) and the particle comes in a frozen position early in the sentence. It

---

[13] I put 'non-deictic' in quotes since C5 involves a metaphorical extension of deixis.

also seems likely that for some instances of C3 and C5 the particle can be syntactically independent from the clause that follows (and thus probably set off by a pause).

With the exception of C4b, the particles are used only with positive statements in the NT. That most uses are restricted to positive statements follows from the typical function of deictic constructions, which is (normally) to point out an entity or state of affairs that really exists or is happening. Although one might expect with more data to find more negative tokens with certain uses, I believe that C1 in particular is only compatible with positive statements.

An emotive element (e.g., surprise) is obvious in many uses of ἰδού, but not necessarily part of the meaning of all uses. In C4, where ἰδού in particular is used as an emphatic constituent-focus marker, the emotive element is most consistently present.

4

An In-depth Discussion of the Five Sets of Uses

We now turn to an in-depth discussion of each of the five sets of uses. It is hoped that the liberal illustrations in the pages that follow will be helpful for translators. I also include many vernacular translations (besides English, also French, Italian, German and occasionally Russian), noting when they are good models and when they are not.

An arrow (→) flags the primary list of passages under discussion in each section. The number of NT tokens (i.e., occurrences of a specific construction) is also given in the first paragraph of each major section. Since some tokens have more than one interpretation, if these subtotals were added together, the result would be greater than the absolute NT totals (ἰδού 200x and ἴδε 29x).

4.1 C1 – ἰδού and ἴδε as deictic thetic particles

In this use, ἰδού and ἴδε function as **deictic thetic** particles. In the NT, there are at least eleven C1 tokens with ἰδού and at least eight tokens with ἴδε.

C1 is central to all of the thetic uses (C1 and C2 and subconstructions), but I reason that C3, or some historically similar predecessor, is more basic to all uses (C1 through C5). In C1, the particle followed by a nominative case NP forms a simple predication: ἰδού/ἴδε–NP_{NOM} where NP_{NOM} is the subject. That the NP is not the grammatical object of the clause is unambiguously shown by its nominative case (at least for masculine and feminine nouns).[1] The construction is used to point out

---

[1] In other words, C1 ἰδού/ἴδε–NP_{NOM} is not an instance of the **perception imperative + object** construction (e.g., Luk 24:39 ἴδετε τὰς χεῖράς μου καὶ τοὺς πόδας μου [see! the.A.p.f hands.A.p.f and the.A.p.m feet.A.p.m] 'Look at my hands and feet!'). Although both constructions can be used in somewhat

to the hearer the presence of an entity in a here-and-now situation. The most plausible syntactic analysis of ἰδού and ἴδε is that they are **morphologically invariable monovalent verbs**, analogous to common uses of Italian *ecco* and French *voilà* (illustrated below),[2] in which case I would expect that there would be no pause between the Greek particle and NP_{NOM}, but instead this combination would have been uttered as a single intonation unit (Bailey 2009:321–323).[3]

Historically, I assume that this construction would have been based on a construction like *Look! (pause) Water!* which I have described elsewhere as a '**perception (verb) imperative + fragment**' construction (Bailey 2009:82–84, 315, 322–323). But, because of frequent use, this form was then grammaticalized into a single clause and (I would expect) spoken as one intonation unit, that is, without a pause. Thus, it would be analogous to *Look water!* and not *Look! (pause) water!* (There are many examples cross-linguistically of the imperative of a perception verb becoming a dedicated deictic thetic particle; see Bailey [2009:85] for examples from various languages, besides French *voilà* and *voici*, which

---

similar situations, there are important differences in their (a) syntax and (b) use conditions: (a) Besides the difference in case, the object construction could presumably (i) be negated, and (ii) the object itself could come before the verb. Although neither (i) nor (ii) are attested in the NT with an imperative of εἶδον/ὁράω, these assumptions are reasonable because preverbal objects occur occasionally with other moods (especially when contrastive, e.g., Act 22:9), and because other perception imperatives can have a preverbal object (e.g., Mat 21:33 Ἄλλην παραβολὴν ἀκούσατε. [another.A.s.f parable.A.s.f hear!] 'Hear another parable!'). (b) Concerning their use in discourse, while the perception imperative + object construction functions as a command, the deictic thetic construction is comparable to a demonstration (which is achieved by means of its pointing function), that is, the speaker shows the hearer what to view rather than ordering the hearer to view it. (For other differences in use, see Bailey 2009:82–84.)

[2]Bailey (2009:84–89) summarizes some basic uses of Italian *ecco* and French *voilà*. Hall (1953) described *ecco* (and Latin *ecce* and its other descendants) as 'morphologically invariable verbs' (*ecco* derives from the Latin demonstrative *ĕccu(m)* and not from a verb like 'see'). Lambrecht (2001:468) describes *voilà* as a 'predicator' that is 'monovalent'.

[3]Without native speakers it would be unwise to insist that ἰδού/ἴδε-NP_{NOM} could not have involved a pause after the particle. But if this Koine construction was comparable to the French and Italian constructions, then it would have lacked a pause. Generally speaking, in discourse studies, a pause is viewed as evidence for a syntactic disjuncture, but there are languages in the world where clause constructions and even NP constructions necessarily include a pause.

Lambrecht [2000:646] explains as frozen forms based on the imperative of *voir* 'to see' plus the demonstratives *là* 'there' and *(i)ci* 'here'.)

Unlike English *here/there* and French *voilà/voici*, Greek ἰδού and ἴδε are unmarked for near and far deixis, as is also Italian *ecco*.[4]

Mat 25:6[5] and **Act 8:36** illustrate two instances of C1:

Mat 25:6 μέσης δὲ νυκτὸς κραυγὴ γέγονεν·   ἰδοὺ ὁ
             mid- -   night   shout   3s.happened *   the.N

νυμφίος,   ἐξέρχεσθε εἰς ἀπάντησιν [αὐτοῦ].
bridegroom.N come.out!   to   meeting   him

nab: But at midnight there was a shout, 'Here's the
    bridegroom![6] Come out to meet him.'
GNB: Here is the bridegroom! ...
BFC: Voici le marié !
GND: Der Bräutigam kommt, ...
NRS: Look! Here is the bridegroom! ...
NVBTO & NRV: Ecco lo sposo, ...
LUT: Siehe, der Bräutigam kommt!

---

[4]Hebrew *hinnēh* (הִנֵּה) is also unmarked for near and far deixis (compare the nearby 'fire and wood' in Gen 22:7 with the far off but still visible city in Gen 19:20). When used as a deictic thetic particle in here-and-now situations, *hinnēh* also clearly functions as a predicator, forming a simple clause with its grammatical subject. That *hinnēh*+NP forms a syntactic unit (a simple clause) is clear because, when the NP is expressed pronominally, it becomes a suffix on *hinnēh*: thus הִנְנִי *hinənî* (or a pausal form, e.g., הִנֵּנִי *hinnēnî*), which is morphologically *hinnēh* + *nî* (הִנֵּה +1sg, e.g., Gen 22:1). Even though such suffixes are normally coreferential with an object (hence they are commonly called 'object suffixes'), I assume with Andersen (2003:53–54) that they are the real subject (i.e., express the grammatical relation of subject). Finally, as additional possible evidence that ἰδού/ἴδε-NP$_{NOM}$ forms a simple predication, it is noteworthy that the single Hebrew word, *hinənî* ('Here I am') was often rendered by the LXX as ἰδοὺ ἐγώ (e.g., Gen 22:1).
[5]In Mat 25:6, the text in Robinson & Pierpont reads ἰδοὺ ὁ νυμφίος ἔρχεται [behold the bridegroom comes], which would be an instance of C2a.
[6]In the context, other natural English renderings could include *It's the BRIDE-GROOM!* (Rich Rhodes, p.c.) and *The BRIDEGROOM's here!* Both renderings are functionally thetic but involve nuances that differ somewhat from those of the deictic thetic construction *Here's the BRIDEGROOM!*

Act 8:36 καί φησιν ὁ   εὐνοῦχος· ἰδοὺ ὕδωρ,   τί   κωλύει
and 3s.says the eunuch   *   water.N what 3s.prevents
με βαπτισθῆναι;
me to.be.baptized

nab: And the eunuch said, 'Here's water! (There's some
water!) What's to stop me from being baptized?'
GNB: Here is some water.
CEV: Look! Here is some water.
BFC, NVS78, FBJ: Voici de l'eau.
GND: Hier gibt es Wasser!
LUT: Siehe, da ist Wasser;
NIV: Look, here is water.
RSV: See, here is water!
LND, NVBTO, NRV: Ecco dell' acqua.
EIN: Siehe, hier ist Wasser.
ELB: Siehe, <da ist> Wasser!

Assuming in C1 that ἰδού/ἴδε–NP_{NOM} counts as a simple clause
spoken under one intonation contour (i.e., ἰδού would not be separated
from NP_{NOM} by a pause), and that ἰδού/ἴδε is its predicator (i.e.,
verb) and that NP_{NOM} is the subject, then this construction functions
as a prototypical deictic thetic construction (i.e., a sentence-focus
construction). Therefore, it would normally be quite appropriate to
render such clauses by an analogous deictic thetic construction in the
target language, such as, for the last example, by English *Here's (some)
water*. Furthermore, it seems unnecessary and redundant to preface the
English *Here's X* construction with *Look!* or *See!* (e.g., NRS, NIV, CEV,
RSV), or to preface the German *Hier/Da ist X* with *Siehe* (e.g., LUT, ELB,
EIN). These are actually 'double-translations' (or 'over-translations'). If
a translator is attempting to translate the meaning of **the construction**,
then it is usually enough to say *Here's X* or *There's X* (or *Hier/Da ist X*).[7] In
contrast, the Italian and French translators have done better. The cited
translations consistently make use of their standard deictic thetics (e.g.,
Act 8:36, *Voici de l'eau, Ecco dell' acqua*).

    Part of the confusion about C1's structure originates in a false
assumption held by some grammarians, that the copula εἰμί is expected
but unexpressed ('due to Semitic influence') even though, as BDF admits,
one finds ἰδού/ἴδε–NP_{NOM} in Classical Greek (BDF § 128; Robertson

---

[7] I am not saying a translator should never use two (or more) words in
English for one in Greek. It is just that many double-translations reveal
indecision and confusion on the part of translators. Since these particles are
plagued by such confusion, it is helpful to be strict with renderings until one
is clear on the major uses.

1934:391, 394–396; Turner 1963:296; Hf&S § 256d; a few examples will be illustrated below). This confusion is also revealed in how some call NP_{NOM} a 'nominal clause' (i.e., 'Nominalsatz', Fiedler 1969:21, 24, 31, etc.), which assumes a copula is missing. I would contend that *this construction never had and never needed a copula*. And this makes sense if we assume C1 developed from an *imperative+fragment* construction. To be sure, we will later discuss ἰδού sentences with εἰμί, but none are here-and-now deictic thetics (C1), and so ἰδού involves a different type of syntactic function (see e.g., Luk 2:25, C2c-FiniteV, in § 4.2.4.3; and Luk 13:30, C5, in § 4.5.3).

Typically in C1, NP_{NOM} is simple (noun +/–article), as in Mat 25:6 and Act 8:36 above. Occasionally, it may embed a relative clause that can either serve (i) to sufficiently identify the entity, as in **Mrk 16:6** (i.e., with a restrictive relative clause), or (ii) to make a subsequent predication about the newly introduced entity, as in **Luk 19:20** (i.e., it is incidental to the entity's identification).[8]

Mrk 16:6 οὐκ ἔστιν ὧδε· ἴδε ὁ   τόπος ὅπου ἔθηκαν αὐτόν.
         not 3s.is here * the.N place.N where 3p.put him

nab: He is not here. <u>There's the place where they laid him.</u>

Luk 19:20 κύριε, ἰδού ἡ   μνᾶ   σου ἣν   εἶχον
          sir   *   the.N mina.N of.you which I.had

ἀποκειμένην   ἐν σουδαρίῳ·
being.put.away in napkin

GNB: Sir, here is your gold coin; I kept it hidden in a handkerchief.

As a characteristic of deictic thetics, while uttering C1, the speaker can simultaneously point to the entity being presented. But like *ecco* in Italian, ἰδού and ἴδε are **underspecified** for near and far deixis. Thus, it is perfectly natural for translators of languages like English and French, whose deictic thetic systems *are* specified, to have to come down on one side of the fence or the other (*here's X* or *there's X*; *voilà* or *voici*).[9] This fact, that ἰδού and ἴδε are neutral in respect to distance, follows from the semantics of their parents, the imperatives meaning 'see/look', which are also neutral. If a Greek speaker needed to be more precise,

---

[8] Other tokens with a relative clause are Mat 12:18; Jhn 1:47; Heb 2:13. In Jhn 1:29, an arthrous participial clause is used in much the same way.

[9] *Voici* and *voilà* are both common renderings of ἰδού and ἴδε in BFC. For deictic thetics, *voici* is most frequently used (for ἰδού: Mat 25:6; Luk 19:20; Act 8:36; Act 9:10; for ἴδε: Mrk 16:6 (with *regardez*); Jhn 1:29; Jhn 1:36; Jhn 1:47; Jhn 19:26; Jhn 19:27), but *voilà* is only occasionally used (ἰδού: Jhn 19:5, ἴδε: Jhn 19:14).

he could add a locative adverb to C1 (see Luk 22:38, discussed in § 4.2.1: ἰδοὺ μάχαιραι ὧδε δύο. [behold swords here two]).

To be sure, C1 can be used in ways beyond merely pointing out to the hearer the presence of an entity in the here-and-now. Here I must mention some special **idiomatic** or **rhetorical uses**. For example, in the LXX version of **1Sa 22:12**, although on the surface Ahimelech might appear to be pointing out his presence to King Saul, it is clear that, like Hebrew הִנֵּנִי (hinənî, see footnote 4), so ἰδοὺ ἐγώ 'Here I am!' is being used as a polite way to say something like 'I am listening and paying attention to you.' Since the context implies that Ahimelech is already standing before Saul, literal translations like NRS (and NET, etc.) are inappropriate, as they imply that Saul is unaware of Ahimelech's presence. In contrast to the NRS, the paraphrases in GNB, NJPS, and NIV are better models as they attempt to translate the function of the utterance in natural English.

1Sa 22:12 καὶ εἶπεν   Σαουλ Ἄκουε δή,   υἱὲ Αχιτωβ.   καὶ εἶπεν
         and 3s.said Saul   listen! now son of.Ahitub and 3s.said

         Ἰδοὺ ἐγώ· λάλει, κύριε.
     *   I   speak! lord

> NRS: [11] The king [Saul] sent for the priest Ahimelech son of Ahitub and for all his father's house, the priests who were at Nob; and all of them came to the king. [12] Saul said, "Listen now, son of Ahitub." He answered, "Here I am, my lord."
>
> GNB: "At your service, sir,"
> NJPS, NIV: "Yes, my lord,"

See also Gen 37:13 where the construction is used by a speaker (Joseph) to indicate his agreement (affirmation) to obey his father's command.

The same use is recognizable at several points in the Jewish pseudepigraphical story *Joseph and Aseneth*,[10] which is in a LXX-style Koine.[11] The clearest examples occur in **J&A 4.3** and **J&A 4.6**, where

---

[10]There are different views about the form and history of the Greek text, as well as its relation to the various early translations, but several authorities date the Greek to sometime between 100 B.C.E. and 200 C.E. See Burchard (1985:187–188) and Cook (1984:468–470). Cook's translation follows Philonenko's edition (1968); both use a system of versification different from the one in Burchard's edition (Burchard et al 2003). See also Burchard (2005).

[11]Many have underscored the influence of the LXX on *Joseph and Aseneth* (see e.g., Humphrey 2000:31–32). In comparison to NT writers, the way ἰδού is used in *Joseph and Aseneth*, especially in Burchard's edition, resembles most closely Matthew's use. As illustrated here and in subsequent sections, we

Pentephres wishes to get the attention of his daughter, Aseneth, in order to tell her something. In the edition of Burchard et al. (2003, hereafter 'Burchard's edition'), she answers her father twice by saying ἰδοὺ ἐγώ. Since both occurrences come in the same scene where her father is already aware of his daughter and interacting with her, it is clear that the construction is meant to indicate the speaker's attention and readiness and not to point out her presence. Thus, Burchard's translation (1985), cited below, is unnatural.

J&A 4.3 καὶ εἶπε   Πεντεφρῆς τῇ θυγατρὶ   αὐτοῦ Ἀσενέθ·
and 3s.said Pentephres to daughter of.him Aseneth

"τέκνον μου". ἡ   δὲ εἶπεν· "ἰδοὺ ἐγώ κύριε".
child   of.me she -   3s.said *   I   lord

4.6 καὶ κατεφίλησεν αὐτὴν καὶ εἶπεν   αὐτῇ· "τέκνον μου
and 3s.kissed   her   and 3s.said to.her child   of.me

Ἀσενέθ". ⁶ καὶ <αὐτὴ> εἶπεν "ἰδοὺ ἐγώ κύριε. λαλησάτω
Aseneth and she   3s.said *   I   lord 3s.speak!

δὴ ὁ   κύριός μου καὶ πατήρ μου".
now the lord   of.me and father of.me

1. And she [=Aseneth] hurried and went down the stairs from the upper floor, and came to her father and mother and greeted them and kissed them. And Pentephres and his wife rejoiced over her[12] daughter (with) great joy, because they saw her adorned like a bride of God. [...] ¶ 3. And Pentephres said to his daughter Aseneth, "My child." And she said, "Behold, (here) I (am), my lord." 4. And he said to her, "Sit down between us, and I will tell you what I have to say." ¶ 5. And Aseneth sat between her father and mother. And Pentephres, her father, with his right hand grasped the right hand of his daughter and kissed it and said to her, "My child, Aseneth." 6. And she said, "Behold, (here) I (am), lord. Let my lord and my father speak up." (Burchard 1985)

Nevertheless, it is certain that Hebrew הִנֵּנִי (hinənî) and LXX ἰδοὺ ἐγώ can also be used by a speaker to *both* point out his presence and convey readiness (to listen or obey, etc.). This is clear in **1Sa 3:4–10**, where the Lord repeatedly calls out to Samuel, who is sleeping in the temple, and Samuel repeatedly answers by saying הִנֵּנִי / ἰδοὺ ἐγώ. Since

---

find clear instances of C1 (with ἐγώ), C2b, C2c-NP, C2c-FiniteV, C3, and C5, all of which are well represented in Matthew. In contrast, I found no clear instances of C4a and C4b in either *Joseph and Aseneth* or Matthew.
[12] 'Her' is evidently a slip in the translation as all the editions read αὐτῶν 'their'.

Samuel does not yet recognize the voice of the Lord (see v 7), he runs
to the priest Eli (v 5), who is asleep in another room. In the first
instance (v 4), since Samuel is apparently still in his bed, it may be
that the construction more purely indicates his attention and readiness,
equivalent to 'Yes, sir'. But once Samuel rises and runs off to Eli's room
to present himself to Eli (from v 5 on), it is easier to see the deictic sense
of the construction, while recognizing that it simultaneously indicates
Samuel's attention and readiness.

1Sa 3:4 καὶ ἐκάλεσεν κύριος Σαμουηλ Σαμουηλ·   καὶ εἶπεν
         and 3s.called Lord   Samuel   Samuel   and 3s.said

Ἰδοὺ ἐγώ.
*   I

5 καὶ ἔδραμεν πρὸς Ηλι καὶ εἶπεν Ἰδοὺ ἐγώ, ὅτι
   and 3s.ran   to   Eli and 3s.said *   I   because

κέκληκάς με·
2s.called.Prf me

NRS: [1] Now the boy Samuel was ministering to the Lord under
Eli. The word of the Lord was rare in those days; visions were
not widespread. [2] At that time Eli, whose eyesight had begun
to grow dim so that he could not see, was lying down in his
room; [3] the lamp of God had not yet gone out, and Samuel
was lying down in the temple of the Lord, where the ark of
God was. [4] Then the Lord called, "Samuel! Samuel!" and he
said, "<u>Here I am</u>!" [5] and ran to Eli, and said, "<u>Here I am</u>, for
you called me." But he said, "I did not call; lie down again." So
he went and lay down. [6] The Lord called again, "Samuel!"
Samuel got up and went to Eli, and said, "Here I am, for you
called me." But he said, "I did not call, my son; lie down
again." [7] Now Samuel did not yet know the Lord, and the
word of the Lord had not yet been revealed to him. [8] The
Lord called Samuel again, a third time. And he got up and
went to Eli, and said, "Here I am, for you called me." Then Eli
perceived that the Lord was calling the boy. [9] Therefore Eli
said to Samuel, "Go, lie down; and if he calls you, you shall
say, 'Speak, Lord, for your servant is listening.' " So Samuel
went and lay down in his place. [10] Now the Lord came and
stood there, calling as before, "Samuel! Samuel!" And Samuel
said, "Speak, for your servant is listening."

Returning to the NT, in Act 9:10, when the Lord first calls to Ananias
in a vision, Ananias answers with ἰδοὺ ἐγώ, κύριε. Assuming this answer
reflects the LXX idiom (and ultimately the Hebrew idiom), Ananias

would be primarily indicating his readiness to listen and serve, in which case *Here I am, Lord!* in English is infelicitous (NRS, NET, GNB, CEV; contrast *Yes, Lord,* in NLT and NIV).

Luk 1:38 (equally 'Hebraic') presents a somewhat different special use of C1. In response to the angel who has been addressing her (and well aware of her presence), Mary indicates her readiness to submit to the Lord's will by referring to herself in the third person: Ἰδοὺ ἡ δούλη κυρίου literally, 'Here (is) the slave of the Lord' (compare 2Sa 9:6 and 1Sa 25:41). The NRS clarifies the referent by adding *I am*, but the translation is still unnatural, in contrast to the GNB, which is more appropriate.

Luk 1:38 ἰδοὺ ἡ   δούλη κυρίου· γένοιτό   μοι
       sir   the.N slave.N of.Lord 3s.may.it.happen to.me

       κατὰ   τὸ ῥῆμά σου.
       according.to the word of.you;

> NRS: [31] And now, you will conceive ... and bear a son, and you will name him Jesus. ... [37] For nothing will be impossible with God." [38] Then Mary said, "<u>Here am I, the servant of the Lord</u>; let it be with me according to your word."
>
> GNB: "<u>I am the Lord's servant</u>," said Mary; "may it happen to me as you have said."

→ With ἰδού, there are at least eleven C1 tokens in the NT—the footnotes indicate some other special uses: Mat 11:19 and ‖Luk 7:34[13] (following BDAG, ἄνθρωπος φάγος is one NP, 'a glutton'); Mat 12:18 (LXX quote); Mat 12:49; Mat 25:6; Luk 1:38; Luk 19:20; Jhn 19:5; Act 8:36; Act 9:10; Heb 2:13 (LXX quote).

→ With ἴδε, C1 occurs at least eight times: Mrk 3:34; Mrk 16:6; Jhn 1:29; Jhn 1:36; Jhn 1:47 (with a relative clause); Jhn 19:14; Jhn 19:26;[14] Jhn 19:27.

C1 tokens occur in both Classical and secular Koine texts, some of which are cited in the literature. Several mention ἰδοὺ χελιδών 'behold a swallow' (e.g., Meisterhans and Schwyzer 1900:203), which is an impressive token from an Attic vase dated from about 510 B.C.E. (Kim

---

[13] Although Mat 11:19 and ‖Luk 7:34 (ἰδοὺ ἄνθρωπος φάγος καὶ οἰνοπότης 'Here is a glutton and a drunkard') at face value function to introduce into the audience's awareness someone who is 'a glutton and a drunkard', they are really being used rhetorically in order to ridicule Jesus.

[14] Jesus' two statements from the cross to his mother and to 'the disciple whom he loved' (Jhn 19:26 'Here's your son', and Jhn 19:27 'Here's your mother') are best seen as performative speech acts, in that by making these statements, the speaker causes something to happen (e.g., the first can be paraphrased as 'I hereby declare this man from now on to be your son'). Many manuscripts read ἰδού instead of ἴδε in one or both of these tokens.

2017), illustrated in **figure 2** in photographs and a line drawing of the same scene (parts A, B and C):

A

B

C

Figure 2. The 'Swallow Vase': photograph and line drawing.
(A) and (C) photograph and close-up: Attic red-figure pelike, circa
510 BCE. The State Hermitage Museum, St. Petersburg, Inv. no. GR-8057
(B-2352). Photograph © The State Hermitage Museum.
Photo by Yuri Molodkovets.
(B) line drawing by H. Anh Thu Nguyen, reproduced with permission
from Kim 2017, fig. 9(b).

The clause in question on the vase is undoubtedly intended as the first utterance of a rapid dialogue. It is uttered by the male youth seated on the left, who is pointing out the appearance of a bird: ΙΔΟ ΧΕΛΙΔΟΝ = ἰδοὺ χελιδών '(Look) There's a swallow!' (where χελιδών is feminine and nominative); there is no doubt that the utterance is meant to convey wonder and surprise. Then the bearded man, in the center, exclaims in agreement: ΝΕ ΤΟΝ ΗΕΡΑΚΛΕΑ = νὴ τὸν Ἡρακλέα '(Yes) by Heracles!' And the young boy standing on the right makes his own observation, using a pronoun to refer to the now activated entity: ΗΑΥΤΕΙ = αὐτηΐ[15] 'There she is!' Finally, tucked between the bearded man and the boy is the important recognition of the arrival of spring, which sums up the scene; in harmony with Kim (2017:163) and others, this would be a title or comment offered by the vase painter: ΕΑΡ ΕΔΕ = ἔαρ ἤδη '(It's) spring already!'[16]

Fiedler (1969:17–18) mentions **Aristophanes' *Lysistrata* 925**. The speaker, Myrrhine, has just said she would run off and fetch a sleeping mat (*cushions* in Lindsay's translation). When she returns, she presents them to Cinesias, her husband, saying:

Lys. 925 ἰδοὺ ψίαθος: κατάκεισο
*   sleeping.mat.N.s.f   lie.down!

<u>Here the cushions are</u>. Lie down … (Lindsay, Perseus)

One finds three tokens in a row in **Epictetus' *Discourses* 3.23.20** (written down by Arrian early second century C.E.). 'Sounds' and 'disposition' are atypical because they are 'second order' entities, that is, they are not 'first order' (i.e., concrete) entities but events or states of affairs[17] (these examples also involve a rhetorical use since Epictetus is quoting the praises that his conceited audience would like to hear).

---

[15]The form αὐτηΐ is the demonstrative pronoun αὕτη plus 'the deictic suffix -ί,' which adds 'emphasis' (Smyth § 333g). This utterance functions as a deictic thetic hybrid (it is a hybrid because, although it is presentational, the subject is a 'ratified topic', i.e., fully activated and topical; see footnote 143 in ch. 4). See the similar use in Aristophanes' *Clouds* 213–214 (Στρεψιάδης - ἀλλ' ἡ Λακεδαίμων ποῦ 'σθ'; Μαθητής - ὅπου 'στίν; αὐτηΐ. 'Strepsiades: But where is Lacedaemon [on the map]? Disciple: Where is it? Here it is!' [Hickie, Perseus]).

[16]As a statement indicating the arrival of spring, see the discussion in Bailey (2009:206–212) of 'time and atmospheric thetics' in Greek and the literature cited there.

[17]See Bailey (2009:46–52) for literature and discussion of different types of entities, including first order, second order, third order, and fourth order entities.

Ep. 3.23.20 ἰδοὺ φωναὶ   φιλοσόφου,   ἰδοὺ διάθεσις
           *   sounds.N.p.f of.philosopher *   disposition.N.s.f
           ὠφελήσοντος   ἀνθρώπους: ἰδοὺ
           aiding.Prt.Fut.G.s.f men.A   *
           ἀκηκοὼς   ἄνθρωπος λόγου,
           having.heard.Prt.Prf.N.s.m man.N.s.m word.G

> <u>Here is the language of a philosopher!</u> <u>Here is the</u>
> <u>disposition of one who is to be beneficial to mankind!</u>
> <u>Here is the man, attentive to discourses</u>, who has read the
> works of the Socratic philosophers … (Higginson, Perseus)

(At the end of § 4.3, I mention two more instances of C1 from the Koine novel by Chariton.)

What is the difference between ἰδού and ἴδε in C1? Given the etymology of ἰδού, one might expect C1 to involve wonder, surprise, or some other emotive element, and that ἴδε would lack such feelings. But I have found no clear pattern in the NT data to support such a claim. In fact, John (who generally avoids ἰδού) uses ἴδε in contexts that seem emotional or where something unexpected is being introduced. This is illustrated by John the Baptist's bold statement in **Jhn 1:29** (see also Jhn 1:36; Jhn 1:47; perhaps Jhn 19:14).

Jhn 1:29 ἴδε ὁ   ἀμνὸς τοῦ θεοῦ   ὁ   αἴρων   τὴν
         *   the Lamb -   of.God the.one taking.away the
         ἁμαρτίαν τοῦ   κόσμου.
         sin   of.the world

> NRS: The next day he saw Jesus coming toward him and declared, "<u>Here is the Lamb of God</u> who takes away the sin of the world!"

Nor do all instances of C1 with ἰδού clearly involve surprise or another strong emotion, even if such nuances are often present. To be sure, 'Here's the language of a philosopher!' (Epictetus) entails (feigned) wonder, and 'Here's the bridegroom!' (Mat 25:6) entails surprise (for the sleeping maidens). But 'Sir, here's your gold [which you requested]' (Luk 19:20), 'Here's a sleeping mat [that I said I would fetch]' (Aristophanes), and 'Here's the fire and wood' (Gen 22:7)[18] do not seem to involve

---

[18] In a recent article, Miller-Naudé and van der Merwe (2011) propose that Hebrew *hinnēh*, in its most basic (i.e., 'central') use, is 'mirative' (i.e., indicates surprise or unexpectedness), although they admit that in about a third of the tokens, including even tokens that are examples of the basic use (p. 64), there is no clear sense of surprise or unexpectedness. My take on Hebrew *hinnēh* is much more in lines with Andersen's (2003) proposal that in its most basic function it is a 'perspectival presentative predicator' (see

unexpectedness, surprise, or any other marked emotion. Thus, I conclude that surprise and other emotions are conversational implicatures (to be inferred from context on a case-by-case basis).

In contrast, clear patterns emerge when we look at the distribution of ἴδε and ἰδού in C1 tokens among NT writers. In Matthew, Luke, and Acts only ἰδού is used, and in Mark only ἴδε is used. This includes one set of parallel passages ('Here are my mother and my brothers'): in Mat 12:49 ἰδού occurs, but in Mrk 3:34 ἴδε.[19] The difference seems to be a matter of register or idiolect, or, as Fiedler and Johannessohn argued, the choice of ἰδού may be an attempt to imitate LXX style.

In John, however, ἴδε occurs six times and ἰδού once (at least according to the Nestle-Aland text). The sole use of ἰδού, Jhn 19:5 ('Here is the man!') occurs when Pilate presents Jesus before the angry crowd. It stands out because Pilate later presents Jesus again to the people using

---

also Lambdin's statement [1971 § 135] that 'the clearest and most basic use of הִנֵּה is as a predicator of existence ... [where] ... it emphasizes the immediacy, the here-and-now-ness, of the situation'). In other words, in its most basic use *hinnēh*, like ἰδού, functions as the 'predicator' (i.e., a morphologically invariable monovalent verb) of a deictic thetic construction (i.e., it has deictic-presentational function). Moreover, as with Koine C1, any sense of surprise with *hinnēh* is a conversational implicature (i.e., due to the specific context it is used in and not inherent to the meaning of the construction—thus, in some tokens it is there and in others it is not). But, despite such similarities between *hinnēh* and ἰδού (and ἴδε) in their most basic uses and in some extended uses, there are many differences. For example, a common (extended) use of *hinnēh* that I have not found clearly represented in the NT is where (as Miller-Naudé and van der Merwe convincingly show [2011:74–77]), *hinnēh* functions to establish the logical grounds for a (usually subsequent) utterance (Lambdin [1971:169–171] makes a similar point; the use of *hinnēh* to set up a condition, translatable by 'if', also seems related—e.g. see Lev 13:5 and many more verses in that chapter, where *hinnēh* is woodenly translated by the LXX as ἰδού). This grounds-establishing function of *hinnēh* is even attested with some frequency with the most basic use (what I am calling a deictic thetic), as illustrated by Gen 22:7, which I cited above: הִנֵּה הָאֵשׁ וְהָעֵצִים וְאַיֵּה הַשֶּׂה לְעֹלָה׃ = *hinnēh hāʾēš wǝhāʿēṣîm wǝʾayyēh haśśeh lǝʿōlâ* [behold the-fire and-the-wood and-where the-lamb for-burnt.offering]. NET: *Isaac said to his father Abraham, "My father?" "What is it, my son?" he replied. "Here is the fire and the wood," Isaac said, "but where is the lamb for the burnt offering?"* The LXX expressed this by a typical C1 construction: Ἰδοὺ τὸ πῦρ καὶ τὰ ξύλα· ποῦ ἐστιν τὸ πρόβατον τὸ εἰς ὁλοκάρπωσιν; [* the fire.N and the.N woods.N where 3S.is the sheep the for burnt.offering].

[19] For non-C1 uses, compare also Mat 12:2 with ‖Mrk 2:24, and Mat 24:23 with ‖Mrk 13:21. Note that Mark uses in close succession both ἰδού (Mrk 3:32) and ἴδε (Mrk 3:34) in similar statements, but only the latter is C1.

ἴδε (Jhn 19:14: 'Here is your king'). Various reasons for the difference have been suggested. If understood ironically (Danker 1970:511), ἰδού in Jhn 19:5 could be an attempt at mock pageantry, while simultaneously alluding to a LXX passage (unbeknownst to Pilate!; see Isa 40:9, Zec 6:12, and Exo 24:8, all with ἰδού).[20]

4.2 C2 – Other thetic constructions

C2 covers various **thetic** constructions that syntactically or conceptually diverge from the more basic construction, C1.[21] Given the variety and number of subconstructions, this turns out to be the most complex set of the five sets of uses. In the NT, there are about eighty-five tokens with ἰδού and at most one token with ἴδε.

Syntactically, I find two types of C2 constructions: (i) ones like C1, where ἰδού alone functions as the predicator; and (ii) more complex ones, which in addition to ἰδού contain a typical predicator, such as a finite verb or locative predicate.

The **conceptual** resemblance to C1 varies. C2a is most like C1 because it is used deictically to introduce here-and-now states of affairs, where the speaker can (normally) point at the entity being introduced. Most other constructions in the C2 family can be described as 'semi-deictic' or 'imagined deictic'. The imagined deictic use is in fact the most common, what I call the **narrative deictic thetic** or C2c.

There is at most only one instance of C2 with ἴδε (Jhn 11:3, discussed in § 4.2.3). But see § 4.4.4 on Mrk 13:21, which is a hybrid involving a C2a skeleton overlaid by a constituent-focus structure.

4.2.1 C2a – Deictic thetics with a finite verb or locative predicate

C2a tokens share with C1 that they introduce here-and-now states of affairs into the discourse. But unlike C1, they all have a typical predicator, either a finite verb or locative predicate. → There are only five possible tokens: Mat 7:4; Mat 12:2; Mat 21:5 (LXX quote); Luk 22:38; Jhn 12:15 (LXX quote).

Jhn 12:15, a LXX quote, illustrates a case where I assume that the predicator is a finite verb and that ἰδού functions as just a deictic

---

[20] These passages are suggested in Walter Bauer's John commentary, according to Fiedler (1969:39).

[21] While nearly all subtypes resemble C1 in having thetic subjects, one rare construction, '*ἰδού+clause with Ø subject*' (§ 4.2.4.4), lacks a subject altogether.

particle (analogous to an adverb) and not as a predicator. The GNB
makes use of a deictic thetic, as does the French FBJ.[22]

Jhn 12:15 ἰδοὺ ὁ   βασιλεύς σου   ἔρχεται, καθήμενος ἐπὶ πῶλον
          *   the king   of.you 3s.comes sitting   on foal
          ὄνου.
          of.donkey

> GNB: <u>Here comes your king</u>, riding on a young donkey.
> FBJ: Voici que ton roi vient, monté sur un petit d'ânesse.

Other tokens are open to multiple interpretations. For example, **Mat
12:2** can be interpreted in various ways: (i) as a deictic thetic (C2a): *Here
are your disciples doing what is not lawful on the Sabbath!* (compare the use of
C1 in Mat 11:19, another implicit rebuke);[23] (ii) as an instance of C3: ἰδού
would be deictic (comparable to *There!*) but syntactically independent
from what follows (a topic-comment structure, with topical subject);
this interpretation is most clearly reflected by JBP. A translation like
Look in the NRS (also NIV) is ambiguous since it could be interpreted as
either C3 or C5.[24]

Mat 12:2 ἰδοὺ οἱ   μαθηταί σου   ποιοῦσιν ὃ   οὐκ
          *   the disciples of.you 3p.do   what not
          ἔξεστιν   ποιεῖν ἐν σαββάτῳ.
          3s.is.permitted to.do on Sabbath

> NRS: [1] ... Jesus went through the grainfields on the sabbath;
> his disciples were hungry, and they began to pluck heads of
> grain and to eat. [2] When the Pharisees saw it, they said to

---

[22] This token is actually used in an extended way in that in both John and
its original context (Zec 9:9), it presumably counted as a prophecy about
the future. However, for our purposes we can assume that it is used as if it
were pointing to something in the here-and-now. (So, this use is comparable
to C2c.)

[23] Although FBJ renders Mat 12:2 as a *voilà* deictic thetic (*Voilà tes disciples qui
font ce qu'il n'est pas permis de faire pendant le sabbat !*), Paul Solomiac (p.c.)
informs me that this construction is not ideal here since it may suggest
the Pharisees just accused Jesus of being careless about the law and so this
voilà sentence would be an illustration thereof. BFC's *regarde* seems more
appropriate (*Regarde, tes disciples font ce que notre loi ne permet pas le jour du
sabbat !*).

[24] Interpreting this as (iii) an instance of C5 (the attention pointer, 'take
note') is suggested by GNB ('Look, it is against our Law for your disciples
to do this on the Sabbath!'). But this interpretation seems least likely to
me assuming that both the Pharisees and Jesus can presently see what the
disciples are doing.

him, "<u>Look, your disciples are doing what is not lawful to do</u>
<u>on the sabbath.</u>"
　JBP: "<u>There, you see</u>," they remarked to Jesus, "your disciples
　　are doing what the Law forbids them to do on the Sabbath."
　In another example, **Luk 22:38**, we have the locative ὧδε 'here',
which is presumably the main predicate. Since ἰδού is unspecified for
near/far deixis, ὧδε specifies near deixis.

Luk 22:38 οἱ　δὲ　εἶπαν,　κύριε,　ἰδοὺ μάχαιραι ὧδε δύο.
　　　　　they and 3p.said Lord　*　　swords　here two

　CEV: <u>The disciples said</u>, "Lord, <u>here are two swords!</u>"
　BFC: "Seigneur, voici deux épées."

　Mat 7:4 appears to be another deictic thetic with a locative predicate
constituent:

Mat 7:4 ἄφες ἐκβάλω　τὸ κάρφος ἐκ　τοῦ ὀφθαλμοῦ σου,　καὶ
　　　　allow I.take.out the speck　from the eye　　　of.you and

　　ἰδοὺ ἡ　δοκὸς　　ἐν τῷ ὀφθαλμῷ σοῦ;
　　*　 the beam.of.wood in the eye　　of.you?

　RSV: [3] Why do you see the speck that is in your brother's eye,
　　but do not notice the log that is in your own eye? [4] Or how
　　can you say to your brother, 'Let me take the speck out of
　　your eye,' <u>when there is the log in your own eye</u>?
　NIV: ... when all the time there is a plank in your own eye?
　CEV: ... when you don't see the log in your own eye?

　This token is atypical because the identity of ἡ δοκός 'the beam'
and its presence in the eye of one of the communicators has just been
established (v 3). Therefore, given the context, this token functions as a
'reminder' (paraphrasable as *Aren't you forgetting something?! There's the*
beam ...). Some translations gloss over this subtlety, using *a* instead of
the (e.g., NIV, GNB). The CEV's circumlocution is noteworthy: *you don't*
see plus perception report. The RSV effectively uses an English reminder
construction, which, technically speaking, is not deictic. Replacing *the*
beam in RSV by *that beam* (Tony Pope, p.c.) could rescue the deictic
element, but a pure deictic thetic in English would not be very idiomatic:
Here's the beam in your own eye.

4.2.2   C2b – Thetics involving spatial or temporal proximity

Occasionally, ἰδού thetics introduce something that is either spatially or
temporally near.[25] These tokens diverge from the prototype, C1, in that

---

[25] The linguistic relationship between time and space is well known; times
are often treated linguistically as metaphorical spaces (Lakoff and Johnson
1980 and Lakoff 1987). In this section, we will see that sometimes it is hard

the states of affairs are not quite here-and-now, yet they are still in some sense 'near'. There are ten C2b tokens. Most are not readily translated by deictic thetics in English.

Five NT tokens introduce a state of affairs that is **located nearby**. → Two have a verb as its predicator (Mat 26:46 and ||Mrk 14:42), and three have a locative phrase. In one, the locative by itself is the predicate, but in two, there is also a finite verb: Mat 12:47 and ||Mrk 3:32; Act 5:9 (locative predicate).

For example, in **Mat 12:47**, Jesus' mother and brothers are asserted to be standing outside (presumably out of sight);[26] and in **Act 5:9** (a warning), another set of entities (also out of sight) are said to be nearby, that is, 'at the door'. In Act 5:9, what is spatially near is also, by implication, temporally near: what is at the door will soon come in and confront the hearer. From the hearer's perspective, the (nearby) presence of the entity is unexpected. The NRS uses *Look* in these, which is emotionally flat. The GND has inverted order, which encourages a focal reading of the postverbal subject *die Leute*. Such inversion also works well in English; my translation (nab) is an example of Lakoff's 'Presentational Deictic', which with the addition of *very*, conveys the surprise and vividness often associated with ἰδού.

Mat 12:47 ἰδοὺ ἡ   μήτηρ   σου   καὶ οἱ ἀδελφοί σου   ἔξω
     *   the mother of.you and the brothers of.you outside

ἑστήκασιν   ζητοῦντές σοι λαλῆσαι.
3p.are.standing.Prf seeking   you to.speak

NRS: [46] While he was still speaking to the crowds, his mother and his brothers were standing outside, wanting to speak to him. [47] Someone told him, "Look, your mother and your brothers are standing outside, wanting to speak to you."

Act 5:9 ἰδοὺ οἱ   πόδες τῶν   θαψάντων   τὸν ἄνδρα   σου
     *   the feet of.those having.buried the husband of.you

ἐπὶ τῇ θύρᾳ καὶ ἐξοίσουσίν   σε.
at the door and 3p.will.carry.out you

NRS: Look, the feet of those who have buried your husband are at the door, and they will carry you out.

nab: There at the door are the very men who just buried your husband.

---

to distinguish what is spatially near from what is temporally near, the two merging into each other.

[26]The parallel passages differ in interesting ways. ||Mrk 3:32 has not *intransitive* 'stand' but *transitive* ζητοῦσίν 'they are asking for'. ||Luk 8:20 lacks ἰδού altogether, and the locative follows the verb: ... ἑστήκασιν ἔξω.

GND: Vor der Tür stehen schon die Leute, die deinen Mann
   begraben haben.

BFC: Écoute, ceux qui ont enterré ton mari sont déjà à la porte.

Mat 26:46 (and ‖Mrk 14:42 with preverbal subject) has the perfect
verb ἤγγικεν as its predicator. Some translations (GNB and NIV) have
used deictic thetics, although the GNB is problematic. The GNB (and
CEV) suggests that the one who would betray Jesus was already present
and visible (e.g., GNB: *here is the man*), which would require this to be
C2a (pure here-and-now). But as Tony Pope has noted (p.c.), the perfect
form ἤγγικεν more likely means that Judas 'is almost here' (Z&G suggest
'*virtually* have come' for v 45), or colloquially, 'is just around the corner',
and it would imply that the situation must be addressed immediately;
in this case we can speculate that Jesus may not have been able to see
the approaching crowd, but he may have heard it and then inferred who
would be leading it. The GNB (and NIV) interpretation of the present
participle ὁ παραδιδούς is also problematic (GNB: *is the man who is
betraying me*). Rather than referring to the true present, here and in v 25
it refers to the immediate future: 'the one who is to betray' (Zerwick
§ 283, similarly CEV). In this case, a translation like *Here comes the one
who will betray me* would work if it could be construed as one of Lakoff's
'Perceptual' deictic constructions (e.g., *Here comes the beep*). But a clearer
English rendering would be something like (nab) *There, the one who will
betray me is about to appear.*

Mat 26:46 ἰδοὺ ἤγγικεν   ὁ   παραδιδούς με.
   *   3s.has.drawn.near.Prf the.one betraying   me

   GNB: [46] Get up, let us go. <u>Look, here is the man who is
      betraying me!</u> [47] Jesus was still speaking when Judas, one
      of the twelve disciples, arrived.

   NIV: Here comes my betrayer!

   CEV: The one who will betray me is already here.

In *Joseph and Aseneth*, there are two tokens with verbal predicators
in Burchard's edition, both announcing the arrival of Joseph, who is
near but out of sight: J&A 5.1 (with perfect ἔστηκεν: 'Behold, Joseph
is standing before the doors of our court'); and J&A 19.1 (with present
ἵσταται: 'Behold, Joseph is standing at the doors of our court').

There is also one token with a locative predicate in Burchard's
edition, **J&A 24.7**. Pharaoh's son presents to Gad and Dan what is both
an offer and a warning, as he wants to trick them into killing Joseph so
he can take Aseneth as his wife. Pharaoh's son essentially claims that
'Blessing and Death' are near (physically and/or temporally).[27]

---

[27] Philonenko's edition lacks ἰδού but is still thetic: εὐλογία καὶ θάνατος
πρόκειται πρὸ προσώπου ὑμῶν. [blessing.N.s.f and death.N.s.m 3S.are.pre-

J&A 24.7   "ἰδοὺ εὐλογία   καὶ θάνατος   πρὸ
Burchard   *   blessing.N.s.f and death.N.s.m before

             προσώπου ὑμῶν.
             face.G   you.G.p

             [4] And Dan and Gad [...] said to [Pharaoh's son] "Let our
             lord say to his servants what he wants [...]" [5] And
             Pharaoh's son rejoiced exceedingly [...] 7. [and ...
             then] lied to them and said "<u>Behold, blessing and
             death (are set) before your face</u>. Take now rather the
             blessing and not the death, because you are powerful
             men and will not die like women, but be brave and
             avenge yourself on your enemies [i.e., on Joseph]."
             (Burchard 1985)

There are five NT tokens that introduce states of affairs that the
speaker asserts will **certainly** come about in either the imminent or
more distant **future:** → Luk 23:29; Jhn 16:32; Heb 8:8 (LXX quote); Jas
5:9;[28] Rev 9:12. All these tokens have finite verbs. States of affairs that
belong to the certain future are unlike the prototype since they are not
here-and-now and so cannot be seen. Yet, they resemble the prototype
in that they are certain and will inevitably be 'here'. 'Certainty' seems to
be implied in the prototypical use of every deictic thetic (see on example
(6) in § 2.2). (Besides these NT tokens, see also J&A 18.1b, with ἔρχεται,
which refers to the near future: 'Behold Joseph the Powerful One of God
is coming to us today.')

Rev 9:12 introduces a set of 'second order' entities (the events, 'two
woes') that will certainly happen in the future (present tense ἔρχεται
refers to the future).[29] In two other tokens, it is a time entity itself ('hour'
or 'days') that is being introduced, and the time in turn indicates when
some state of affairs will occur in the future (Luk 23:29; Jhn 16:32): In

---

sented before face.G you.G.p]. Both editions could be translated by inverted
constructions in English: *(Here) before you are (two choices,) blessing and death.*
[28]Jas 5:9 is a warning (ἰδοὺ ὁ κριτὴς πρὸ τῶν θυρῶν ἔστηκεν. [* the.N judge.N
before the doors 3S.is.standing.Prf] NLT: *look—the Judge is standing at the
door!*). According to Louw and Nida (1988 § 67.58) πρὸ τῶν θυρῶν is an idiom
that indicates that something will happen 'soon' or 'very soon' (see GNB:
The Judge is near, ready to appear). In contrast, the phrase ἐπὶ τῇ θύρᾳ in Act
5:9, another warning that we just discussed, refers to a real door, and so I
categorized this with the other tokens that introduce a state of affairs that
is located nearby.
[29]See Zerwick § 278 on the present (especially with ἔρχομαι) with future
meaning; see Pope (1988) for a more detailed discussion of the present with
future meaning as well as for the present used for inevitable states of affairs
(pp. 31–33). The particle ἰδού here undoubtedly underscores that certainty.

Luk 23:29, the (probably distant) time is introduced when people will say something (note NRS's *surely*, which brings across the certainty of the states of affairs). In English, there is no deictic thetic construction compatible for either passage. But NVS78 makes use of *voici* in Rev 9:12.

Rev 9:12 Ἡ οὐαὶ ἡ μία ἀπῆλθεν· ἰδοὺ ἔρχεται   ἔτι δύο
     the woe - first passed.Aor *   3s.comes.Pres yet two

οὐαὶ μετὰ ταῦτα.
woes after these.things

> Rich Rhodes (p.c.): The first horror is past; <u>two more horrors are right behind</u>!
>
> GNB: The first horror is over; <u>after this there are still two more horrors to come</u>.
>
> NVS78: Le premier malheur est passé. <u>Voici que</u> deux malheurs viennent encore après cela.
>
> BFC: Le premier malheur est passé; après cela, deux autres malheurs doivent encore venir.

Luk 23:29 ὅτι   ἰδοὺ ἔρχονται   ἡμέραι ἐν αἷς
     because *   3p.are.coming.Pres days   in which

ἐροῦσιν· μακάριαι ...
3p.will.say blessed

> NRS: <u>For the days are surely coming</u> when they will say, 'Blessed are the barren, and the wombs that never bore, and the breasts that never nursed.'

4.2.3 C2d – Other thetic constructions with ἰδού

Before treating the most common thetic use of ἰδού, *narrative deictic thetics*, I shall first dispense with **C2d**, which involves a handful of heterogeneous tokens. They introduce states of affairs that resemble C1 in that they belong to the '**now**', but they differ in being either not quite 'here' or not visible. Several of these could be taken as C5, and perhaps C2d is the closest thetic use to C5, where the physical deictic element is completely gone.

→ Likely instances of C2d include Act 10:19, Act 13:11, and Rev 21:3. If not C5, Mat 26:45 ('the hour has arrived') and perhaps Act 5:25 (apparently periphrastic; see footnote 123) may be two more. Jhn 11:3, another possibility, is the only possible C2 token with ἴδε, although C5 ('listen' or 'pay attention') is also a possible interpretation.

The state of affairs in **Act 10:19** (with participle)[30] is 'now' but not 'here': it is simultaneous with the speech time but refers to a location other than the hearer's immediate one, into which 'three men' are introduced. This use of ἰδού is very similar to that in the narrative deictic thetic. Although the GNB adds *here*, Peter cannot see them. The GNB has used a double-translation, assuming both *here* and *Listen* stand for ἰδού.

Act 10:19 εἶπεν [αὐτῷ] τὸ πνεῦμα· ἰδοὺ ἄνδρες τρεῖς ζητοῦντές
3s.said to.him the Spirit   *   men   three looking.for

σε,
you

> GNB: when the Spirit said [to Peter], "<u>Listen</u>! Three men are <u>here</u> looking for you."

Another possible instance is the single-sentence message in **Jhn 11:3** (ἴδε), which introduces a surprising state of affairs. Predicates like *sick* that indicate non-permanent conditions are very common in thetic constructions in many languages (Bailey 2009:54). Alternatively, ἴδε could be C5 ('listen' or 'pay attention'). Many English translations render ἴδε here as Ø.

Jhn 11:3 κύριε, ἴδε ὃν   φιλεῖς ἀσθενεῖ.
Lord   *   the.one.whom you.love 3s.is.sick

> NRS: [Mary and Martha's brother Lazarus was very ill.] 3 So the sisters sent a message to Jesus, "Lord, he whom you love is ill." 4 But when Jesus heard it, he said, "This illness does not lead to death; ..." 6 [and] he stayed two days longer in the place where he was.
> GNB: "Lord, your dear friend is sick."

Act 13:11,[31] with a locative predicate, is special because it appears that Paul is not describing a state of affairs but causing one to come to pass by virtue of uttering it. That is, the utterance functions as a 'performative' (i.e., akin to a curse, e.g., *I hereby declare that the Lord's hand is on you*; for more on performative-like instances, see on Exo 34:10 in § 4.5.1 and footnotes 14 and 103 in ch. 4). Given the future form of

---

[30] Instead of the participle ζητοῦντές, many manuscripts read the indicative ζητοῦσιν. This is the only token with a participle as the main predicator in a present tense thetic clause with ἰδού. See below for the discussion of participles in subsequent predications, which often occur with C2c (narrative deictic thetics).

[31] Act 13:11, which lacks εἰμί, resembles several εἰμί 'event-central' thetics that lack ἰδού (e.g., Luk 1:66; Act 4:33; Act 10:38; Act 11:21 etc.). The absence of εἰμί in Act 13:11 may be explained in that ἰδού is the here-and-now predicator.

the next clause, 'you will be (blind)', some translations (e.g., GNB, CEV)
also render the ἰδού clause as future, but this weakens the performative
effect. If this construction is truly to be understood as a type of deictic
thetic, then the literal sense might be suggested by *Now, here is (comes)
the Lord's Hand on you.*

Act 13:11 καὶ νῦν ἰδοὺ χεὶρ κυρίου ἐπὶ σὲ καὶ ἔσῃ
         and now *   hand of.Lord on you and you.will.be

    τυφλὸς
    blind

> GNB: [10] and [Paul] said, "You son of the Devil! You are the
> enemy of everything that is good. ... [11] The Lord's hand <u>will</u>
> come down on you now; you will be blind ..."
> NRS: And now listen—the hand of the Lord is against you,
> and you will be blind ...

Rev 21:3, also with a locative predicate, is variously interpreted:
(i) ἰδού is rendered by the NVS78 as deictic thetic *voici* 'here is' and by the
NRS as *see!* Under this interpretation, this token introduces something
that is 'now', but assumedly not entirely visible—and so it could be
an instance of C2d. But if it is truly visible (e.g., if 'the tabernacle'
is equated with 'the new Jerusalem'), then it could be C2a. (ii) Other
translations render ἰδού as 'now' (GNB, CEV, French BFC).[32] In that case,
the clause could be an instance of C5 where 'the tabernacle' could be
understood as a topic expression (e.g., the CEV is paraphrasable as *As for
God's home, it is now with his people*). Like Act 13:11 above, this utterance
resembles a performative; since John is apparently still witnessing the
new Jerusalem descending from heaven (v 2), it may serve as an official
proclamation of that event.

---

[32] The 1984 edition of the NIV has *now*, but the 2011 edition has *Look!*

Rev 21:3 καὶ ἤκουσα φωνῆς μεγάλης ἐκ   τοῦ θρόνου λεγούσης·
and I.heard voice   loud   from the throne saying

ἰδοὺ ἡ   σκηνὴ   τοῦ θεοῦ   μετὰ τῶν ἀνθρώπων, καὶ
*   the dwelling -   of.God with the men   and

σκηνώσει   μετ᾽ αὐτῶν,
3s.will.dwell with them

NRS: [1] Then I saw a new heaven and a new earth; ... [2] And I
saw the holy city, the new Jerusalem, coming down out of
heaven from God, prepared as a bride adorned for her
husband. [3] And I heard a loud voice from the throne saying,
"See, the home of God is among mortals. He will dwell with
them as their God; they will be his peoples, and God himself
will be with them; ..."
NVS78: Voici le tabernacle de Dieu avec les hommes !
CEV: God's home is now with his people.
GNB: Now God's home is with people!
    In § 4.5.3, tokens will be discussed that may be thetic (e.g., 2Co 5:17) or
thetic-like, but where I categorize ἰδού as C5. Those utterances involve
elements that make them even less like C1 than any of the C2d tokens.

4.2.4   C2c – Narrative deictic thetics

Tokens with ἰδού occurring in narrative (including narrative embedded
in direct speech) are frequent, numbering about 69.[33] All but four are
probably thetic,[34] and I designate the remaining 65 thetic uses, including
subtypes, as **C2c**. (At least eleven of these tokens are not preceded
by καί.)
    What is the function of ἰδού in thetic clauses in narrative? If one
considers English translations, one could conclude its meaning is too
subtle to bother with.
    Part of the answer to this question concerns its **syntactic** function.
Below I will note (a) certain uses where I assume ἰδού functions as a
predicator and (b) others where it is a frozen thetic particle, in which
case it is not a proper predicator.
    The other part of the answer concerns the **semantic** or **conceptual**
function. A general portrayal of narrative ἰδού would be that it serves
to 'enliven' the narrative or add **vividness** and **immediacy** to it. But

[33] A few occur in narratives embedded in speech (e.g., past tense: Act 10:30;
present habitual: Luk 9:39).
[34] The following tokens are excluded as C2c because they have topical
subjects: Mat 8:29 and Mat 8:32, both occurring midstream in narrative; and
Mat 13:3 and ‖Mrk 4:3, which begin a parable. See § 4.5.5 where they are
treated as a special type of C5.

this characterization requires more precision. The fact is that there are many constructions in Greek and other languages that can be claimed to add vividness and immediacy to a narrative, including, for example, perception reports,[35] direct speech, 'direct thoughts', the historical present, and constructions that emphasize nearness (*right in front of X*) or suddenness and surprise ('mirative' constructions and adverbs like *suddenly*). And in section § 2.2, certain thetic constructions were briefly illustrated from English that had a similar function. Lakoff (1987) identified two subtypes (based on English's 'central' deictic thetic) used in this way in **narrative**: (i) the 'Narrative Focus' and (ii) 'Presentational Deictic'. A third construction (iii) that is relevant to us and common in English narrative is a non-deictic thetic, what Lakoff calls the 'Presentational Existential'. I will refer to these three constructions as 'Lakoff's narrative constructions':

Table 3: Lakoff's narrative constructions

(i) Narrative Focus (Deictic)	There I was in the middle of the jungle ...
(ii) Presentational Deictic	(There) in the alley had gathered a large crowd of roughnecks.
(iii) Presentational Existential	Suddenly there burst into the room an SS officer holding a machine gun.

Constructions (i) and (ii), with *there* used as a deictic, are used to create a vivid picture in an imagined scene, where the locative adverb refers to a location in that scene. Moreover, (ii) indicates 'a discovery, thus introducing [...] the referent [...] into the discourse' (Lakoff p. 521). Construction (iii), with non-deictic *there*, is also used to create a vivid scene into which a new entity is introduced.

So, with this background in mind, BDAG's brief note (summarized in § 3.1) that ἰδού can 'enliven' a narrative is useful to a certain extent as a general portrayal but begs for refinement, since there are other constructions in Koine that can be so described. In fact, a similar portrayal of the **historical present** is given in BDF § 321, where it is stated that it is used in 'a vivid narrative at the events of which the narrator imagines himself to be present.' And this portrayal of the Koine historical present has also been shown to be in need of refinement,[36]

---

[35] For an in-depth discussion of perception reports, see Bailey 2009 (especially § 2.4.4. and chapter 5).

[36] Although many assume the function of the historical present is to create vivid or dramatic effect (BDF § 321; Hf&S § 197d; Dana & Mantey § 174.3; Wallace 1996:526), Porter (1994:30–31) rejects this portrayal 'because of

although it will be illustrated shortly that Mark occasionally uses the historical present in parallel passages where Matthew uses ἰδού. For my part, a starting assumption will be that C2c, the historical present, as well as other constructions mentioned above (perception reports, *suddenly*, etc.) share a degree of functional overlap, but I will not assume that any of them are fully synonymous. Since none of them are formally identical structures, presumably each can have its own effects and unique ways of adding vividness and immediacy, while also diverging in function.

Can we therefore add precision to such generic portrayals of 'enlivening' a narrative or adding vividness or immediacy?

First of all, the most obvious point is that in up to 63 out of 65 narrative tokens the statement is **thetic**. These thetics serve to introduce both 'first order' entities (especially people, but occasionally also things) and 'second order' entities (states of affairs, events) that tend to be providential or supernatural, or introductions that will lead to events or speeches of spiritual significance (thus, following Johannessohn and Fiedler, there is a potential 'theological' component).[37] In contrast, the historical present is much less frequently used in thetics (more on this below).[38]

its outdated view of tense functions, the lack of indication in the text of such a perspectival shift, and the resulting clumsiness in perspective when tenses are seen as shifting so quickly.' Porter instead portrays its function as 'draw[ing] added attention to' or 'highlight[ing]' events or contexts. Much in line with Porter, Levinsohn (2000:200–203) describes it as a highlighting device, and 'particularly in Mark and John, what is highlighted [...] is not so much the speech or act to which it refers but the event(s) that follow', i.e., it functions *cataphorically*. More recently, Runge (2008), following Levinsohn, has described it as a means to give prominence to what immediately follows. Similarly, Robar (2016) has suggested recasting the traditional description of 'vividness' in terms of 'thematic prominence'; concerning Matthew's discourse, she concludes (p. 350) that it is 'an aid to the reader or listener to discern the hierarchy of themes present, and in particular to know which themes are of intrinsic interest to the author.' For my part, I assume that the two parameters, vividness and highlighting (i.e., marking thematic prominence), often overlap but are clearly not identical.

[37] It would seem wrong to claim that all of these introductions are of providential nature or of spiritual significance. However, when they are, it is clear that the use of ἰδού does not merely add vividness as an end in itself, as if the narrator just wanted to tell a good story, but, instead, its use highlights what 'the Hand of God' is orchestrating, which would in turn be something truly exciting for the audience. So, in this sense, there can certainly be an emotive (affective) component in the use of C2c.

[38] From my preliminary study of the HP (=historical present) in Mark (who is known for using the HP frequently), I find that it is used only occasionally

Second, I propose that C2c shares with C1 some element of deictic
meaning, and so we can expect some functional similarity between C2c
and the comparable English constructions (à la Lakoff). More precisely,
I propose that C2c resembles C1 in that the entity is introduced into an
imagined world (of some other time and place) that is to be treated as
if it were the real here-and-now. This amounts to an invitation to the
audience to imagine being on stage where the events are happening
right before them (one might compare this to how certain shots in a film
more successfully draw the audience into a scene). But this portrayal
requires qualification:

> (a) It is only in some tokens (roughly half) that we can claim that
> the audience is being invited to take **the perspective of a
> story-internal character**. In these, we can call ἰδού a
> 'personal perspective marker'.
> (b) In many tokens, **the perspective is relatively 'omniscient'**
> rather than that of a story-internal character. In such tokens,
> ἰδού is better characterized as a generic marker of vividness
> or immediacy.[39]

To illustrate (a), consider **Luk 22:47**. According to the above proposal,
the audience is being invited to imagine themselves on stage with the
cast. They are to view the introduction of the 'crowd' and 'Judas' as if
they were appearing before them in the here-and-now of the story. In
this context, it is natural for the audience to take Jesus' perspective (as

---

with thetics. More typically the subject is topical. The most common HP
verb is λέγω 'say' (Wallace 1996:529), which is not a typical thetic verb. For
ἔρχομαι 'come', a verb that is often used in thetics, I find the following:

18x = HP and non-thetic (all but one have a non-lexical topical subject):
Mrk 2:3 (non-referential subject); Mrk 2:18; Mrk 3:20; Mrk 5:15; Mrk 5:35;
Mrk 5:38; Mrk 6:1; Mrk 6:48; Mrk 8:22; Mrk 10:1; Mrk 10:46; Mrk 11:15;
Mrk 11:27; Mrk 14:17; Mrk 14:32; Mrk 14:37; Mrk 14:41; Mrk 16:2.

6x = HP and thetic: Mrk 1:40; Mrk 3:31; Mrk 5:22 (with the variant reading of καὶ ἰδοὺ ἔρχεται); Mrk 11:27; Mrk 12:18; Mrk 14:66.

4x = thetic, in past narrative, but not HP (verb is past or participial): Mrk
4:4; Mrk 12:42; Mrk 14:3; Mrk 15:43.

[39] Follingstad (2001) makes many insightful comments about הִנֵּה (hinnēh)
'behold' in terms of viewpoint (i.e., perspective) and mental space. His
discussion was inspirational for me when I began studying perception
reports and ἰδού/ἴδε, although my approach and terms differ from his in
several respects. Most relevant to us here is the fact that he similarly notes
that הִנֵּה may coincide with different viewpoints, including not just that of a
story-internal character (pp. 512–513, 585).

main character), although they might also identify with the disciples.[40]
(See § 4.2.4.1 below on the translation of this token.)

Luk 22:47 Ἔτι αὐτοῦ λαλοῦντος ἰδοὺ ὄχλος, καὶ ὁ
    yet him speaking * crowd and the.one

    λεγόμενος Ἰούδας εἷς τῶν δώδεκα
    being.called Judas one of.the twelve

    προήρχετο   αὐτοὺς καὶ ἤγγισεν τῷ Ἰησοῦ
    3s.was.leading.Impf them and 3s.drew.near to.the Jesus

    φιλῆσαι αὐτόν
    to.kiss him

> NRS: [Just before his arrest, Jesus is praying while nearby his
> disciples have fallen asleep, being overcome with sadness.]
> 46 and he said to them, "Why are you sleeping? Get up and
> pray that you may not come into the time of trial." 47
> While he was still speaking, <u>suddenly a crowd came, and
> the one called Judas, one of the twelve, was leading them</u>.
> He approached Jesus to kiss him;

(b) A more omniscient perspective is illustrated in **Luk 23:50** where
a new scene begins (in nearly all consulted translations, v 50 begins
a new paragraph). The previous context, Luk 23:26–49, narrates the
events of the crucifixion and the reactions of the crowd present. But
when Joseph of Arimathea is introduced in v 50, it does not seem that
it is from any particular character's perspective in the scene (e.g., the
women or soldiers, etc.). Instead, the audience is expected to view the
introduction from a more general perspective. This would mean that,
assuming Joseph was actually present at the crucifixion, ἰδού would be
referring to that, and an appropriate translation could be *Now there was
a man there (= at the crucifixion) named Joseph* ... Alternatively, but perhaps
less likely, Joseph might have been elsewhere in Jerusalem but aware of
Jesus' crucifixion and death; if so, then the intended sense would be *Now*

---

[40] While Luke's highlighting of the introduction of the 'crowd' and 'Judas' by
the use of ἰδού presumably invites the audience to take the perspective of
the story-internal characters, it seems just as important, if not more so, that
this introduces a key step in the direction of the narrative, Judas's betrayal
of Christ.

there in Jerusalem was a man named Joseph ... [41] (Other passages requiring an omniscient perspective are discussed below, e.g., Mat 27:51.)[42]

Luk 23:50 Καὶ ἰδοὺ ἀνὴρ ὀνόματι Ἰωσὴφ βουλευτὴς   ὑπάρχων
     and *   man by.name Joseph council.member being

    [καὶ] ἀνὴρ ἀγαθὸς καὶ δίκαιος
    and man good   and righteous

NRS: [vv 26–49, crucifixion scene.] ¶ [50] Now there was a good and righteous man named Joseph, who, though a member of the council, had not agreed to their plan and action. He came from the Jewish town of Arimathea, and he was waiting expectantly for the kingdom of God. [52] This man went to Pilate and asked for the body of Jesus.

Finally, I note in passing that C2c seldom coincides with the **historical present**. In only two past narratives is a present finite verb so used (Mat 2:13 and Mat 2:19).[43] Both recount the appearance of an angel of the Lord in a dream to Joseph.

But it is noteworthy that, occasionally, when Matthew (and sometimes Luke) has an ἰδού clause, the parallel passage in Mark has a historical present. While this too might suggest the meanings of the two constructions overlap, we cannot make too much of this since such parallels are infrequent, and, as noted above (footnote 38), *the historical present is not very common with thetics.* Compare **Mat 8:2** (and ‖Luk 5:12) with **Mrk 1:40**. Incidentally, the GNB, NRS, and NIV appear to have made

---

[41] Whether or not Joseph actually saw Jesus die on the cross, it is clear that, for the narrative as a whole, Joseph's introduction here, highlighted by ἰδού, together with what he subsequently does (give Jesus an honorable burial) comprise an important step in Luke's narrative, since, as a respected member of the Jewish establishment, Joseph would count as a witness to Christ's character as well as to his death and burial.

[42] The following tokens require an omniscient perspective (**bold** tokens are illustrated in these sections; underlined ones have a finite verb): Mat 9:3; Mat 9:20; **Mat 27:51**; Mat 28:11; Luk 2:25; Luk 5:12; Luk 7:37; Luk 19:2; Luk 23:50; Luk 24:13; Act 8:27; Act 10:17; Act 16:1. Probably also Mat 2:1; Mat 8:34; Mat 9:10; Mat 20:30; Mat 26:51.

[43] See also the variant reading of Mrk 5:22 (καὶ ἰδοὺ ἔρχεται) discussed in footnote 145.

One case also occurs in J&A 26.7 (Burchard), where Aseneth is fleeing and is suddenly met by her enemy and his riders: Καὶ ἔφυγεν Ἀσενὲθ ἔμπροσθεν καὶ ἰδοὺ ὁ υἱὸς Φαραὼ ἀπαντᾷ αὐτῇ καὶ πεντήκοντα ἄνδρες ἱππεῖς μετ' αὐτοῦ. [and 3S.fled.Aor Aseneth ahead and * the.N son.N of.Pharaoh 3S.meets.Pres her and fifty men.N horsemen.N.p.m with him] 'And Aseneth fled ahead and behold the son of Pharaoh meets her and fifty horsemen with him' (nab). Philonenko's edition has aorist ὑπήντησεν '3S.met.Aor'.

no attempt to handle either ἰδού or the historical present. For other parallels, compare Mat 8:24 with Mrk 4:37; Mat 9:2 and Luk 5:18 with Mrk 2:3; and (to some extent) Mat 8:34 with Mrk 5:15.

Mat 8:2 καὶ ἰδοὺ λεπρὸς προσελθὼν
and * leper having.approached.Aor

προσεκύνει   αὐτῷ
3s.was.worshiping.Impf him

Mrk 1:40 Καὶ ἔρχεται   πρὸς αὐτὸν λεπρὸς παρακαλῶν αὐτὸν
and 3s.comes.Pres to   him   leper   begging   him

[καὶ γονυπετῶν] ...
and kneeling

Mat GNB: Then a man suffering from a dreaded skin disease came to him, ...
Mrk GNB: A man suffering from a dreaded skin disease came [Greek: 'comes'] to Jesus, knelt down, and begged him for help.
Mat NRS: and there was a leper who came to him and knelt before him, ...
Mrk NRS: A leper came to him begging him, and kneeling he said to him, ...
Mat NIV: A man with leprosy came and knelt before him...
Mrk NIV: A man with leprosy came to him and begged him on his knees, ...

Other close parallels in narrative between the Synoptic Gospels reveal that where Matthew or Luke use an ἰδού thetic, Mark uses a thetic construction without either ἰδού or the historical present: (i) aorist of γίνομαι 'happen': Mrk 9:7 (∥Mat 17:5); (ii) imperfect of εἰμί 'be': Mrk 3:1 (∥Mat 12:10) and Mrk 2:6 if not periphrastic (∥Mat 9:3); (iii) aorist participle of ἔρχομαι 'come', Mrk 15:43 (∥Luk 23:50); and (iv) *object+participle* complement of perception report, Mrk 1:10 (∥Mat 3:16).[44]

The following sections group C2c tokens according to syntactic complexity. We find simple constructions (ἰδού-NP$_{NOM}$) where I take ἰδού to be a predicator as in C1, as well as constructions with a finite verb predicate. Tokens with participles (ἰδού-NP$_{NOM}$ ... *participle*) are listed separately, although they are probably best analyzed as instances of the simple construction. Finally, there are a few tokens in narrative that are treated separately, two of which lack a subject altogether (C2c-∅-subject, § 4.2.4.4), and up to three that could be categorized as instances of left-detachment (§ 4.2.5).

---

[44] Outside of narrative, one finds the (negated) perception report in Luk 6:42 paralleled by Mat 7:4 with ἰδού.

4.2.4.1 ἰδού + NP$_{NOM}$: the simple construction: C2c-NP

Syntactically, C2c-NP is identical to C1, being composed of ἰδού–NP$_{NOM}$. BDAG's subentry ἰδού.2 ('used w. a noun without a finite verb') lists both C1 and C2c-NP tokens. As in C1, I take ἰδού to be the predicator (i.e., a morphologically invariable verb).

As in **Luk 22:47**,[45] illustrated shortly before but now repeated with more vernacular translations, so in Rev 6:2, the form ἰδού–NP$_{NOM}$ is followed by καί, which indicates the end of the thetic clause. In the latter passage, the idiom καὶ ἰδού occurs in conjunction with the perception report formula 'X saw'. This is a common LXX/Hebrew idiom, especially for recounting visions and dreams (Johannessohn 1937).[46]

Luk 22:47 Ἔτι αὐτοῦ λαλοῦντος ἰδοὺ ὄχλος, καὶ ὁ
  yet him   speaking   *   crowd and the.one

λεγόμενος Ἰούδας εἷς τῶν δώδεκα
being.called Judas one of.the twelve

προήρχετο   αὐτοὺς καὶ ἤγγισεν   τῷ Ἰησοῦ
3s.was.leading.Impf them   and 3s.drew.near to.the Jesus

φιλῆσαι αὐτόν
to.kiss him

NRS: While he was still speaking, <u>suddenly a crowd came</u>, and the one called Judas, one of the twelve, was leading them. He approached Jesus to kiss him;

CEV: While Jesus was still speaking, <u>a crowd came up</u>.

CAS: While these words were still being uttered, <u>a crowd appeared all of a sudden</u>.

nab: While he was still speaking, <u>there in front of him appeared a crowd</u>.

NRV: Mentre parlava ancora, <u>ecco una folla</u>;

NVBTO: Mentre egli ancora parlava, <u>ecco giunse una folla di gente</u>;[47]

---

[45] I assume ὁ λεγόμενος Ἰούδας 'and the one called Judas' is not governed by ἰδού.

[46] Johannessohn (1937:179–181, 235) notes how the Hebrew construction 'X looked/saw and behold' (e.g., ‏וירא...והנה‎) slowly exited the Hebrew historical books in the Bible but remained in use in prophetic visions (e.g., Amos, Zechariah, Daniel). In Revelation, this idiom with ἰδού occurs eight times.

[47] In the NRV and NVBTO, *ecco* has the same function I am claiming for ἰδού here. NRV's *ecco una folla* 'ecco a crowd' is more dramatic sounding than the NVBTO, which has added *giunse* 'came' (Marco Librè, p.c.).

Rev 6:2 καὶ εἶδον, καὶ ἰδοὺ ἵππος λευκός, καὶ ὁ   καθήμενος ἐπ
and I.saw and *   horse white   and the sitting   on

αὐτὸν ἔχων τόξον
it   having bow

NRS: I looked, <u>and there was a white horse</u>! Its rider had a
   bow; ...

In **Rev 6:2**, the audience is clearly invited to share John's perspective,
as indicated by the perception report formula 'X saw'. And in Luk 22:47,
the audience is to take the perspective of Jesus, in front of whom the
crowd appears.

Many tokens in this set are immediately followed by one or
more subsequent predications, that is, by clauses (often verbless) that
predicate something about the newly introduced topic (e.g., a background
description). This is illustrated in **Luk 19:2** by ὀνόματι καλούμενος
Ζακχαῖος, 'being called Zacchaeus by name' and in Luk 5:12 by πλήρης
λέπρας 'full of leprosy', etc.[48] As illustrated here, most C2c-NP tokens are
followed by some background description before the narrative resumes.
So the perspective is often relatively omniscient: Luk 19:2 concerns the
general location of Jericho (something brought out by *here* in KNX and
JBP, and by *là* in BFC). **Luk 5:12** concerns 'one of those cities'; since it is
the man with leprosy who apparently sees Jesus first, it is unlikely the
ἰδού clause is to be taken from Jesus' perspective.

Luk 19:2 Καὶ ἰδοὺ ἀνὴρ ὀνόματι καλούμενος Ζακχαῖος, καὶ αὐτὸς
   and *   man by.name being.called Zacchaeus and he

ἦν   ἀρχιτελώνης
3s.was chief.tax.collector

NRS: [1] [Jesus] entered Jericho and was passing through it. [2]
   <u>A man was there named Zacchaeus</u>; he was a chief tax
   collector and was rich. [3] He was trying to see who Jesus was,
   but on account of the crowd he could not, ... [4] So he ...
   climbed a ... tree to see him, ... [5] When Jesus came to the
   place, he looked up and said to him, "Zacchaeus, ..."
GNB: There was a chief tax collector <u>there</u> named
   Zacchaeus, ...
NET: <u>Now</u>[49] a man named Zacchaeus <u>was there</u>; ...
KNX: and <u>here a rich man</u> named Zacchaeus, the chief
   publican, was trying to distinguish which was Jesus, ...

---

[48] On identifying clause breaks after thetics, see Bailey (2009:65–69) for a
general introduction with English examples, and pp. 146–153 and 338–342
for discussion of Greek.

> JBP: And <u>here we find</u> a wealthy man called Zacchaeus, a chief collector of taxes, wanting to see what sort of person Jesus was.
>
> NJB: and <u>suddenly</u> a man whose name was Zacchaeus <u>made his appearance</u>;
>
> BFC: <u>Il y avait là un homme</u> appelé Zachée; c'était le chef des collecteurs d'impôts et il était riche.
>
> FBJ: Et <u>voici un homme</u> appelé du nom de Zachée; c'était un chef de publicains, ...
>
> LND: ed <u>ecco un uomo</u>, chiamato Zaccheo il quale era il capo dei pubblicani ed era ricco.

Luk 5:12 καὶ ἰδοὺ ἀνὴρ πλήρης λέπρας·   ἰδὼν   δὲ τὸν
and *   man full   of.leprosy having.seen and -

'Ιησοῦν, ...
Jesus

> NRS: Once, when he was in one of the cities, <u>there was a man</u> covered with leprosy. When he saw Jesus, he bowed with his face to the ground and begged him, "Lord, if you choose, you can make me clean."

Translation issues: Most English translations use flat-sounding constructions to render such tokens, as illustrated above by GNB's *there was a chief tax collector there* in Luk 19:2 and CEV's *a crowd came up* in Luk 22:47. Both are common and neutral non-deictic thetic constructions (even with GNB's addition of deictic *there*). Such translations say less than the Greek, since they lack immediacy and vividness and fail to bring across any possible deictic element or, where relevant, that something is surprising or providential.[50] But unlike most of the other English translations, JBP manages to add vividness and draw in the audience by its use of *here we find* in Luk 19:2.

In contrast, Italian and French translations manage to use *ecco/voilà/voici* fairly frequently in these tokens, as illustrated in Luk 19:2 above by *ecco* in LND and *voici* in FBJ. However, in this particular passage, *ecco* is neither colloquial nor perfectly natural but still good written Italian and effective in making the introduction more dramatic and vivid (Marco Librè, p.c.). Similarly, French *voici* in this same passage

---

[49] The NET includes a footnote here about καὶ ἰδού, stating that ἰδού was left untranslated 'because it has no exact English equivalent here' and that καὶ is rendered by *now* in order 'to indicate the introduction of a new character'. Although not in this passage, elsewhere the NIV also seems to occasionally handle καὶ ἰδού in the same way (Luk 2:25; Luk 23:50; Luk 24:13).

[50] See Andersen (2003:33 note 14) for a similar point on הִנֵּה, which translators often leave untranslated.

is awkward (Paul Solomiac, p.c.). Thus, there is a tendency in Italian and French for translators to overuse *ecco/voilà/voici*.

While there may be no perfect equivalent in English, Lakoff's narrative constructions (see table 3) can sometimes approximate the Greek. For example, when there is a location,[51] the '**Presentational Deictic**' can be used, since this construction requires a locative to immediately follow the deictic adverb. Such a locative can be personal if the perspective is personal. For example, in Luk 22:47, where the events unfold primarily from Jesus' perspective, 'in front of him (Jesus)' can serve as the locative. One could say (using deictic *there*) *While he was still speaking, there in front of him appeared a crowd* ... But when the perspective is more omniscient, an impersonal location, if evoked, can sometimes serve that function, as in the case of 'Jericho' in Luk 9:2: *There in Jericho was a man named Zacchaeus*.

However, when a location seems irrelevant, Lakoff's '**Presentational Existential**' (which does not require an explicit location to be named but does require a content verb) can sometimes work. This construction seems especially successful when used together with an adverb that brings out some relevant nuance of ἰδού. For example, in Luk 22:47 (again) one could use the adverb *suddenly* together with this construction (with non-deictic *there*): *suddenly there appeared a crowd*; and in Luk 19:2 (again) the providential element could be emphasized as follows: *There (providentially) happened to be a man named Zacchaeus*; besides other possibilities.

As several of the above translations illustrate, translators sometimes add a phrase that indicates **surprise** or **suddenness** in order to represent ἰδού.[52] Now, in § 4.1, I argued that the emotive elements of surprise and wonder are not always present for C1 and I believe the same is true of C2c constructions. Therefore, surprise (suddenness or wonder), while very common with C2c, is only a conversational implicature: it depends on the degree to which the appearance may be judged unexpected or extraordinary for the audience or narrative-internal characters. Therefore, adding *suddenly* is not always appropriate, although it can be one way to add vividness in English. Interestingly, in at least two places where Matthew has ἰδού, one finds instead εὐθύς 'immediately, just then' in Mark (compare Mrk 14:43 and ‖Mat 26:47; Mrk 7:25 and ‖Mat 15:22).[53] But since such

---

[51] Lakoff's 'Presentational Deictic' construction is appropriate when there is a locative that is topical (part of the common ground). See also footnote 65.

[52] For example, the NRS and CEV occasionally add the word *suddenly*, as already illustrated above by *suddenly a crowd came* in the NRS of Luk 22:47. See also C2 tokens with aorist participles: NRS Mat 9:20 and CEV Mat 15:22; and with finite verbs: NRS in Mat 3:16 and Mat 4:11; see also *just then* in Luk 14:2 and *at that moment* in Mat 27:51.

[53] For Mat 15:22, KNX, by the use of deictic *here*, underscores the deictic component rather than the component of suddenness or surprise: *After this, Jesus left those parts and withdrew into the neighbourhood of Tyre and Sidon. And here*

parallels are the exception, claims about the semantic overlap between
ἰδού and εὐθύς should not be exaggerated.[54]

One more translation strategy worth mentioning would be to use
a rhetorical device that slows down the narrative and suggests that
something special is about to happen. In one translation project I have
consulted for, the translators concluded that, in especially Matthew and
Luke, if they preceded the introduction by *(and then) it happened that*,
the reader would typically expect that something special was about to
happen, such as something miraculous or otherwise providential. For
example, a back-translation of Luk 22:47 (C2c-NP) reads *While Jesus was
speaking, it thus happened that a crowd of people came up to him*, and Luk
7:12 (C2c-FiniteV) reads *As they neared the city gate, it thus happened that a
dead man was being taken out.*

→ In the NT, there are at least thirteen likely C2c-NP tokens: Luk
5:12; Luk 7:37;[55] Luk 19:2; Luk 22:47; Luk 23:50; Act 8:27; Act 10:17
(a hearer-old set of entities is situated in the general scene); Rev 6:2;
Rev 6:5; Rev 6:8; Rev 7:9; Rev 14:14; Rev 19:11. Other tokens may also
belong here: Mat 2:9; Mat 26:47 (and possibly Luk 24:13); in each the
subject is followed immediately by some descriptive material and then
comes a finite verb (see § 4.2.5 for discussion); all three, as well as Act
10:17 in the primary set, introduce hearer-old entities, something that
distinguish these from the norm. For C2c-NP in *Joseph and Aseneth*, in
Burchard's edition, see J&A 14.9 (καὶ ἰδοὺ ἀνήρ ... 'and behold a man ...')
and J&A 10.16 with locative (καὶ ἰδοὺ πηλὸς πολὺς ... εἰς τὸ ἔδαφος 'and
behold mud.N much.N ... on the floor').

4.2.4.2 ἰδού + NP$_{NOM}$ + (X)-participle-(X): C2c-NP+Prt

In this section, I briefly treat examples of narrative ἰδού–NP$_{NOM}$ that are
followed by a (nominative) **participial phrase** (+/– X = optional predicate elements). Elsewhere[56] I have presented reasons why the participial
phrase should most likely be counted as a subsequent predication that
is syntactically separate from ἰδού–NP$_{NOM}$, that is, outside of the thetic
clause (just like the verbless subsequent predications illustrated in the
last section, e.g., 'called Zacchaeus by name' in Luk 19:2). In other words,

---

a woman, a Chanaanite by birth, who came from that country, cried aloud, Have pity
on me, Lord ...

[54] That ἰδοὺ ἐξαυτῆς 'behold immediately' can coincide (Act 11:11) also
suggests ἰδού is not synonymous with 'immediately' or 'suddenly' (contra
Johannessohn [1942:58] and Fiedler [1969:38] who imply the opposite).

[55] For Luk 7:37 (with an omniscient perspective), by simply adding deictic
there, the GNB's rendering can be transformed into Lakoff's 'Presentational
Deictic': '[There] in that town was a woman who lived a sinful life.'

[56] See Bailey (2009:338–342).

this combination is just another type of narrative ἰδού + NP_{NOM} that was described in the previous section.

Mat 12:10 is one example of C2c-NP+Prt, which BDAG, by means of its English gloss, also suggests represents two separate clauses (i.e., the ἰδού clause followed by the participial clause). Notice that if ἰδού is not counted as an independent indicative verb, then the sentence would lack one, in which case this would be a sentence fragment. But that is obviously not the case.

Mat 12:10 καὶ ἰδοὺ ἄνθρωπος χεῖρα ἔχων   ξηράν. καὶ
          and *   man   hand having.Pres withered and

          ἐπηρώτησαν   αὐτὸν
          3p.questioned him [=Jesus]

  BDAG: 'καὶ ἰ. ἄνθρωπος *and there was a man*' [having (i.e.,
     who had) a withered hand, and the people questioned
     Jesus, saying, 'Is it lawful to heal on the Sabbath?']

Besides tokens with a transitive participle as in the above example, I assume that intransitive participles, as illustrated by the aorist ἐλθών[57] 'having.come' in **Mat 9:18**,[58] are also subsequent predications and therefore separate from ἰδού–*NP_{NOM}* (in other words, verb transitivity makes no difference). Still, all of the English translations I have consulted treat the aorist participle as a finite verb *came*. But the literal sense of the Greek would be something like *as he was saying these things, (suddenly) here's a ruler who has come in, who is bowing to him, saying ...*

Mat 9:18 Ταῦτα   αὐτοῦ λαλοῦντος αὐτοῖς, ἰδοὺ ἄρχων εἷς
          these.things he.G speaking.G to.them *   ruler one

          ἐλθὼν   προσεκύνει   αὐτῷ λέγων ὅτι
          having.come.Aor 3s.was.bowing.Impf to.him saying that

          ἡ   θυγάτηρ μου ἄρτι   ἐτελεύτησεν·
          the daughter of.me just.now died

---

[57] In the ἰδού–*NP_{NOM}* + *participial phrase* construction, the participle can be present, aorist, or perfect. Following normal rules for interpreting participles, the **aorist** is used for states of affairs that are complete or perfective in relation to another event (e.g., Mat 9:18, ἰδοὺ ἄρχων εἷς ἐλθὼν προσεκύνει αὐτῷ [here's ruler one having.come 3S.was.bowing to.him]). **Present** forms are for simultaneous actions (e.g., λέγουσα [saying] in Mat 3:17) and lasting states (e.g., Mat 12:10, ἰδοὺ ἄνθρωπος χεῖρα ἔχων ξηράν [here's man hand.A having withered]) and **perfect** forms for lasting resultant states (e.g., Rev 4:1 ἰδοὺ θύρα ἠνεωγμένη ἐν τῷ οὐρανῷ [here's door opened in the heaven]).
[58] In Mat 9:18, the subject is modified by εἷς '(a certain) one' (see also Mat 19:16), which is presumably analogous to Luke's use of τις. But Luke only uses τις with ἰδού in C2c-FiniteV (Luk 10:25; Luk 14:2; Act 16:1). On τις and theticity, see Bailey (2009:174–181).

NRS: While he was saying these things to them, <u>suddenly a leader of the synagogue came in</u> and knelt before him, saying, "My daughter has just died; ..."

→ There are seventeen instances of C2c-NP+Prt: Mat 3:17; Mat 8:2; Mat 9:10; Mat 9:18; Mat 9:20 (listed under BDAG ἰδού.1.b.β); Mat 12:10; Mat 15:22; Mat 17:5; Mat 19:16; Mat 20:30; Mat 26:51 (anchored subject); Mat 28:11 (anchored subject); Luk 5:18; Luk 13:11; Rev 4:1; Rev 12:3; Rev 14:1. With the exception of two anchored[59] entities, all of the entities introduced are hearer-new.

4.2.4.3 ἰδού + subject-phrase + finite verb: C2c-FiniteV

This now leaves us to discuss tokens where narrative ἰδού occurs with a finite verb, C2c-FiniteV.[60] Consider **Mat 4:11** and **Mat 3:16**, where in the latter the finite verb follows ἰδού.

Mat 4:11 Τότε ἀφίησιν αὐτὸν ὁ   διάβολος, καὶ ἰδοὺ ἄγγελοι
          then   leaves   him   the devil   and *   angels

          προσῆλθον   καὶ διηκόνουν   αὐτῷ
          3p.came.Aor and 3p.served.Impf him

NRS: Then the devil left him [=Jesus], <u>and suddenly angels came</u> and waited on him.

Mat 3:16 βαπτισθεὶς   δὲ ὁ Ἰησοῦς εὐθὺς
          having.been.baptized and - Jesus immediately

          ἀνέβη   ἀπὸ τοῦ ὕδατος· καὶ **ἰδοὺ**
          came.up.Aor from the water   and *

          ἠνεῴχθησαν   [αὐτῷ] οἱ οὐρανοί,
          3p.were.opened.Aor to.him the heavens

NRS: [Jesus comes to John to be publicly baptized.] And when Jesus had been baptized, just as he came up from the water, <u>suddenly the heavens were opened to him</u> and he saw the Spirit of God descending like a dove and alighting on him.

---

[59] The subject in Mat 26:51, 'one of those with Jesus', is not entirely new because it is 'anchored' in the sense that 'one', which by itself refers to a hearer-new entity, is nevertheless identified in relation to 'Jesus', who is hearer-old. See footnote 19 in ch. 2.

[60] In most tokens, the finite verb is aorist. Other forms include present tense forms (besides the two historical present forms discussed in § 4.2.4, see Luk 9:39), imperfects (Luk 7:12; Luk 9:30; Rev 4:2; and the instances of ἦν, discussed later in this section), and pluperfects (Mat 12:46; Act 1:10).

Several things suggest that ἰδού here holds a different type of syntactic relationship with its clause than when no finite verb immediately follows (i.e., with ἰδού–NP$_{NOM}$ in C1, C2-NP, and C2-Prt):

(i) Both orders, ἰδού–*subject-verb* and ἰδού–*verb-subject*, occur (unlike C2-Prt where in our data the subject always immediately follows ἰδού).[61]

(ii) A finite verb is syntactically independent, unlike the nominalized clauses following ἰδού–NP$_{NOM}$, such as the participial type we saw in the last section or a relative clause in Luk 19:20 (C1) illustrated earlier.

(iii) If we omit ἰδού from C2c-FiniteV, we still have a complete clause.

(iv) Finally, as will be illustrated shortly, the finite verb may even be εἰμί 'be', something that was argued to be unnecessary in constructions like C1.

For these reasons, ἰδού does not appear to be a predicator, but instead holds a weaker relation to its clause, functioning as a **frozen thetic particle**. Its position in the sentence is not free but frozen at or near the clause beginning, that is, always before the subject, verb, and other core constituents. Thus, its position still mimics the other thetic structures (C1, C2-NP etc.). The clause structure of C2c-FiniteV is represented

---

[61] I have discussed constituent order in ἰδού and ἴδε clauses elsewhere (Bailey 2009:376–384, § 6.7.3). In the dedicated thetic uses—C1 and C2— the particle comes early in the clause and the subject immediately follows. The primary exception to this generalization involves rare instances of C2c-FiniteV, like the one at hand, which has the order ἰδού–*verb-subject*, instead of the more common order ἰδού–*subject-verb*, which I take to be a default order (i.e., pragmatically unmarked). Briefly, I suggest that this marked order, ἰδού–*verb-subject*, is used when the entity or state of affairs being introduced is overtly marked as 'demoted' (i.e., 'backgrounded') relative to other things (this observation does not necessarily apply to the introduction of times). For example, in Luk 8:41 ἀνήρ (a man came up whose name is Jairus) is introduced postverbally evidently in anticipation of the switch of attention to the woman suffering from hemorrhages. In Luk 7:12 τεθνηκώς (a man who has died and is being carried out of the city) is introduced postverbally in anticipation of the switch of attention to his mother for whom Jesus, moved by pity, raises her son. And in Mat 17:3 'Moses and Elijah' are introduced postverbally in the Transfiguration story; in this example it may be that the backgrounding is both anaphoric, in relation to Jesus' transfiguration, and cataphoric, in relation to the switch of attention to the shining cloud and heavenly voice, which in fact confirm Jesus' rank over Moses and Elijah. (Constituent order in thetic Koine constructions not involving ἰδού and ἴδε are discussed at length in Bailey 2009:233–279.)

by (18) (subject and verb may be optionally inverted). This structure contrasts with (19), which represents C1, C2c-NP, and C2c-NP+Prt.

(18) C2c-FiniteV: [ἰδού-PARTICLE NP-SUBJECT (X) finite verb-PREDICATOR (X)]

(19) C1, C2c-NP etc.: [ἰδού-PREDICATOR NP-SUBJECT] [subsequent predication]

Concerning the translation of the above illustrated passages, Mat 4:11 and Mat 3:16, there is some question about what perspective the audience should take (both introduce supernatural events). Commentators are divided about Mat 3:16, whether Jesus alone sees the heavens open and the dove descend, or if John and others present see this. In Mat 4:11, there is no mention of anyone besides Jesus being present, so one interpretation is that the perspective is that of Jesus. However, it seems likely that an omniscient perspective is more relevant here since, assuming Jesus already realizes he is the Messiah, the supernatural appearance of angels would not be so surprising to him as to the 'omniscient' reader.

Consider now **Mat 28:9**, where the perspective is clearly personal. The clause serves to bring Jesus into the awareness of the characters, the women who had visited Jesus' grave, whose perspective the audience is invited to share. Meeting someone you knew had died would be very surprising, so *suddenly* is one way to handle ἰδού (GNB, CEV, NRS, NIV, NJB).[62]

Mat 28:9 καὶ ἰδοὺ Ἰησοῦς ὑπήντησεν αὐταῖς λέγων· χαίρετε.
     and * Jesus met them saying hello
     NRS: <u>Suddenly Jesus met them</u> and said, "Greetings!"

Mat 27:51–52 contains five thetics expressed by five finite verb[63] clauses—the Temple curtain tears, the earth shakes, the rocks split, the tombs open, and many of the dead are raised. These (unexpected and supernaturally timed) events are portrayed as occurring as a result of Jesus' death (v 50). Ἰδού, which occurs only once, introduces all five thetics. Again, there is no reason to view ἰδού as a predicator here,

---

[62] That the proper name Ἰησοῦς 'Jesus' is anarthrous (i.e., lacks the definite article) makes sense because it is both focal and prominent in this first post-resurrection appearance. Levinsohn (2000:155) notes that, in the Synoptic Gospels, once Jesus is established as the main character, when reactivated he is usually referred to with the article, except in his reappearances after his resurrection, as illustrated here in Mat 28:9 (see also in Luk 24:15, UBS text).
[63] All five verbs are technically speaking 'unergative' but here obviously function as thetics (i.e., each introducing an unexpected event). See Bailey (2009:53–57) on verb types that are cross-linguistically preferred in thetics.

but instead each clause has its own finite verb as predicator. Since the perspective is relatively omniscient, the audience must step onto the larger stage of Jerusalem to view the five events. Translating ἰδού by *at that moment* (e.g., NRS, also NIV, NLT, etc.) is appropriate if attached to the first three events.[64] But ἰδού can be rendered in more effective ways. The supernatural nuance could be captured by *amazingly*, or more dramatically by an 'inverted' construction (i.e., the subject is postverbal and part of the predicate is preverbal): *And down came the veil of the Sanctuary splitting in two from top to bottom, the ground shook, rocks split apart and tombs opened up!*

Mat 27:51 Καὶ ἰδοὺ τὸ   καταπέτασμα τοῦ   ναοῦ   ἐσχίσθη
           and *   the curtain   of.the temple 3s.was.torn

           ἀπ' ἄνωθεν ἕως κάτω εἰς δύο καὶ ἡ   γῆ
           from above to below in two and the earth

           ἐσείσθη   καὶ αἱ πέτραι ἐσχίσθησαν,
           3s.was.shaken and the rocks 3p.were.split

        52 καὶ τὰ μνημεῖα ἀνεῴχθησαν   καὶ πολλὰ σώματα
           and the tombs   3p.were.opened and many bodies

           τῶν   κεκοιμημένων   ἁγίων ἠγέρθησαν,
           of.the having.fallen.asleep saints 3p.were.raised

> NRS: [50] Then Jesus cried again with a loud voice and breathed his last. [51] <u>At that moment</u> the curtain of the temple was torn in two, from top to bottom. The earth shook, and the rocks were split. [52] The tombs also were opened, and many bodies of the saints who had fallen asleep were raised. [53] After his resurrection they ... appeared to many.

Unlike C1, which is by definition restricted to the true here-and-now present and never employs εἰμί 'be', C2c-FiniteV allows εἰμί. There are three tokens with imperfect ἦν: Luk 2:25, Luk 14:2 and Act 16:1 (see also Mat 8:24 and Mat 28:2 with ἐγένετο). Consider **Luk 2:25**. If ἰδού's function were predicative (as an 'existential predicate'), ἦν would be redundant. So ἰδού's function must instead be to lend this (otherwise non-deictic) thetic a special vividness presumably because of the providential role Simeon plays: he, being a holy man, 'just happens' to show up and prophesy about the baby.

---

[64]The phrase *at that moment* should not be applied to the events of v 52, especially that many of the dead are raised, since that event belongs to the same scene as v 53, where after Jesus' resurrection the risen saints appear to many.

Luk 2:25 Καὶ ἰδοὺ ἄνθρωπος ἦν   ἐν Ἰερουσαλὴμ ᾧ   ὄνομα
and * man   3s.was in Jerusalem   to.whom name

Συμεὼν
Simeon

NRS: [22] ... [Joseph and Mary] brought him [=baby Jesus] up to
Jerusalem to present him to the Lord ... [24] and they offered a
sacrifice ... [25] <u>Now there was a man in Jerusalem</u> whose
name was Simeon; this man was righteous and devout,
looking forward to the consolation of Israel, and the Holy
Spirit rested on him. [26] It had been revealed to him by the
Holy Spirit that he would not see death before he had seen
the Lord's Messiah. [27] Guided by the Spirit, Simeon came
into the temple; and when the parents brought in the child
Jesus, ... [28] Simeon took him in his arms and praised God, ...

The perspective here (as well as in Act 16:1 with ἦν) is relatively
omniscient (the introduction is not from the parents' perspective,
despite possible first impressions). Thus, Simeon is introduced onto the
larger stage of Jerusalem (v 27 finally brings Simeon into the temple
before the parents). One of Lakoff's 'Presentational Deictic' sentences
would work here (*There in Jerusalem*[65] *was a man named Simeon*), but by
itself would not succeed in bringing across any of the providential nature
('wonder') that is relevant here. To capture this nuance, it would seem
reasonable to translate this as *There in Jerusalem (there) just so happened
to be a man named Simeon*, or by (without deictic *there*) *Providentially, there
was a man in Jerusalem, named Simeon*.

The third instance with ἦν comes in **Luk 14:2**. 'In front of him'
indicates that it is Jesus' perspective that is primary (rather than that of
others in the Pharisee's home, v 1). If, as in the last example, we again
take ἦν to be thetic (i.e., 'existential'), then the adjective ὑδρωπικός
'having dropsy' must be either a split element of the subject or a
subsequent predication. If ὑδρωπικός is part of the subject NP, then
the entire sentence is one clause (where, as suggested by the English
renderings, ἔμπροσθεν αὐτοῦ 'in front of him' could be a topical element
rather than a subsequent predication).[66] In any case, the construction is

---

[65] Lakoff's 'Presentational Deictic' construction works well here because
the locatives in these ἰδού + ἦν/ἐγένετο passages (e.g., ἐν Ἰερουσαλὴμ 'in
Jerusalem') are non-predicative and topical. On the different syntactic
functions of locative phrases in εἶναι constructions, see Bailey (2009, § 4.1,
especially pp. 130–132).

[66] In Bailey (2009:158), I argue for a similar split-subject structure for Luk
16:1: ἄνθρωπός τις ἦν πλούσιος ὃς εἶχεν οἰκονόμον [man.N certain.N was
rich.Adj.N who 3S.had steward] 'There was a *rich man* who had a steward.'

readily expressed by a 'Presentational Deictic', as illustrated by the NAS
and NET. The NRS uses *just then* to add immediacy. The addition in the
NET of *right* (*in front of him*) is also effective in adding immediacy.

Luk 14:2 Καὶ ἰδοὺ ἄνθρωπός τις   ἦν   ὑδρωπικὸς
         and *   man   a.certain 3s.was having.dropsy.Adj

         ἔμπροσθεν αὐτοῦ.
         in.front.of him

> NAS: And <u>there in front of Him</u> was a man suffering from
>   dropsy.
> NET: There <u>right</u> in front of him was a man suffering from
>   dropsy.
> NRS: <u>Just then</u>, in front of him, there was a man who had
>   dropsy.

There are a handful of C2c-FiniteV tokens in *Joseph and Aseneth*. In
J&A 14.1–2, after a week of fasting, Aseneth receives a hopeful sign as
she watches the morning star appear, the heavens tear in two, and a
bright light appear. The second instance of ἰδού (14.2) introduces two
thetic clauses, the first of which begins with a topical locative ('near the
morning star'). (See also J&A 18.1a and J&A 28.8.)

J&A 14.1 Καὶ ὡς   ἐπαύσατο Ἀσενὲθ ἐξομολογουμένη τῷ
         and when 3s.stopped Aseneth confessing.Pres.N to.the

         κυρίῳ ἰδοὺ ὁ   ἑωσφόρος ἀστὴρ ἀνέτειλεν ἐκ   τοῦ
         Lord *   the.N morning.N star.N 3s.rose.Aor from the

         οὐρανοῦ κατὰ ἀνατολάς.
         heaven   in   east

    14.2 καὶ ἔτι ἑώρα   Ἀσενὲθ καὶ ἰδοὺ ἐγγὺς
         and still 3s.was.looking.Impf Aseneth and *   near

         τοῦ   ἑωσφόρου ἐσχίσθη   ὁ   οὐρανὸς καὶ
         to.the morning.star 3s.was.torn.Aor the.N heaven.N and

         ἐφάνη   φῶς   μέγα καὶ ἀνεκλάλητον.
         3s.appeared light.N great.N and inexpressible.N

> 1. And when Aseneth had ceased making confession to the
>   Lord, <u>behold, the morning star rose out of heaven in the
>   east</u>. And Aseneth saw it and rejoiced and said, "So the Lord
>   God listened to my prayer, because this star rose as a
>   messenger and herald of the light of the great day." 2. And
>   Aseneth kept looking, and <u>behold, close to the morning star,
>   the heaven was torn apart and great and unutterable light
>   appeared</u>. (Burchard 1985)

→ There are up to thirty tokens of C2c-FiniteV in the NT.[67] A few have multiple thetic clauses. About a quarter have hearer-old subjects: Mat 1:20;[68] Mat 2:1; Mat 2:13; Mat 2:19; Mat 3:16; Mat 4:11; Mat 8:24; Mat 8:34; Mat 9:3 (?); Mat 12:46; Mat 17:3; Mat 17:5; Mat 27:51 (five thetics); Mat 28:2 (two thetics, the second with γάρ); Mat 28:9; Luk 2:25; Luk 7:12 (ὄχλος ... ἦν σὺν αὐτῇ with εἰμί is probably a second thetic); Luk 8:41; Luk 9:30; Luk 9:38; Luk 9:39 (description, 'habitual narrative', present tense); Luk 10:25; Luk 14:2; Luk 24:4; Act 1:10; Act 10:30; Act 11:11;[69] Act 12:7 (two thetics); Act 16:1; Rev 4:2.

Of these thirty, four tokens have postverbal subjects (see footnote 61 on the significance): Mat 3:16; Mat 17:3; Luk 7:12; Luk 8:41. In one, Mat 28:2, the subject is split, straddling its verb.[70]

Finally, we might wish to ask what the difference is between this construction, C2c-FiniteV and C2c-NP+Prt. While more research is needed, C2c-NP+Prt appears to be secondary or backgrounded in relation to a foregrounded finite verb clause that usually follows. Moreover, unlike the C2c-NP+Prt, C2c-FiniteV occasionally introduces hearer-old entities, especially in Matthew's Gospel (Mat 3:16; Mat 8:34; Mat 12:46; Mat 17:3; Mat 27:51 [5x]; Mat 28:9). This last fact also suggests that C2c-FiniteV is better integrated into the event line as foregrounded material.

4.2.4.4 ἰδού + clause with Ø subject: C2c-Ø-subject

Two ἰδού tokens in narrative lack a lexical subject: **Mat 9:2** and **Mat 9:32**.

Mat 9:32 Αὐτῶν δὲ   ἐξερχομένων ἰδού προσήνεγκαν   αὐτῷ
         they.G and going.out.G   *   3p.brought.Aor to.him

         ἄνθρωπον κωφὸν δαιμονιζόμενον.   [33] καὶ
         man   mute   being.demon-possessed   and

         ἐκβληθέντος   τοῦ δαιμονίου ἐλάλησεν ὁ   κωφός.
         had been cast.out the demon   3s.spoke the mute

         NRS: [32] After they had gone away, <u>a demoniac who was mute
         was brought to him</u>. [33] And when the demon had been cast
         out, the one who had been mute spoke; ...

---

[67] The variant reading in Luk 2:9 of καὶ ἰδού instead of καί would count as another instance of C2c-FiniteV.
[68] Bill Neumann (p.c.) pointed out to me that Mat 1:20 comes in the middle of an intricate chiasm.
[69] Act 11:11 is unique in that temporal ἐξαυτῆς 'immediately' intervenes between ἰδού and the subject.
[70] For a discussion of Mat 28:2, see Bailey (2009:383).

Mat 29:2 καὶ ἰδοὺ προσέφερον   αὐτῷ παραλυτικὸν ἐπὶ
and *   3p.were.bringing.Impf to.him paralytic   upon

κλίνης βεβλημένον. καὶ ἰδὼν   ὁ Ἰησοῦς τὴν
stretcher lying   and having.seen the Jesus   the

πίστιν αὐτῶν εἶπεν τῷ   παραλυτικῷ·
faith of.them, 3s.said to.the paralytic

NRS: <u>And just then some people were carrying a paralyzed man lying on a bed</u>. When Jesus saw their faith, he said to the paralytic, "Take heart, son; your sins are forgiven."

Both tokens resemble other C2c uses in that they introduce a new entity, but they differ in that the new entity is expressed by the object. And, since they lack a lexical subject, they do not qualify as cases of (sentence-focus) thetic constructions. So, these two tokens represent another syntactic step away from the prototype, C1. Nevertheless, given the 'impersonal' or 'quasi-passive'[71] use of transitive προσφέρω 'bring' in both tokens, both essentially function as intransitive thetic clauses, that is, as typical C2c clauses. (In Mat 9:32 the semantic agent is completely suppressed as the clause subject is never identified, and in Mat 9:2 it is equally suppressed except for the reference to τὴν πίστιν αὐτῶν 'their faith' later in v 2.)

For the sake of comparison, **Luk 5:18**, which is a parallel passage to Mat 9:2, is a more typical thetic (C2c-NP+Prt). It has an explicit subject ἄνδρες 'men' (which persists in the next clause as a topic).

Luk 5:18 ἰδοὺ ἄνδρες φέροντες ἐπὶ κλίνης ἄνθρωπον ὃς   ἦν
         *   men   carrying on pallet man   who 3s.was

παραλελυμένος καὶ ἐζήτουν   αὐτὸν εἰσενεγκεῖν
paralyzed   and 3p.were.seeking him   to.carry.in

---

[71] Such an impersonal or quasi-passive use of active forms, especially with the third person plural, is mentioned in some grammars. For example, BDF § 130.2 discusses this under the rubrics of the 'omission of the subject' and 'the impersonal passive'; and Moule (1988:28–29) describes this as 'the use of the 3rd person plural with a vague and unexpressed subject, "they", as in our phrase "they say", which is equivalent to a Passive [...]'. Although this use is not considered by BDF to be very common in the NT, what I find noteworthy in regard to theticity is the relative frequency of transitive προσφέρω 'bring' to introduce new entities via the object onto a well-established narrative stage, where, as illustrated by these two instances in Mat 9 with ἰδού, the identity of the subject entities is irrelevant to the story (see also Mat 4:24, Mat 8:16, Mrk 10:13, and Luk 18:15, all without ἰδού). In all these tokens, the thetic-like object is postverbal, which is the pragmatically unmarked ('default') position for focal objects. See chapter 5 of Bailey 2009 (pp. 280–313) for a discussion of the unmarked position of focal objects, including thetic-like ones.

NRS: <u>Just then some men came</u>, carrying a paralyzed man on a
bed.

4.2.5 C2e and C2c – ἰδού–NP$_{NOM}$ as left-detachment

Occasionally, ἰδού–*NP*$_{NOM}$ comes very close to looking like a left-detached
topic expression.[72] Examples occur in both narrative and non-narrative.
All introduce hearer-old entities (unlike most cases of C2c-NP and C2c-
NP+Prt). As in C1 and C2c-NP etc., I assume that ἰδού and NP$_{NOM}$ form a
syntactic unit.

In **narrative**, there are three tokens, → Mat 2:9, Mat 26:47, and Luk
24:13; they are apparently a type of C2c-NP. In each, a phrase intervenes
between the subject and the finite verb, which is either descriptive or
adverbial. In **Luk 24:13**, the adverb ἐν αὐτῇ τῇ ἡμέρᾳ 'on that same day'
intervenes, probably to emphasize this element. (I assume with Z&G,
Björck p. 45, and Aerts p. 53 that ἦσαν πορευόμενοι is periphrastic.)
The perspective is omniscient, and by adding *we find*, JBP draws in the
audience. **Mat 2:9** follows with a restrictive relative clause ('which they
saw in the east'). The perspective is that of the magi, and the sentence is
readily rendered by a 'Presentational Deictic', as the NRS illustrates.

Luk 24:13 Καὶ ἰδοὺ δύο ἐξ αὐτῶν ἐν αὐτῇ τῇ ἡμέρᾳ ἦσαν
and * two of them on same the day 3p.were

πορευόμενοι εἰς κώμην
traveling to village

NRS: Now on that same day <u>two of them</u> were going to a
village called Emmaus, ...

JBP: Then on the same day <u>we find two of them</u> going off to
Emmaus,

Mat 2:9 καὶ ἰδοὺ ὁ ἀστήρ, ὃν εἶδον ἐν τῇ ἀνατολῇ,
and * the star which 3p.saw in the east

προῆγεν αὐτούς,
3s.went.before.Impf them

NRS: When they [=the magi] had heard the king, they set out;
<u>and there, ahead of them, went the star</u> that they had seen at
its rising, until it stopped over the place where the child was.

In **non-narrative**, there are at least two tokens, → Luk 1:36 and
Jas 3:4, again, both with hearer-old entities ('Elizabeth' and the generic
class of 'ships'). It might be possible to take ἰδού as an instance of C5,
meaning 'listen' or 'take note', in which case ἰδού would be syntactically

---

[72] For a general introduction on left-detached expressions, see Bailey
(2009:32–34) and for a discussion of some Greek examples, see pp. 181–186.

(and intonationally) separate from NP$_{NOM}$. But it would seem clumsy; in any case, no English translations I have consulted suggest this interpretation. Instead, I suggest that this is an extended use of structure C1, which I designate **C2e**. Although it is not physically deictic like C1, it nevertheless points to something, in this case to a concept in long-term memory.

In **Luk 1:36**, by means of ἰδοὺ Ἐλισάβετ, the speaker introduces the new topic of 'Elizabeth' in order to illustrate another case of a miraculous pregnancy. Following the descriptive phrase, ἡ συγγενίς σου 'your relative', comes the main predication, 'SHE ALSO has conceived a son in her old age'. Since the main predicate is an instance of constituent-focus, 'Elizabeth' is referred to again lexically (by καὶ αὐτή 'she also').[73]

Luk 1:36 καὶ ἰδοὺ Ἐλισάβετ ἡ   συγγενίς σου   καὶ αὐτὴ
　　　　and *   Elizabeth   the relative of.you also she

συνείληφεν   υἱὸν ἐν γήρει   αὐτῆς
3s.has.conceived son in old.age of.her

NRS: And now, your relative Elizabeth in her old age has also conceived a son; ...

GNB: <u>Remember your relative Elizabeth</u>. It is said that she cannot have children, but she herself is now six months pregnant, even though she is very old.

CEV: Your relative Elizabeth is also going to have a son, ...

Concerning **Jas 3:4**, James has just mentioned a horse and its bit as an analogy for a man and his tongue (v 3). He then introduces another topic by means of the construction 'ἰδού also ships', thereby raising another analogy, ships and their rudders (GNB and NIV are reasonable translations but not NRS's *look at*). The idea of 'ships' is new to the discourse but old to the hearer (the readers are expected to know what ships are). Following the descriptive phrases comes the main predicate, μετάγεται ὑπὸ ἐλαχίστου πηδαλίου 'are guided by a very small rudder'.

Jas 3:4 ἰδοὺ καὶ τὰ πλοῖα τηλικαῦτα ὄντα καὶ ὑπὸ ἀνέμων
　　　　*   also the ships so.great   being and by winds

---

[73] Italian translations also use *ecco* (NVBTO *Ed ecco, Elisabetta, tua parente, ha concepito anche lei un figlio nella sua vecchiaia*; LND; NRV), although they sound a bit awkward or old fashioned (Marco Librè, p.c.).

The FBJ uses *voici* (*Et voici qu'Élisabeth, ta parente, vient, elle aussi, de concevoir un fils dans sa vieillesse*), which is somewhat awkward (Paul Solomiac, p.c.) and which does not match the Greek in the function or structure I am proposing (it introduces a clause, not a NP). In contrast, some modern French translations use imperatives that instruct the hearer to pay mental attention, like *look!* (BDS: *Vois :*) or *listen!* (PDV: *Écoute !*).

σκληρῶν ἐλαυνόμενα, μετάγεται   ὑπὸ ἐλαχίστου πηδαλίου
hard   being.driven 3s.is.guided by   very.small rudder

NRS: <u>Or look at ships</u>: though they are so large that it takes
  strong winds to drive them, yet they are guided by a very
  small rudder ...
GNB: <u>Or think of a ship</u>: big as it is ... it can be steered by a very
  small rudder, ...
NIV: <u>Or take ships as an example.</u>

These last two tokens resemble **reminders** in that they introduce
hearer-old entities. For Luk 1:36, the GNB actually reads *Remember your
relative Elizabeth.* Jas 3:4 could be paraphrased *Recall what ships are like.*

4.3   C3 – Deictic particles in non-thetic constructions

In C3, ἴδε and ἰδού are used as here-and-now deictic particles, but the
clause lacks sentence-focus structure because the subject is topical. In
the NT, the ἴδε tokens (6x) are more frequent and generally clearer
examples of the category than ἰδού tokens (up to 5x) (one finds clear
ἰδού tokens outside of the NT; a few are discussed below). Since C3 is
deictic, there is a close resemblance with C1 in that in both constructions
the particle refers to something in the here-and-now and could be
accompanied by a pointing gesture. In some tokens, C3 also resembles
C1 in that it introduces an entity into the discourse either implicitly or
explicitly via the clause's object.

Syntactically, the particles always occur at the beginning of a
sentence involving a typical predicator (verb or locative predicate); so
it appears they come in a frozen clause-initial position that mimics the
position their ancestors would have normally taken as imperatives of
'see' (in the NT, they never occur with a conjunction, but twice they
follow a vocative: Mrk 11:21; Mrk 13:1; in one textual variant of Tob
2:8, ἰδού follows καὶ πάλιν).[74] What is not clear is whether or not the
particle may be followed by a pause and thus (in some cases at least) be
syntactically independent from the rest of the clause, like a vocative or
imperative (this question is taken up below with some examples from
the novel by Chariton, as well as early in § 4.5 and in footnote 119). And
for translation purposes it might be helpful to think of them as instances
of a perception verb imperative that is followed by a pause (e.g., *Look!*).
But insofar as the particle use is distinct from the true imperative use, I
assume that the C3 particle may often be integrated syntactically into its

---

[74] The same analysis seems to be true of C5, except that C5 occurs much more
often with conjunctions and other initial elements, as will be shown later.

clause. (To be sure, there are some instances of ἴδε where it is debatable if it is an instance of the particle or the imperative.)

Consider **Mat 25:20**, with topical subject 'I'.

Mat 25:20 κύριε,   πέντε   τάλαντά   μοι   παρέδωκας·
master five.A.p.n talents.A.p.n to.me you.gave

ἴδε ἄλλα   πέντε   τάλαντα   ἐκέρδησα.
*   more.A.p.n five.A.p.n talents.A.p.n I.gained

NRS: Then the [servant] who had received the five talents came forward, bringing five more talents, saying, 'Master, you handed over to me five talents; <u>see, I have made five more talents</u>.'

GNB: Look! Here are another five thousand that I have earned.

The master wants to know how much the servant given five talents has earned. So the servant's answer presupposes the open proposition 'I have gained X', and the informative part of the answer is expressed by the (preverbal) constituent-focus object ἄλλα πέντε τάλαντα 'five more talents'. (The same analysis applies to 'two talents' in Mat 25:22.) Here, ἴδε is clearly used as a here-and-now deictic since the speaker is showing something to his master.[75] Although I assume that ἴδε is most likely syntactically integrated into the clause (and not a true imperative nor simply an interjection), nevertheless, for English it seems that the closest translation would be an independent phrase like *Here!* or *Look (here)!* followed by a pause (Z&G suggest *look!*). The NRS, cited above, has a similar rendering, *see*, but the GNB actually uses a dedicated deictic thetic (plus *Look!*), which, for all practical purposes, seems to have the same effect for this token. (For another possible instance of C3 with constituent-focus, see Act 10:21, discussed in § 4.4.4.)

Ἴδε is also used deictically a few verses later, in **Mat 25:25** (Z&G also say ἴδε means *here!*). This too fails the test for sentence-focus because, again, the subject is topical. But this token is not an instance of constituent-focus. To be sure, it is also readily restructured in English as a deictic thetic (e.g., GNB, with double translation: *Look! Here is what belongs to you*; also CEV, NIV). But if ἴδε is really intended to point to the act of returning the talent, the NRS would better reflect the Greek structure, where the subject is topical: *Here you have what is yours*. Alternatively, if ἴδε by itself is taken instead to be a shorthand for 'here is your talent', then ἔχεις τὸ σόν can be interpreted as a personal defense whereby the servant suggests he has fulfilled his responsibility; present tense ἔχεις [2s.have.Pres] could

---

[75] Although it is difficult to prove since the addressee is singular, I assume with BDAG that ἴδε here is an instance of the particle and not the imperative.

be rendered as 'you are holding (what is yours)' (Rutger Allan, p.c.), or the clause as a whole could be paraphrased as 'you have not lost your property' (Tony Pope, p.c.), or as in 'nab' below.

Mat 25:25 Ἴδε ἔχεις   τὸ σόν.
*   you.have.Pres the yours

> NRS: Here you have what is yours.
> GNB: Look! Here is what belongs to you.
> nab: Here! You have back your property.

For **Mrk 11:21**, the consulted English translations unanimously render ἴδε as *look*, separated from what follows by some punctuation (! or ,). The subject, ἡ συκῆ ἦν κατηράσω 'the fig tree that you cursed', expresses the clause topic (a recent topic of conversation—the day before, v 13), and the predicate expresses the informative comment. It is difficult to construe the clause as a deictic thetic in English translation. For example, Peter can hardly be saying 'Here is the fig tree that you cursed, it has withered'. Finally, ἴδε here clearly involves an emotive element (surprise or wonder), as it also does in the next example, Mrk 13:1.

Mrk 11:21 ῥαββί, ἴδε ἡ   συκῆ   ἦν   κατηράσω
Rabbi *   the fig.tree which you.cursed

ἐξήρανται.
has.been.withered

> GNB: [20] Early next morning, as they walked along the road, they saw the fig tree. It was dead all the way down to its roots. [21] Peter remembered what had happened and said to Jesus, "<u>Look, Teacher, the fig tree you cursed has died!</u>"
> NRS: Rabbi, look! The fig tree that you cursed has withered.

It is possible to interpret ἴδε+NP$_{NOM}$ in **Mrk 13:1** in different ways. At first glance, it might appear to be (**i**) an instance of C1.

Mrk 13:1 διδάσκαλε, ἴδε ποταποὶ   λίθοι καὶ ποταπαὶ
teacher   *   what.sort.of stones and what.sort.of

οἰκοδομαί.
buildings

> NRS: [1] As he came out of the temple, one of his disciples said to him, "<u>Look, Teacher, what large stones and what large buildings!</u>" [2] Then Jesus asked him, "Do you see these great buildings? Not one stone will be left here upon another; all will be thrown down."
> GNB: "Look, Teacher! What wonderful stones and buildings!"
> BFC: Maître, regarde ! Quelles belles pierres, quelles grandes constructions !

But what distinguishes this construction from C1, as well as from a typical instance of C3, is the addition of the question word ποταποί 'what kind of', which makes this an **exclamative** construction. Following Michaelis (2001), an exclamative construction represents *an emotional judgment about a state of affairs that the speaker feels is surprising*, and so it necessarily expresses the speaker's perspective and feelings.[76] By adding ἴδε, the speaker explicitly invites the hearer (i.e., Jesus) to share the same judgment. (More will be said about exclamatives in the section on C4.) So, as a second interpretation **(ii)**, this token can be viewed as a C3-exclamative hybrid construction. All English and French translations I have consulted render it as *look* or *regarde*, set off by a comma or an exclamation mark, and this seems like a good way to handle this in translation (in which case this use of ἴδε is indistinguishable from the imperative). To interpret this clause as **(i)** a deictic thetic, such as *Here are such wonderful stones ...*, strikes me as odd, as if the speaker (or hearer) would be noticing the stones and buildings for the first time ever. Rather, the stones and buildings are to be taken as given (topical): it is their impressive nature that is being asserted and marveled at. **(iii)** A third possible interpretation is C4b (see § 4.4.3).

Outside of the NT, there are clear instances of ἰδού used as C3. Consider the use of ἰδού in what is known as the shorter Greek text of **Tob 7:13** (the longer Greek text lacks ἰδού). Here in what is a formal transaction, much as we saw above in Mat 25:25 where something 'changes hands', Raguel presents his daughter, Sarah, to Tobias, at which point she becomes Tobias' wife (there on the spot in Raguel's home).

Tob 7:13 καὶ εἶπεν Ἰδοὺ κατὰ   τὸν νόμον Μωυσέως
and he.said * according.to the law   of.moses

κομίζου αὐτὴν
take!   her

> NETS: Then [Ragouel] called Sarra his daughter, and taking her hand, he gave her over to Tobias as wife, and he said, "Behold, according to the law of Moyses take her, and lead her away to your father." And [Ragouel] blessed them.

---

[76] In her cross-linguistic study, Michaelis defines an exclamative utterance as an emotional judgment about a state of affairs that the speaker feels is surprising (2001:1039). The utterance lexically evokes an open proposition where the open variable is a degree. Against that presupposition, the utterance asserts 'a particular scalar degree' that the speaker feels emotional about (e.g., an extreme degree of temperature: *Man(,) it's hot in Dallas!*; of intelligence: *What a genius!*; or of deliciousness: *What delicious desserts John bakes!*). In the current passage, Mrk 13:1, the disciple is apparently exclaiming about the amazing size or beauty of the temple stones and buildings.

Another interesting C3 token, **Tob 2:8**, may be a case of an extended (rhetorical) use.[77] The clause is also conjoined by καί. Tobit had previously fled for his life because he was discovered secretly burying Israelites murdered by the Assyrian emperor, Shalmaneser. Sometime later, when his son reported to him that an Israelite had just been murdered and left in the market, he recovered the body and buried it. When his neighbors see what he has done, they ridicule his behavior among themselves, using ἰδού to point out his behavior, where 'he' is the topical subject (GNB changes third person to second person in order to make the rebuke direct). It is easy to imagine that the gossiping neighbors are uttering this after the fact, in which case ἰδού would not be purely here-and-now but used rhetorically. In either case, it is readily translated by deictic *here* (see NRS and GNB). The order καὶ πάλιν ἰδού occurs in the longer text, which suggests that πάλιν 'again' is to be read emphatically and that perhaps it is syntactically dislocated; the shorter text has καὶ ἰδοὺ πάλιν.

Tob 2:8 καὶ   πάλιν   ἰδοὺ   θάπτει   τοὺς νεκρούς.
         and   again   *   he.is.burying the   dead.A.p.m

> NRS: [7] When the sun had set, I went and dug a grave and buried him. [8] And my neighbors laughed and said, "Is he still not afraid? He has already been hunted down to be put to death for doing this, and he ran away; yet here he is again burying the dead!"

> GNB: [8] My neighbors thought I was crazy. "Haven't you learned anything?" they asked. "You have already been hunted down once for burying the dead, and you would have been killed if you had not run away. But here you are doing the same thing all over again."

In the secular Koine novel by Chariton, there are a handful of instances of ἰδού that I take to be cases of C3 and C1, although these differ from the NT use in that often the speech word, φησὶ(ν) '3s.says', or in one case a vocative, immediately follows ἰδού. The examples below are from the novel about Chaereas and Callirhoe, written by Chariton about the time the NT was being written or somewhat later.[78] (The explanations in square brackets in the translations are my additions. The Greek text is from Perseus.)[79]

---

[77] Thanks to Michael Aubrey (p.c.) for pointing this instance out to me.

[78] See Reardon (1989:17), Goold (1995:2), and Trzaskoma (2010:xxiv).

[79] In this novel, there are two more instances of ἰδού, one in 3.9.8 and another in 7.5.2. All examples in Chariton occur in reported speech.

2.11.1[80] καὶ 'ἰδοὺ' φησὶ 'τρεῖς γεγόναμεν, ἀνὴρ καὶ
and * 3s.says three we.have.become.Prf man and

γυνὴ καὶ τέκνον.
woman and child

Reardon: Callirhoe went up to her room and shut the door. She held Chaireas's picture [which was on a ring on her finger] to her womb. "Here are the three of us," she said, "husband, wife and child; let us decide what is best for us all."

Trzaskoma: "Look, there are three of us: husband, wife, and child."

5.5.2[81] ἰδού, Τύχη, καὶ κρίνομαι.
* Fortune also I.am.being.put.on.trial

Reardon: "Oh," she [=Callirhoe] cried, "that was all I needed, in my misfortunes—to be taken to court! I have died and been buried; I have been stolen from my tomb; I have been sold into slavery—and now, Fortune, on top of that I find myself on trial! You were not satisfied with traducing me to Chaereas; you have led Dionysius to suspect me of adultery!"

Goold: and now, here I am, on trial! Was it not enough for you, Fortune ...?

Trzaskoma: Look, Fortune—now I'm on trial too!

---

[80] It is helpful to briefly summarize some of the novel's plot. Handsome Chaereas and beautiful Callirhoe, from leading families in Syracuse, fall in love and then marry to the great disappointment of Callirhoe's other suitors. But when the disgruntled suitors trick Chaereas into believing that Callirhoe has been unfaithful, he in anger kicks her so hard that she appears to have died. Callirhoe is then buried in a tomb but later discovered alive by grave robbers (pirates), who kidnap her and take her to Miletus, where she is sold to an important citizen, Dionysius, who was recently widowed.

The specific context of 2.11.1 is that Callirhoe has just discovered she is pregnant by her husband Chaereas, and now her master, Dionysius, wants to marry her. She wonders whether to kill herself or to abort the child and marry. Alone in her room, she utters this ἰδού sentence as she addresses her husband's image on her ring.

[81] Callirhoe is recounting her misfortunes and voices her complaint to 'Fortune'.

1.9.7 [82] 'ἰδού' φησὶν 'ὁ   δαίμων, ὃν   ἐφοβοῦ:
  *   3s.says the.N spirit.N whom you.were.afraid.of

> Trzaskoma: So he [=the pirate leader, Theron] took her
> [=Callirhoe] by the hand and led her outside. ¶ Calling his
> accomplice over, he said, "<u>Here's the spirit you were afraid of</u>.
> Some pirate you are—afraid even of a woman!"
>
> Reardon: "There you are—there's the spirit you were afraid of."

1.14.6 [83] ''Ιδού' φησὶν 'ἄλλος   τάφος,
  *   3s.says another.N tomb.N

> Reardon: So they [the pirates] left hurriedly, where the wind
> took them; Callirhoe, left to herself, was free now to lament
> her own lot. "<u>There!</u>" she said. "<u>Another tomb</u>, in which
> Theron has shut me up! It is more lonely than the first!"
>
> Trzaskoma: "Look! Another tomb!"

The first two passages cited above, 2.11.1 and 5.5.2, contain clear instances of C3. Neither are thetic since both have a topical subject (which is in both cases Callirhoe, who is talking about herself). But unlike in our NT examples, in both tokens, something intervenes between ἰδού and the main clause. In 2.11.1 the intervening element is φησί(ν) '3s.says', and in 5.5.2, it is a vocative, Τύχη 'Fortune'.

That such elements, especially a vocative, can intervene might be viewed as evidence that ἰδού in C3 can (at least sometimes) be syntactically independent from what follows, and that in such cases ἰδού might have been followed by a pause and separated off intonationally. But this conclusion is not certain. The fact is that discontinuous phrases are common in Greek, and 'postpositives' (i.e., certain words, including some enclitics, as well as forms of φημί) regularly come after the first word or first phrase in a sentence, just as we find φησί(ν) and the vocative Τύχη doing in these examples.

The last two examples cited above, 1.9.7 and 1.14.6 (both with nominative case NPs) are clear instances of C1 (here-and-now deictic

---

[82] In the preceding context, a henchman pirate had broken into the tomb of Callirhoe, who was presumed dead, but when she threw herself at his feet, he ran out in fear. Then Theron, the chief pirate, enters the tomb, finds Callirhoe and brings her out. (Theron at first had thought he would kill her but then decided to take her along with all the grave goods and sell her.) Once they exit the tomb, Theron says this ἰδού sentence to his henchman.

[83] Having sold Callirhoe as a slave, the pirates have now sailed away, and Callirhoe is alone reflecting on her lot. She is in a fine bedroom in the house of her master as she talks to herself. Theron's 'locking' is figurative; Callirhoe is probably referring to the fact of being sold into slavery, which was a terrible misfortune for a highborn Greek woman.

thetics), except that, again, φησί(ν) intervenes. If we could prove that ἰδού was truly separated syntactically in these tokens, then they would represent a slight variation of C1, that is, **ἰδού + nominative fragment** (which would be comparable to the 'perception (verb) imperative + fragment' construction discussed in § 4.1).

In summary, C3 resembles C1 in that ἴδε and ἰδού have here-and-now deictic reference, but it differs in that the main clause is not a bona fide sentence-focus thetic. In the Chariton data, an element, φησί(ν) or a vocative, often comes in between the particle and the rest of the clause.

→ Possible NT instances of C3 number no more than eleven and all ἰδού tokens in the NT are somewhat debatable. Mat 12:2 (ἰδού; or C2a or C5; see § 4.2.1); Mat 25:20; Mat 25:22; Mat 25:25; Mrk 11:21; Mrk 13:1 (or C4); Jhn 11:36 (or C4); Act 10:21 (ἰδού; or C2; see § 4.4.4); Heb 10:7 and ||Heb 10:9 (ἰδού; or C5); Rev 21:3 (ἰδού; or C5 or C2; see § 4.2.3). (See also J&A 16.10 [Burchard; 16.5 in Philonenko].)

4.4   C4 – The emotively emphatic constituent-focus marker

As C4, I count those instances of ἰδού and ἴδε which immediately precede a phrase that is simultaneously a case of constituent-focus and emotively emphatic.[84] In this use, the particle forms a syntactic unit with the constituent-focus phrase (e.g., a noun phrase or adverbial phrase) and can be described as an **'emphatic focus marker'**. In the NT, there are up to fifteen tokens with ἰδού and up to seven with ἴδε.

To be sure, there are a handful of instances where ἰδού/ἴδε begins a sentence where later in the sentence, but not immediately, a constituent-focus phrase occurs and where there seems to be an emotive component. But the clearest examples of emotive constituent-focus involve immediate adjacency, and so I consider immediate adjacency to be a requirement of C4. There are of course other constructions in the language that seem to reinforce such a structure involving immediate adjacency: First, there is the fact that in C1 the focused (thetic) subject always immediately follows the particle (thus forming a syntactic unit, in this case a simple clause: ἰδού/ἴδε+NP$_{NOM}$). Second, there is the parallel use of adverbial καί, which (probably) always immediately precedes the

---

[84] As will be noted below, I have doubts about a C4 analysis for some of the instances of ἴδε-*focused-constituent-X*, since alternative interpretations (C5 or C3) may also be possible. Incidentally, there is no clear instance of ἴδε-*X-focused-constituent*, that is, where the focused constituent comes later in the clause.

constituent it modifies.[85] From an information structure point of view, one typical use of adverbial καί is as an ('additive') constituent-focus marker (often rendered as *also* or *too*).

In the following three sections, I treat three different varieties of C4. All three sets involve **emotive emphasis**, a part of the meaning that, in at least the case of ἰδού, was presumably inherited from its middle verb ancestor (§ 3.1). The focused constituent may be the subject or, in contrast to prototypical thetic constructions, another part of speech (object, time phrase, verb, or other predicative element). While a few tokens may alternatively be viewed as having deictic or semi-thetic properties, most cannot. Assuming that the particles indicate emotive emphasis, renderings like *Look* or *Listen* must be rejected. In § 4.4.4 (and § 4.5.2), other tokens with constituent-focus are discussed that are simultaneously instances of C3, C5, or C2.

4.4.1 C4a – ἰδού and emotively emphatic time durations

C4a involves tokens where ἰδού immediately precedes a focused constituent and where that constituent expresses a duration of time that is emotively emphatic, that is, the speaker is essentially **exclaiming** over what seems to be a surprising length of time (there are no tokens with ἴδε). The construction in mind, ἰδού + *time phrase*, is in fact noted by BDAG (ἰδού.1.b.ε), Moulton and Howard (1929:447), and Fiedler (1969:20) (besides others—see on p. 31 for Fiedler's references) who assume ἰδού 'emphasizes' the time. Moreover, they note that the time phrase is in the **nominative**. This is striking since in Greek time durations are normally expressed by the accusative (BDF § 161.2; Smyth § 1580–1587). Thus, we have essentially the same structure as ἰδού–NP_{NOM} in C1, except that the NP refers to an abstract (second order) time entity rather than to a concrete (first order) entity.

Examples cited in the literature from outside the NT include ones from papyri, **PM.3 203.9** (early second century C.E.), **PP.2 98.17** (fourth century C.E.), and **BGU 948.6** (from a Christian letter from the fourth century C.E.).[86]

---

[85] In NT Greek, adverbial καί is assumed to always modify an immediately following word or phrase (Levinsohn 2000:101, Heckert 1996:64, Titrud 1992:244). In Classical Greek, it also usually modifies what immediately follows, 'but sometimes also a preceding word when that word stands first in its clause' (Smyth § 2881).

[86] **PM.3 203.9** = P. Michigan III, cited by Fiedler (1969:20) and Zilliacus (1943:38). http://papyri.info/ddbdp/p.mich;3;203 (retrieved November 24, 2015);

  PP.2 98.17 = P. Princeton II, cited by BDF § 144 and Fiedler 1969:20. http://papyri.info/ddbdp/p.princ;2;98 (retrieved November 24, 2015);

PM.3 203.9 γεινώσκιν σε   θέλω ὅτι εἰδοῦ τρεῖς μῆνες
to.know   you.A I.want that (=ἰδού) three.N months.N

ἀφ' ὅτε   ἤλαγμαι εἰ[ς] Ψέλκιν
since when I.moved to   Pselkis

nab: I want you to know that it has been <u>three months</u>
  since I moved to Pselkis.[87]

PP.2 98.17 ἐθαύμασά   σε   οὖν   ἰδοῦ δύο   μῆνες
I.was.amazed at.you so/then *   two.N months.N

σήμερον οὐδὲν   δέδωκάς   μοι
today   nothing.A you.have.given to.me

nab: So I was amazed at you (that) it has been <u>two months</u>
  today that you have not given me anything.

BGU 948.6 γινώσκιν ἐ[θ]έλω ὅτι εἶπέν σοι   ὁ πραγματευτ[ὴς
to.know   I.want that 3s.said to.you the businessman

ὅ]τι … ἡ μήτηρ σου   Κοφαήνα ἀσθενεῖ,
that   the mother of.you Kofaina 3s.is.sick

ἰδοὺ, δέκα τρεῖς   μῆνες
*   ten three.N months.N

nab: I would like (you) to know that the businessman said to
  you that … your mother Kofaina has been sick <u>for thirteen
  months</u>.

→ In the NT, there appear to be three instances of this construction,
Luk 13:16, **Luk 15:29**, and **Luk 13:7**. To be sure, all three involve
ἔτη 'years', which is neuter and thus ambiguous in respect to the
nominative/accusative distinction. But given the above illustrated Koine
construction, it is reasonable to assume that ἔτη is nominative in each
(BDF § 144 suggests this for at least Luk 3:16).

Luk 13:16 ταύτην δὲ θυγατέρα Ἀβραὰμ   οὖσαν, ἣν   ἔδησεν
this.one but daughter of.Abraham being whom 3s.bound

ὁ   σατανᾶς ἰδοὺ **δέκα καὶ ὀκτὼ ἔτη**, οὐκ
the Satan   *   ten and eight years not

BGU 3.948.6 = Ägyptische Urkunde aus den königlichen Museen zu Berlin,
Griechische Urkunden I-VIII, 1895–1933, cited by BDF § 144, Moulton
(1908:11), and Moulton and Milligan 1930:299. I quote here the fuller
citation from Moulton and Milligan. http://papyri.info/ddbdp/bgu;3;948
(retrieved November 24, 2015).

[87] Arzt-Grabner et al. (2006:501) translate this line as 'du sollst wissen, dass
es, sieh da, schon drei Monate her ist, dass ich nach Pselkis gegangen bin.' I
am taking ἤλαγμαι as a middle perfect of ἀλλάσσω.

ἔδει   λυθῆναι   ἀπὸ τοῦ δεσμοῦ τούτου
it.was.needed to.be.set.free from the.G bond.G this.G

τῇ   ἡμέρᾳ τοῦ   σαββάτου;
on.the.D day.D of.the Sabbath

NRS: " ... And ought not this woman, a daughter of Abraham
whom Satan bound for <u>eighteen long years</u>, be set free
from this bondage on the sabbath day?"

FBJ: Et cette fille d'Abraham, que Satan a liée <u>voici dix-huit
ans</u>, il n'eût pas fallu la délier de ce lien le jour du sabbat !

nab (Paul Solomiac, p.c.): Et cette femme, qui est une fille
d'Abraham, <u>voilà dix-huit ans que</u> le Satan la tenait liée, il
n'aurait pas fallu la détacher de ce lien le jour du sabbat ?

NRT: Так не нужно ли было освободить в субботу и эту
женщину, одну из дочерей Авраама, <u>вот уже
восемнадцать лет</u> связанную сатаной?

CRV: А эту женщину, дочь Авраама, которая связана
сатаной <u>вот уже восемнадцать лет</u>, разве не следовало
освободить от этих уз в день субботний?

Luk 15:29 ἰδοὺ **τοσαῦτα ἔτη**   δουλεύω σοι
*   so.many years I.serve   you

CEV: For years I have worked for you like a slave and have
always obeyed you.

GNB: Look, all these years I have worked for you like a
slave, ...

NRS: Listen! For all these years ...

NIV: Look! All these years I've been slaving ...

Tony Pope (p.c.): For years and years I've been at your
service ...

FBJ: Mais il répondit à son père: "Voilà tant d'années que je
te sers, ..."

Luk 13:7 ἰδοὺ **τρία ἔτη**   ἀφ' οὗ   ἔρχομαι ζητῶν
*   three.N years.N since which.G I.come seeking

καρπὸν ἐν τῇ συκῇ   ταύτῃ καὶ οὐχ εὑρίσκω·
fruit   on the fig.tree this   and not I.found

GNB: Look, <u>for three years</u> I have been coming here looking
for figs on this fig tree, and I haven't found any. Cut it down!

NRS: <u>See here!</u> For three years I have come looking for fruit
on this fig tree ...

NIV: For three years now I've been coming ...

nab/Tony Pope: <u>It's been no less than three years</u> that I've
been coming ...

FBJ: <u>Voilà trois ans que</u> je viens chercher des fruits sur ce
figuier, ...

NRT: <u>Вот уже три года</u> я прихожу смотреть, нет ли на
этом инжире плодов, и ничего не нахожу.

CRV: <u>Вот уже три года</u>, как я прихожу сюда, чтобы
посмотреть, не принесла ли смоковница плоды, и не
нахожу ни одного.

Moreover, the context in each of the NT passages clearly supports
an emotively emphatic reading. In Luk 13:16, Jesus is angry with his
opponents and exclaiming about all the years the poor woman has been
sick. In Luk 15:29, the older brother is bitterly complaining about how
long he has served his father. And in Luk 13:7, the speaker complains
that three years is plenty long to wait for a tree to bear fruit—it is time to
chop it down! In each token, the time phrase is an instance of **emotively
emphatic constituent-focus** that identifies a time duration against an
open proposition. Much like an exclamative construction, it emphasizes
an **extreme degree**—what the speaker judges to be an excessive length
of time.[88] For example, in Luk 15:29, the open proposition to be taken for
granted would be 'I have served you [for X time]' and 'so many years'
identifies the amount. Thus, in all three NT passages, as in the papyrus
examples, a time phrase immediately follows ἰδού and is emotively
emphatic.

If we assume ἔτη 'years' in the above is nominative, then, as
pointed out by BDF § 144, we may note a resemblance with certain
time statements lacking ἰδού. Consider, for example, the time durations
expressed with ἡμέραι 'days' (unambiguously nominative): In **Act 24:11**,
the clause has εἰμί as its predicator, but in **Mat 15:32** (‖Mrk 8:2), the
clause is verbless and structurally parallel to ἰδοὺ τρία ἔτη ἀφ' οὗ ... in

---

[88] In footnote 76, I mentioned Michaelis' definition of an exclamative
utterance, i.e., an emotional judgment about a state of affairs that the
speaker feels is surprising (2001:1039). Thus, both C4a and other subtypes
of C4 share much with exclamative constructions like *(Man,) it's so hot!* and
What a fool he was! See also Bailey (2009:372–375) for more comparison of
exclamative constructions and C4 constructions.

Luk 13:7.[89] Mat 15:32 also clearly emphasizes the time (see also Turner's [1963:231] comments on Jos 1:11).[90]

Act 24:11 ἀπολογοῦμαι, ¹¹ δυναμένου σου ἐπιγνῶναι ὅτι οὐ
I.make.my.defense   being.able you to.learn   that not

πλείους εἰσίν μοι **ἡμέραι δώδεκα** ἀφ' ἧς
more.than 3p.are to.me days.N twelve   from which

ἀνέβην προσκυνήσων εἰς Ἰερουσαλήμ.
I.went.up will.be.worshiping to Jerusalem

NRS: ¹⁰ … I cheerfully make my defense, … ¹¹ As you can find out, it is not more than <u>twelve days</u> since I went up to worship in Jerusalem.

Mat 15:32 σπλαγχνίζομαι ἐπὶ τὸν ὄχλον, ὅτι ἤδη **ἡμέραι τρεῖς**
I.feel   for the crowd for already days.N three.N

προσμένουσίν μοι
3p.remain   with.me

nab: I feel for the crowd for <u>it is already three days</u> that they are with me (and have nothing to eat).

BFC: J'ai pitié de ces gens, <u>car voilà trois jours qu'ils</u> sont avec moi et ils n'ont plus rien à manger.

NRT: Мне жаль этих людей, они со Мной <u>вот уже три дня</u>, и у них не осталось еды.

CRV: Жаль Мне людей, ибо <u>вот уже три дня</u> они со Мной, а есть им нечего.

The parallel between Mat 15:32 without ἰδού and Luk 13:7 with ἰδοὺ τρία ἔτη ἀφ' οὗ … in particular suggests that the ἰδού sentence is a **bi-clausal** construction, something resembling a cleft, composed of an ἰδού-time **clause** (where ἰδού is the predicator) plus a relative clause embedded in a prepositional phrase (BDF § 144 actually describes both as 'asyndetic quasi-clausal temporal designation[s] in [the] nom[inative]'). Much as the relative clause in the English **it-cleft** *It's been THREE YEARS*

---

[89] That ἤδη ἡμέραι τρεῖς counts as a separate verbless clause is also suggested by the order προσμένουσίν μοι, where the (non-focal) enclitic pronoun follows the verb. In contrast to this order, within a single clause when a focal noun phrase precedes its verb, an enclitic pronoun would normally immediately follow, resulting in this order: *Focus-enclitic-Verb* (see Bailey [2009:113–114], which reflects observations made by Levinsohn [2000] and others). Such enclitic placement may perhaps be best viewed as essentially prosodic, as underscored by Michael Aubrey (p.c.).

[90] See also Rom 13:11: ὥρα ἤδη ὑμᾶς ἐξ ὕπνου ἐγερθῆναι, [hour.N already for.you from sleep to.wake.up] '(and knowing also that) *now* is the time for you to wake up from sleep'.

that I have been coming ..., so the embedded clause in Greek expresses the part of the proposition that is to be taken for granted (i.e., the open proposition).[91]

But the structures in Luk 13:16 and in Luk 15:29 are less obviously comparable to bi-clausal *it*-clefts in English, even if they too are readily translated by such constructions in English. In any case, in all these cases it is reasonable to assume that ἰδού–*TIME* forms some sort of **syntactic phrase** where ἰδού is a kind of focus marker (thus a phrase and not a full clause). This is especially clear for Luk 13:16 where ἰδού–*eighteen years* comes clause-finally (see below for a comparable structure in Russian). From the LXX, **Deu 8:4** is a comparable token, and this predates the above NT and papyri tokens.[92] Interestingly, in this passage (as well as in Deu 2:7 and Zec 7:5 where ἰδού–*TIME* are sentence-initial), ἰδού translates not הִנֵּה 'behold' but זֶה (*zeh*) 'this' followed by a time phrase, which happens to be the standard Hebrew idiom for emphasizing time durations or multiple occurrences of an event.[93] This

---

[91] See Lambrecht (2001) for a comparable analysis of cleft constructions. See also below my illustrations of what are very similar emphatic constructions in French, including one with and one without *voilà*, which are true clefts, and where the clefted *que* clause expresses the part of the proposition that is to be taken for granted.

[92] See also Gen 27:36, which according to one textual variant (cited by Moulton and Howard 1929:447) reads: ἐπτέρνικε γάρ με ἰδού δεύτερον τοῦτο [3S.has.tricked me ἰδού second this.N/A] 'for [Esau] has duped me *this second time!*' The Masoretic Text reads זֶה.

[93] The Hebrew construction זֶה (*zeh*) + time phrase, which is actually fairly frequent (Gesenius-Kautzsch-Cowley 1910 § 136.d), is used to emotively emphasize a time duration or the number of occurrences that something happens (see Waltke and O'Connor 1990 § 17.4.2 and Holmstedt 2014:8). In my opinion, it should be either viewed as an extended use of the demonstrative or else as an earlier or original use of the form (so Joüon & Muraoka § 143a). In either case, this use with time phrases represents a dedicated construction, one that is typically unrecognized as such by English translators and therefore, much like ἰδού–*TIME*, often mistranslated or under-translated. The question of whether or not its syntax should be viewed as a clefted verbless clause or something else (e.g. adverbial phrase) has been discussed recently (see e.g. Holmstedt 2014 and literature therein). Unlike Deu 8:4, the LXX more typically rendered this construction by a demonstrative followed by a time phrase, as illustrated by Jdg 16:15 (זֶה שָׁלֹשׁ פְּעָמִים הֵתַלְתָּ בִּי [this three times 2sm.deceived.Prf with-me]), where Delilah scolds Samson for deceiving her *three times*: τοῦτο τρίτον παρελογίσω με [this.A.s.n third.A.s.n 2s.deceived.Aor me]. The ESV mistakenly assumes זֶה has its common demonstrative sense (*You have mocked me these three times*) and so does not do justice to the emotionally charged idiom (translations that render זֶה as *now* are not much better, e.g., see CEV's emotionally neutral

suggests the translators were seeking to translate the meaning of the Hebrew construction rather than imitating its 'literal' form.

Deu 8:4 τὰ ἱμάτιά σου οὐ κατετρίβη   ἀπὸ σοῦ,
the clothing of.you not 3s.were.worn.out.Aor from you

οἱ πόδες σου οὐκ ἐτυλώθησαν,
the feet of.you not 3p.became.knobby.Aor

ἰδοὺ τεσσαράκοντα ἔτη.[94]
* forty   years

> nab: Your clothes did not wear out on you and your feet did not become callous <u>for a whole forty years</u>.
>
> NETS:[95] Your clothes were not worn off you; your feet did not become hard; look, <u>for forty years</u>!

Translation issues: Despite the recognition in such standard works as BDAG and BDF that ἰδού–TIME emphasizes a time, many translators have failed to bring this across but instead have fallen back on renderings like *look!* or *listen!* or German *siehe*, etc. Such renderings fail to translate the meaning of the construction. They promote the false assumption that ἰδού has a single sense and a single syntactic function.

The use of a deictic thetic (presentational) particle to emphasize a time duration is not limited to Koine ἰδού. In his cross-linguistic

---

construction: *You've made me look like a fool three times now*). Better translation models can be found in the NIV's use of a cleft clause, which more readily allows for an emotional reading (*This is the third time you have made a fool of me*) and in some Russian and French translations. At least one Russian translation uses a (dedicated) emphatic time construction for this instance (NRT: Вот уже третий раз ты издеваешься надо мной) as do also some French translations (BFC: Voilà trois fois que tu te moques de moi ; see also FBJ). Below, I discuss these emotive constructions in Russian and French.

[94] Editors of these ancient texts have sometimes added a comma before or after ἰδού, but such commas are not original. For example, in BDAG's citation of BGU 948.6, a comma immediately precedes ἰδού; in the online version of this same papyrus, commas both precede and follow it; and in Deu 8:4 in the Rahlf-Hanhart edition of the LXX (but not in Swete's 1901 edition), a comma immediately precedes ἰδού. This editorial habit gives the unfortunate impression that ἰδού is simply an imperative (e.g., *Siehe!, See!, Lo!*) or a syntactically disconnected 'interjection'. The same tendency is true of Robinson and Pierpont, who in their NT text usually include a comma after ἰδού (or ἰδού plus postpositive like γάρ) and ἴδε, but it is not true of the Nestle-Aland/UBS text.

[95] The unnatural translation here is explained by the fact that NETS does not aim to be an idiomatic translation of the LXX, but, as the English translator of Deuteronomy states (Melvin K. H. Peters), 'to signal precisely what is present in Greek'.

study of temporal adverbs, Haspelmath (1997:138–139) briefly mentions
a handful of European languages that use 'presentative particles' with
'noun phrases denoting a time span' in order to emphasize the time
span. He mentions French *voilà*, Russian вот, Lithuanian *štai*, as well as
NT Greek (citing ἰδού in Luk 13:7 and Luk 15:29).

For Russian, Haspelmath cites the two sentences repeated here in
(20). For both (i) and (ii), he gives the same free gloss: 'I have lived in
Paris for five years', and for both he states (p. 139) that 'the presentative
particle emphatically asserts the existence of the time span' of five
years and 'is only felicitous if the time span of five years is perceived
as unusually long.' Such an emotionally emphatic interpretation has
been confirmed for me by several native Russian speakers, who have
also pointed out that the deictic particle вот [*vot*] is only used in this
way when combined with the adverb уже [*uže*] 'already', that is, never
without уже.[96]

(20) (i) Vot uže pjat' let kak ja živu   [lo already five years that I live
          v Pariže   in Paris]
     (ii) Ja živu v Pariže vot uže   [I live in Paris lo already five
          pjat' let.   years].

The construction вот уже + *time phrase* is actually very common in
Russian, and many Russian Bible translators have made use of it in some
of the ἰδού-*TIME* passages in Luke (see cited translations above), as well
as in passages that do not involve ἰδού (see above for the NRT and CRV
renderings of Mat 15:32).

It is also worth noting that Haspelmath describes the first of his
examples (i) as syntactically biclausal and the second (ii) as monoclausal.
In (i), *vot uže pjat' let* is clearly the main clause, as the complementizer

---

[96] I am grateful to Tatiana Mayskaya, Alexey Somov, and Vitaly Voinov (p.c.)
for sharing their native speaker intuitions on the Russian data and
translations. To paraphrase one of their observations, although a time
phrase in some sentences can of course be felt to be emphatic without
вот уже, its presence guarantees that the speaker has (relatively) strong
feelings (of surprise, irritation, anger, etc.) about the length of time (e.g.
the time span is viewed as especially or unduly long). Although no Russian
lexicon I consulted specifically mentions this use of вот (уже) with time
phrases, Alexey Somov (p.c.) suggested to me that it is essentially covered
by the *second* subdefinition of вот in the online Russian language
resource ГРАМОТА.РУ, which states that вот is used to strengthen what
follows usually with a sense of shock or surprise. (In contrast, the *first*
subdefinition illustrates deictic thetic constructions, presumably the
prototypical use of вот: e.g. Вот вам ключ 'Here's the key for you'.)
Retrieved February 13, 2018 at http://gramota.ru/slovari/
dic/?word=%D0%B2%D0%BE%D1%82&all=x

как [*kak*] 'that' subordinates what follows. In (ii), *vot uže pjat' let* comes later in the sentence and presumably functions as an adverbial phrase. The latter structure seems comparable with what I have described above as the quasi-clausal status of ἰδού-*TIME*, especially in Luk 13:16 and Deu 8:4 where it comes later in the sentence.

The use of French *voilà* to emphasize a length of time is also instructive. *Tex's French Grammar*[97] briefly mentions three cleft constructions that may be used to indicate a time duration (i) *il y avait ... que ...*, (ii) *cela faisait ... que...*, and (iii) *voilà ... que ...*, the latter of which is called 'more emphatic', although the editors do not explain. These three clefts are illustrated by (21a–c), to which has been added a fourth possibility, (d), which is not mentioned in the grammar.[98]

(21)   a. Y'a une heure que j't'attends.
       b. Ça fait une heure que j't'attends.
       c. Voilà une heure que j't'attends.
       d. Une heure que j't'attends !

All four constructions would be instances of constituent-focus (answering 'how long ...?'), and all could be rendered in English by *It's been an hour that I've been waiting* or *I've been waiting for an hour*. Moreover, all four of these may be used in an emotively emphatic context, where, for example, the speaker is irritated for having to wait so long. But there are subtle semantic differences between these constructions. For our purposes, what stands out is that (c) *voilà ... que ...* guarantees an emphatic connotation that (a) and (b) do not. This can be shown in that the associated feeling of irritation may be cancelled in (a) and (b) by adding *seulement* 'only' or by following them by a phrase like *mais qu'est-ce qu'une heure* 'but what's an hour'. In (a) and (b), such an addition would indicate that either the speaker is not irritated or that he or she is being sarcastic, but in (c) (and [d]), it could only indicate sarcasm.

(22) a. Y'a seulement une heure que j't'attends.	speaker is either not irritated or sarcastic
b. Ça fait seulement une heure que j't'attends.	speaker is either not irritated or sarcastic
c. Voilà seulement une heure que j't'attends.	speaker is only sarcastic
d. (seulement) une heure (seulement) que j't'attends !	speaker is only sarcastic

---

[97] Blyth et al. 2006. Retrieved February 3, 2009 at http://www.laits.utexas.edu/tex/gr/pred2.html and http://www.laits.utexas.edu/tex/gr/pred1.html
[98] I am especially grateful to Paul Solomiac (p.c.) for sharing his native speaker intuitions on these sentences.

Although not all French translations I have consulted use the *voilà* construction in the passages discussed above, several do. For example, as shown above, the FBJ used it for Luk 15:29 and Luk 13:7. *Voila ... que ...* would also work in Luk 13:16 (as illustrated by 'nab' above), although the FBJ actually uses a different construction, with sentence internal *voici*. (The BFC uses *voila ... que ...* in Mat 15:32, above, which lacks ἰδού.)

In contrast, *Écoute* in the BFC's rendering of Luk 15:29 as well as the NRS's *Listen* miss the mark, as does also *Look!* in the GNB and NIV. Equally inappropriate is deictic *here is this woman/ descendant* in the REB and GNB for Luk 13:16 and *See here!* in the NRS for Luk 13:7.

Of course many languages do not use deictic thetic particles like Greek ἰδού, French *voilà*, and Russian вот to emphasize time durations, so other means must be sought. Although none of the standard English translations use it-clefts, the clause-initial phrases *for years* in Luk 15:29 (CEV) and *for three years* in Luk 13:7 (GNB, NRS, NIV) would have the same effect if read with emphatic stress. But how is a reader to know these are to be read with emphatic stress? Thus, English translations that also add words like *all, long* or *no less than* that tend to 'attract' emphatic stress and suggest a semantic extreme are surer means of guaranteeing an emphatic reading (see *long* in the NRS and NIV of Luk 13:16 and *all these* in the GNB and NRS of Luk 15:29, despite their additions of *look* and *listen* which make double-translations of ἰδού).

It might appear that another possible candidate of C4a occurs in 2Co 12:14. BDAG lists it with tokens that carry 'emphasis on the size or importance of someth[ing].' But τρίτον τοῦτο 'this third' (again, allowing either accusative or nominative reading) does not indicate a time duration but a numbered occurrence. What is not obvious from the Greek and some translations (e.g., GNB and RSV) is that this will (most likely) be Paul's third *trip*, not that he had planned twice before to come and then could not (see 2Co 13:1–2 where Paul repeats the phrase 'this third [trip/time]'). But whether or not this token involves emotive emphasis is not clear (although the general context is emotive). An alternative interpretation is to take ἰδού as an instance of C5, meaning 'pay attention', where it modifies the clause as a whole. The NIV appears to opt for *now* (which is weak for C5). The NRS's *Here I am* is impossible from the Greek (see § 4.5.4 on Heb 10:7).

2Co 12:14 Ἰδοὺ **τρίτον τοῦτο** ἑτοίμως ἔχω   ἐλθεῖν   πρὸς ὑμᾶς,
     *   third   this   ready   I.have to.come to   you

NIV: <u>Now I am ready to visit you for the third time</u>, and I will not be a burden to you, ...

RSV: Here for the third time I am ready to come to you.

NRS: Here I am, ready to come to you this third time.

GNB: This is now the third time that I am ready to come to
   visit you

To sum up, tokens in which ἰδού emphasizes a time duration exemplify
a distinct construction, C4a. Where case is unambiguous, the time
phrase is nominative. Conceptually, what the speaker judges to be an
extreme amount of time is emotively emphasized; the emotive element
is readily traced to ἰδού's deriving from a middle verb. Syntactically,
ἰδού-TIME appears to form some sort of phrase, which to some degree
resembles the simple clause structure of ἰδού-NP$_{NOM}$ in C1. As in C1, so
in C4a, ἰδού immediately precedes its focal constituent.

All of the NT tokens cited above are listed under BDAG ἰδού.1.b.ε. There
the editors say ἰδού is used 'w[ith] emphasis on the size or importance of
someth[ing].' But they include other tokens there, including some that
belong to C4b to be discussed in § 4.4.3, but not those that are discussed
in the next section, § 4.4.2.

4.4.2 ἰδού/ἴδε + νῦν 'now', emphasizing a point in time

There are also four tokens where the adverb νῦν 'now' appears to be
emotively emphatic. In each token, νῦν is immediately preceded by either
ἰδού (2Co 6:2, 2x)[99] or ἴδε (Mat 26:65; Jhn 16:29). These tokens appear to be
a closely related construction to C4a but they differ conceptually in that
they emphasize a *point* of time rather than a *duration*; and adverbs are
also caseless. Fiedler also takes these four tokens to be emphasizing νῦν
(1969:23 on Mat 26:65 and Jhn 16:29; 1969:73 on 2Co 6:2).

Ἰδού occurs twice in **2Co 6:2**, which involves an emotional appeal.
The implication is that the time for God's favor is *now* and not some
other time. Assuming ἰδού is an emphatic focus marker forming a
phrase with νῦν, renderings like *see* or *listen* or *gebt acht* (which are in
any case clumsy here) miss the mark. Instead, italics for emphasis are
helpful as illustrated by the GND's use of italics for *jetzt*.

2Co 6:2 ἰδοὺ **νῦν** καιρὸς εὐπρόσδεκτος, ἰδοὺ **νῦν** ἡμέρα
   *   now time   acceptable   *   now day

   σωτηρίας.
   of.salvation

   NRS: See, now is the acceptable time; see, now is the day of
      salvation!
   GNB: Listen! This is the hour to receive God's favor; today is
      the day to be saved!

---

[99] I am less certain if the LXX instances of ἰδοὺ νῦν really emphasize the adverb.
Perhaps worth mentioning here is that two such tokens do not involve הנה but
just עתה 'now': Exo 5:5; 1Ki 12:26. But contrast 2Ki 5:22 (הנה עתה).

NIV: I tell you, now is the time of God's favor, now is the day of
salvation.
WMS: Right now the time of welcome is here; right now it is
the day of salvation.
GND: Gebt acht: *Jetzt* ist die Zeit der Gnade! *Jetzt* ist der Tag der
Rettung!

In my view, tokens with ἴδε are less certain; C5 readings might
be preferred. In any case, in both ἴδε passages, νῦν is an instance of
constituent-focus. The context of Mat 26:65 is strongly emotive ('ἴδε
NOW you have heard his blasphemy!'); that of Jhn 16:29 is perhaps
weaker, involving joy or relief ('ἴδε NOW you are speaking plainly to
us!'). That the latter may be rather a case of C5 might be suggested in
that v 30 begins with νῦν and lacks ἴδε.

4.4.3 C4b – ἰδού/ἴδε + focused constituent, emphasizing an extreme

In this section, I propose a similar analysis for emotively emphatic constituents other than time durations and νῦν. As in C4a, so here ἰδού/ἴδε
immediately precedes a focused constituent. The constituent can be of
any type (subject, object, predicate, etc.) and can occur in any case. I
designate these **C4b**. It functions to emphasize some kind of an extreme
degree, such as a measure, amount, or comparable aspect of an event or
state. On the basis of this analysis, we can challenge many renderings
found in the standard translations. To be sure, there are questions about
some of my proposed examples, and (again) this analysis with ἴδε should
be considered provisional since C5 or C3 readings might be preferred. This
use of ἰδού also seems to be represented in Classical texts.[100]

BDAG's subentry ἰδού.1.b.ε (used 'w[ith] emphasis on the size or
importance of someth[ing]') lists one token, **Luk 19:8**, that I am calling
C4b (besides ones emphasizing time durations discussed earlier). It
emphasizes 'half of my possessions' (no mere pittance for a professional
miser—Marshall [1978] says the normal amount according to the rabbis
would have been only a fifth). Most translations take ἰδού as C5,
rendering it as *Listen* (GNB, *Écoute*, BFC) or metaphorical or physical *Look*
(NRS, NIV). The NIV double translates it as *Look* and *Here and now*—which
are of course deictic, implying Zacchaeus is reimbursing people on the

---

[100] Fiedler (1969:17–19) lists some Classical examples of ἰδού 'strengthening'
imperatives and other verbs, although some of his examples may really be
deictic thetic-like uses: Aristophanes' *Clouds* 255 ἰδοὺ κάθημαι 'There, I'm
seated' (nab); Aristophanes' *Acharnians* 434 ἰδοὺ ταυτὶ λαβέ [* this.A/N
2s.take!] 'Catch hold! here they are.' ('Anonymous' English translation on
Perseus site.)

spot.[101] Given the context, such renderings might seem appropriate, but if taken as C4b, *Look*, *Listen* and *Here and now* are unnecessary. Instead, an effective way to bring out the emphatic sense is to add words that suggest an extreme degree (and which in reading will tend to 'attract' emphatic stress). For example, in the present example, *no less than* could be added.[102] (If the convention is recognized, it is also possible to use typographical means to indicate emphasis, e.g., *italics*, **bolding**, ALL CAPS, but this seems to be a less clear method.)

Luk 19:8 ἰδοὺ **τὰ ἡμίσιά μου τῶν ὑπαρχόντων**, κύριε, τοῖς
*   the half.A.p.n of.me the.G possessions.G Lord to.the

πτωχοῖς δίδωμι,[103] καὶ εἴ τινός τι
poor.ones I.give.Pres and if someone.G something.A

ἐσυκοφάντησα ἀποδίδωμι τετραπλοῦν.
I.defrauded I.pay.back.Pres four.times.A.p.n

nab: Zacchaeus [a noted tax collector and sinner] stood up and said to the Lord, "Lord, I promise to (I will) give to the poor <u>no less than half of my possessions</u>, and if I have cheated anyone, I promise to (I will) pay back four times as much."

GNB: <u>Listen</u>, sir! I will give half my belongings to the poor, ...

NIV: <u>Look</u>, Lord! <u>Here and now</u> I give half of my possessions to the poor, and if I have cheated anybody out of anything, I will pay back four times the amount.

As we shall soon see more clearly, the focused phrase in C4**b** is not restricted to the nominative. So, unlike the nominative time phrases

---

[101] The NIV's taking this as deictic leads to an unfortunate inconsistency. It renders the Greek present verbs δίδωμι and ἀποδίδωμι as different tenses, the first as a present tense (*give*) and the second as a future (*will pay back*). See footnote 103.

[102] Taking ἰδού+'half my possessions' to alone express the focus domain requires the hearer to accommodate the presupposition that 'Zacchaeus would give X to the poor'. Although the passage does not explicitly evoke this presupposition, it is a reasonable inference to make since tax collectors were stereotyped as thieves and the Law required restitution (e.g., Exo 21:37; Exo 22:3–6). An alternative reading would be to take ἰδού+'half my possessions' as an emphatic element in a larger predicate-focus domain, which included 'give to the poor'.

[103] Several English translations (GNB, NAB, NAS, NJB) render the present indicatives, δίδωμι and ἀποδίδωμι, as future English verbs, and the use of the present tense for future sense in certain contexts is well established (BDF § 323; Dana & Mantey § 174.2; so also Marshall 1978 and Z&G on this verse; Pope 1988). But it is also possible to view these as a type of performative speech act (i.e., instances of the so-called 'aoristic present';

found with C4a, I assume ἡμίσια 'half (of my possessions)' is an accusative
object (the neuter noun is ambiguous). But this and other instances of
C4b resemble C4a tokens in the following ways: (i) both occur in contexts
involving strong emotions (e.g., anger, annoyance, exasperation, joy,
amazement); and (ii) the particle immediately precedes a phrase that
(iii) emphasizes an amount that can be characterized as an *extreme
degree* or *measure* in the speaker's estimation. For example, just as to be
sick for eighteen years is judged by the speaker to involve an extreme
(Luk 13:16), so is to give up half of one's possessions.

A nice example is found in the papyrus **PM 217.8** (late third century
C.E.), with accusative object 'three letters'. Pantikos (apparently a
soldier stationed away from home elsewhere in Egypt) is complaining to
his wife, Plutogenia, who will not visit him, let alone write him a single
letter, even though he has written her *three letters.*[104]

PM 217.8 εἰδοὺ **τρεῖς ἐπιστολὰς** ἔπεμψά σοι   καὶ οὐδὲ
        =ἰδοὺ three letters.A   I.sent   to.you and not.even

        μίαν   μοι   ἔγραψας.
        one.A.f.s to.me you.wrote

        nab: *Three letters* I have sent you but not one have you
            written me.

        Zilliacus: Siehe, drei Briefe habe ich dir gesandt, und keinen
            einzigen hast du mir geschrieben.

With emphatic **subjects**, a positive extreme can be emphasized, as
in **Luk 11:41** ('everything') and Jhn 12:19 (ἴδε, 'the [whole] world'), or a
negative extreme can be emphasized, as in **Luk 23:15** ('nothing worthy
of death'). Under a C4b interpretation, the NRS's *and see* in Luk 11:41 and
the NIV's *as you can see* in Luk 23:15 are superfluous and misleading.

Luk 11:41 πλὴν τὰ   ἐνόντα   δότε ἐλεημοσύνην,
        but the.things being.inside give alms

        καὶ ἰδοὺ **πάντα**   καθαρὰ ὑμῖν ἐστιν.
        and *   all.things.N clean   to.you 3s.is

        GNB: But give what is in your cups and plates to the poor,
            and <u>everything</u> will be ritually clean for you.

        NRS: So give for alms those things that are within; and <u>see,
            everything</u> will be clean for you.

BDF § 320; Dana & Mantey § 174.1), where Zacchaeus is making a promise
paraphrasable as 'I promise to give ... and I promise to repay ....'
[104] **PM 217.8** = P. Michigan, cited by Zilliacus (1943:17–18, 38). http://papy-
ri.info/ddbdp/p.mich;3;217 (retrieved November 24, 2015).

Luk 23:15 καὶ ἰδοὺ **οὐδὲν**   **ἄξιον θανάτου** ἐστὶν πεπραγμένον
and *   nothing.N worthy of.death 3s.is been.done

αὐτῷ·
by.him

nab: <u>absolutely nothing worthy of death</u> has been done by
    him!
GNB: There is <u>nothing</u> this man has done to deserve death.
NRS: <u>Indeed</u>, he has done <u>nothing</u> to deserve death.
NIV: <u>as you can see</u>, he has done <u>nothing</u> to deserve death.

It appears that extreme aspects of events or states of affairs can also be
emotively emphasized. In **Act 5:28**, instead of 'not teaching' about Jesus
as the authorities had commanded, the apostles 'fill' Jerusalem with the
Gospel ('fill' contrasts with 'not teaching'; to fill is to do something to an
extreme degree). In Jhn 7:26, rather than hiding because the authorities
are trying to kill him, Jesus speaks 'openly' (with ἴδε; alternatively,
C5, given the doubt about ἴδε tokens). In contrast, the illustrated
translations take these as deictic constructions (e.g., *here, see*).[105]

Act 5:28 [οὐ] παραγγελίᾳ   παρηγγείλαμεν ὑμῖν μὴ διδάσκειν
not with.strict.charge we.charged   to.you not to.teach

ἐπὶ τῷ ὀνόματι τούτῳ, καὶ ἰδοὺ **πεπληρώκατε** τὴν
in the name   this and * you.have.filled -

Ἰερουσαλὴμ τῆς   διδαχῆς ὑμῶν
Jerusalem with.the teaching of.you

NRS: We gave you strict orders not to teach in this name, yet
    <u>here</u> you have filled Jerusalem with your teaching and you
    are determined to bring this man's blood on us.
GNB: ... but <u>see</u> what you have done! You have spread your
    teaching all over Jerusalem, ...
RSV: ... yet <u>here</u> you have filled Jerusalem with your
    teaching ...

---

[105] Gen 34:10 could be an instance: καὶ ἡ γῆ ἰδοὺ πλατεῖα ἐναντίον ὑμῶν
[and the land.N ἰδού wide before you] 'and the land is *very* wide before you
(to choose where you wish to live and support yourselves)'. This token is
interesting because it lacks a typical predicator, ἰδού is not initial (as we
saw in Luk 13:16 and Deu 8:4) but follows the subject, and the Hebrew lacks
הִנֵּה (לִפְנֵיכֶם תִּהְיֶה וְהָאָרֶץ [and-the-land 3Sf.will.be before-you]). Perhaps
הִנֵּה was read for תִּהְיֶה '3Sf.will.be'.

Jhn 7:26 οὐχ οὗτός ἐστιν ὃν   ζητοῦσιν   ἀποκτεῖναι;
not this   3s.is whom 3p.are.seeking to.kill

καὶ ἴδε παρρησίᾳ λαλεῖ
and *   openly   3s.speaks

NRS: [25] Now some … were saying, "Is not this the man whom
they are trying to kill? [26] And <u>here</u> he is, speaking openly,
but they say nothing to him! …"
GNB: <u>Look!</u> He is talking in public, and they say nothing
against him!

Other possible instances include 2Co 6:9 (even though the apostles
are considered to be dying, ἰδοὺ ζῶμεν BFC: *nous sommes bien vivants*
'we are *very much* alive') and Gal 1:20 (Paul is swearing emphatically
ἰδοὺ ἐνώπιον τοῦ θεοῦ 'before God', the highest authority, e.g., perhaps
I swear to God himself [Tony Pope, p.c.]).[106]

Three possible ἴδε tokens—all with exclamative properties—include
Jhn 11:36 ('How [very] fond he was of him!' ἴδε πῶς ἐφίλει αὐτόν),
Mrk 13:1 ('such [wonderful] stones'), and Mrk 15:4 ('How many charges
they bring against you!' ἴδε πόσα σου κατηγοροῦσιν). But all three
tokens could instead be interpreted as C3 or C5, as suggested by typical
renderings like *see, look, here*, etc.

The declaration from the one seated on the throne in **Rev 21:5** may
be another instance, in which case we may translate *I make all things
completely new* (the idea of 'new' summarizes much of vv 1–4). To be
sure, a C5 interpretation also seems possible (GNB and BFC render ἰδοὺ
as *now*, and NRS as *see*).[107] There is little consensus among translations
on this token.

Rev 21:5 Καὶ εἶπεν ὁ   καθήμενος ἐπὶ τῷ θρόνῳ·
and 3s.said the.one sitting   on the throne

Ἰδοὺ καινὰ ποιῶ πάντα,
*   new I.make all.things

NRS: See, I am making all things new.
GNB: And now I make all things new!
[BFC: Maintenant …]
NIV: I am making everything new!
nab C4: I make all things <u>completely new</u>!

---

[106] The construction in Gal 1:20 is an elliptical oath meaning 'I swear/affirm
to God I am not lying': ἰδοὺ ἐνώπιον τοῦ θεοῦ ὅτι οὐ ψεύδομαι [ἰδού before
the.G God.G that not I.lie].
[107] Luk 13:35 ἰδοὺ ἀφίεται ὑμῖν ὁ οἶκος ὑμῶν [behold 3S.is.abandoned to-you
the house of.you] may be another instance (the context is also emotional).
The implication would be 'Although you (Jerusalem) have been hoping for
deliverance, your house *is now abandoned* (i.e., hereby cursed)'.

It must be admitted that it can be sometimes difficult to distinguish cases of C4b from cases of C3 or C5. And there are one or two cases where an extreme value appears to be emphasized, but the focused constituent does not immediately follow ἰδού: **Act 27:24** ('all the ones sailing with you').[108] Thus, this token represents, constructionally speaking, a step away from C4b, where ἰδού does not function as a constituent-focus marker, but as a sentence adverb, that is, C5. (It seems less likely to me that the verb is being emphasized.)

Act 27:24 καὶ ἰδοὺ κεχάρισταί   σοι   ὁ θεὸς **πάντας τοὺς**
          and *   3s.has.given to.you - God all.A   the.A

πλέοντας μετὰ σοῦ.
sailing.A   with you

> NRS: [22] ... keep up your courage, for there will be no loss of life among you, but only of the ship. [23] For last night there stood by me an angel of the God to whom I belong and whom I worship, [24] and he said, 'Do not be afraid, Paul; you must stand before the emperor; and indeed, God has granted safety to all those who are sailing with you.'

We must also distinguish **Act 2:7** from C4b (see Fiedler 1969:33 quoting Foakes Jackson and Lake 1933:18–19), which is the only NT instance of οὐκ/χ ἰδού.[109] Even though the context involves amazement and ἅπαντες 'all' could (in principle at least) be emphasized, nevertheless οὐκ ἰδού is a well-known indicator of rhetorical questions in the LXX[110] (that are paraphrasable as positive assertions).[111] To be sure, the present example is not a prototypical rhetorical question. It actually functions as a hedged assertion, similar to an English 'tag question' (that also involves amazement), since the speakers do not quite believe their ears and are seeking confirmation. Moreover, unlike the present example, not all LXX tokens

---

[108] Somewhat similar is Mat 28:20 (C5). Here I take the subject to be topic, the entire predicate to be in the focus domain and the clause-final element 'all days' as likely emotively emphatic: καὶ ἰδοὺ ἐγὼ μεθ᾽ ὑμῶν εἰμι πάσας τὰς ἡμέρας 'and remember [I]TOPIC [am with you [all days]EMPH]FocusDomain'. The order is unmarked for ἰδού sentences.

[109] Since ἰδού has the smooth breathing, one would normally expect not οὐχ (which actually has good manuscript support) but οὐκ (also well supported) or οὐχί (in one manuscript) (see Nestle-Aland for the various readings).

[110] Bruce (1990:117) notes that οὐκ ἰδού 'is used in LXX in rhetorical questions, and "in time became the recognized equivalent for the classical ἆρ᾽ οὐ;"' (quoting Thackeray 1909:126). Οὐκ ἰδού is a fairly common LXX rendering for Hebrew הֲלֹא 'is it not!' (Gen 13:9; Exo 4:14). Less frequently one finds just ἰδού (Jos 1:9; Jdg 6:14). See Thackeray (1909:126) for more detail.

[111] Rhetorical questions with οὐ and οὐχί 'not' normally expect an affirmative answer. See BDF § 427 and the entries οὐ.3.a.α and οὐχί.3 in BDAG.

clearly involve an emotive element (the formula 'are not X written in Y' in 1Ki 11:41 etc. seems emotionally flat, probably due to overuse). Nevertheless, as with this example, most rhetorical questions have an emotive element, and in this way οὐκ/χ ἰδού's typical use with rhetorical questions (as well as a hedged assertion, like this passage) resembles C4, although what it modifies (or 'emphasizes') is not the constituent it precedes but the **truth value** of the entire proposition.[112] It thus represents another subconstruction (English translators are reluctant to squeeze *look* or *listen* out of this.)

Act 2:7 οὐχ ἰδοὺ ἅπαντες οὗτοί εἰσιν   οἱ   λαλοῦντες Γαλιλαῖοι;
        not *   all   these 3p.are the speaking Galileans

REB: Surely these people who are speaking are all Galileans!
NET: Aren't all these who are speaking Galileans?

4.4.4   Other cases with constituent-focus: C3, C5, and C2

With maybe one or two exceptions (Jhn 18:21 and Mat 19:27), the tokens discussed from here on do not appear to be emotively emphatic, yet each appears to involve constituent-focus. Translators have interpreted these in various ways. Three groups suggest themselves: (i) instances of C3; (ii) instances of C5; and (iii) a few hybrids, **CF+C2a**, where a deictic thetic skeleton (C2a) is overlaid by a constituent-focus structure.

The deictic properties of ἴδε in Mat 25:20 were discussed in § 4.3 ('ἴδε I have made five more talents'). I counted that as an instance of C3 (and not as C4b even though the constituent-focused phrase occurs immediately after ἴδε).

The tokens in **Jhn 18:21** and **Act 10:21** are worth comparing since the subject constituents are focused in both, each answering an implicit question ('Who knows what I have said?' and 'Who are they seeking?').

Jhn 18:21 τί   με   ἐρωτᾷς;   ἐρώτησον τοὺς   ἀκηκοότας
          why me   you.question question! the.ones having.heard

τί   ἐλάλησα αὐτοῖς· ἴδε οὗτοι   οἴδασιν ἃ
what I.spoke to.them *   these.ones know   what.things

εἶπον ἐγώ.
I.said I

NRS: [21] Why do you ask me? Ask those who heard what I said to them; they know what I said. [22] When he had said this,

---

[112] On polarity (or verum) focus (assertions where what is focal is the truth value of a proposition), see Bailey (2009:38–39, 69–72) and Bailey (2011:297, 317–320).

one of the police standing nearby struck Jesus on the face,
saying, "Is that how you answer the high priest?"

Act 10:21 ἰδοὺ ἐγώ εἰμι ὃν   ζητεῖτε
          *   I   am   whom you.are.seeking

NIV: [18] [Three men sent by Cornelius came to a house and]
called out, asking if ... Peter was staying there. [19] While
Peter was ... thinking ... , the Spirit said to him, "[Peter,]
three men are looking for you. [20] ... Do not hesitate to go
with them, for I have sent them." [21] Peter went down and
said to the men, "I'm the one you're looking for. Why have
you come?"

BFC: Je suis celui que vous cherchez. ['I am the one you are
looking for.']

NVS78: Me voici; c'est moi que vous cherchez. ['Here I am;
it's me you're looking for.']

Ἴδε οὗτοι in Jhn 18:21 cannot have here-and-now deictic reference
(C3) assuming the disciples referred to by οὗτοι are absent at Jesus' trial
(with the exception of one or two hiding). Perhaps it is an instance of C5.
Interestingly, most translations leave it untranslated (the NIV has *surely*,
which does not seem right to me, especially with ἴδε). Alternatively,
perhaps it is a type of (emotive) C4 (but without the feature of an
extreme degree); it might contribute to the emotively charged response
Jesus' answer elicits.

In contrast, Act 10:21 looks physically or metaphorically deictic. In
my view, ἰδού means either *Hey!* (C5) or *Here!* (C3) and it is separate
from what follows where ἐγώ is an instance of constituent-focus.[113] Most
translations (e.g., NIV and French BFC above) in fact render this as a
statement compatible with a constituent-focus interpretation, although
they generally do away with ἰδού (see also RSV, NRS, GNB, CEV; but
the NVS78, FBJ, and TOB add *voici* and BDS *voilà*). A deictic thetic
interpretation (C2) seems impossible from the Greek: If Peter wanted to
say, 'Here I am, the one you are looking for' (see NVS78 above, which
double translates ἰδού), then the form ἰδοὺ ἐγώ without the copula εἰμι
would have sufficed (C1), followed by a relative clause (compare ἰδοὺ
ἐγώ in Act 9:10).

The subject in **Mat 19:27** is also likely constituent-focus (also ‖Mrk
10:28 and Luk 18:28). This token comes on the heels of the account about
the rich young leader: Jesus had invited him to sell all he had, give it
to the poor and then follow Jesus, but instead he walks away depressed.

---

[113] Therefore, ἰδού here does not form a syntactic unit with ἐγώ as in C4b,
but instead functions as an adverb that modifies the entire clause, or else
perhaps it should be read as intonationally separate.

Peter then points out that (in contrast to the rich young man) 'WE have left everything and followed you ...' Thus, ἰδού may be an instance of C5, for which *Listen/Écoute, Remember* and (metaphorical) *Look* are appropriate renderings.

Mat 19:27 ἰδοὺ **ἡμεῖς** ἀφήκαμεν πάντα   καὶ ἠκολουθήσαμέν **σοι·**
       *   we   we.left   all.things and we.followed   you

> NRS: Then Peter said in reply, "<u>Look, we</u> have left everything and followed you. What then will we have?"
> CEV: Remember, we have left everything to be your followers!
> NIV: We have left everything to follow you!
> BFC: Écoute, lui dit-il, nous avons tout quitté pour te suivre.

Now consider the information structure hybrids, **CF+C2a**, in **Mrk 13:21.**

Mrk 13:21 Καὶ τότε ἐάν τις   ὑμῖν εἴπῃ· ἴδε **ὧδε** ὁ
       and then if   someone to.you 3s.says * here the

χριστός, ἴδε **ἐκεῖ,** μὴ πιστεύετε·
Christ   *   there not you.believe

> CEV: If someone should say, '<u>Here</u> is the Messiah!' or '<u>There</u> he is!' don't believe it.
> GNB: if anyone says to you, '<u>Look, here</u> is the Messiah!' or, '<u>Look, there</u> he is!'—do not believe it.

Both tokens (with ἴδε; see also ‖Mat 24:23, and Luk 17:21b, Luk 17:23b, and Luk 17:23c, all with ἰδού) have deictic thetic skeletons with predicate locatives (i.e., C2a structures; see e.g., Luk 22:38). Each skeleton is then overlaid by a dominant constituent-focus structure. Both utterances presuppose the question 'Where is the Christ?' The locatives, which come in the marked focus position (pre-subject, in this case), are focal; first ὧδε 'here' and then ἐκεῖ 'there'[114] attempt to answer the question (since the presupposed constituent 'the Christ' is fully activated in the second clause, it is expressed by a null form). If these had instead been straightforward C2a deictic thetics, then we would have expected ἴδε ὁ χριστός ὧδε/ἐκεῖ, where, formally, the subject would be initial, and conceptually, 'the Christ' would be what was asserted as unpredictable (i.e., not in the common ground or 'in the presupposition'). Most English translations render these by a form compatible with a deictic thetic reading, such as *HERE is the MESSIAH* (e.g., CEV and GNB). Crucially, this

---

[114] In ‖Mat 24:26b (ἰδοὺ ἐν τῇ ἐρήμῳ ἐστίν [C5:hey! in the desert 3S.is]) what is focused is 'in the desert' (and 'in the inner rooms' in Mat 24:26d). That εἰμί occurs indicates that this is not C1, which makes sense if we assume that 'in the desert' (and 'in the inner rooms') are locations that cannot be seen or directly pointed to.

form is *equally* compatible with the constituent-focus reading, where *here* would be stressed, but *the Messiah* if relatively activated would be an unstressed lexical NP (*HERE is the Messiah*), a pronoun (*HERE he is*), or unexpressed (*HERE!*). The GNB's *Look* (also NIV, NRS; and BFC *regardez*) is unnecessary. The CEV is the best model.

The token in **Mat 12:41** (similarly in Mat 12:42 and ‖Luk 11:31 and ‖Luk 11:32) is also an information structure hybrid: a deictic[115] C2a thetic skeleton is overlaid by a dominant constituent-focus structure. Unlike Mrk 13:21 above, where the focal locatives come in the marked focus position (following ἴδε), here we find the subject constituent πλεῖον Ἰωνᾶ 'something greater than Jonah' in that position. The utterance evokes the presupposition that 'Here is X in regard to Jonah' (so ὧδε 'here' and part of the subject 'Jonah' are in the presupposition) and asserts that X is 'something greater (than Jonah)'. The CEV makes use of a deictic thetic, but essentially the same effect is achieved by the GNB's non-deictic *there* thetic with deictic *here*.[116]

Mat 12:41 καὶ ἰδοὺ **πλεῖον** Ἰωνᾶ ὧδε.
and * something.greater.than Jonah here

> NRS: The people of Nineveh will rise up at the judgment with this generation and condemn it, because they repented at the proclamation of Jonah, <u>and see, something greater than Jonah is here</u>!
>
> CEV: They turned to God when Jonah preached, and yet <u>here</u> is something far greater than Jonah.
>
> GNB: and I tell you that there is something <u>here</u> greater than Jonah!
>
> BFC: Et il y a <u>ici</u> plus que Jonas !
>
> NVS78: et <u>voici</u> qu'il y a <u>ici</u> plus que Jonas.

4.4.5 Summary comments and counts on C4

In § 4.4, a variety of ἰδού and ἴδε tokens have been surveyed that simultaneously involve constituent-focus. In tokens categorized as C4, I have argued that the focused constituent forms a syntactic unit with the

---

[115] That the underlying construction here is a C2a thetic skeleton with locative predicate is clear from the lack of εἰμί (compare ‖Mat 12:6 with εἰμί and no ἰδού). Incidentally, while this has a deictic thetic skeleton, we should hardly expect that Jesus would be so blatant as to simultaneously point at himself. His words suffice.

[116] The NIV translates Mat 12:41 and parallel tokens by *now* ('and now one greater than Jonah is here'), which I feel weakens the rhetorical effect of Jesus' statement. But *now* is still appropriate insofar as it conveys one element of the here-and-now deictic.

particle and that the focused constituent is emotively emphatic; thus, translations like *see, look,* and *here* are inappropriate.

C4 tokens divide into at least two subtypes: C4a, with ἰδού–*TIME*$_{NOM}$ (which has some cleft-like characteristics and has noteworthy parallels in French and other languages) and C4b, ἰδού + *any other phrase* (in any case). Stretching the category somewhat, a third type would be οὐκ/χ ἰδού, which occurs with rhetorical questions (it emphasizes a proposition's positive truth value). There is a resemblance between C4a and C1 in that both require a focal constituent in the nominative.

We also found instances of constituent-focus that did not involve emotive emphasis and where I do not assume the particle forms a syntactic phrase with the focused constituent. The focused constituent need not immediately follow the particle. In some tokens, the particles were instances of C3 or C5. Other tokens were hybrids that had a deictic thetic skeleton (C2a) overlaid by a constituent-focus structure.

→ Here is a summary list of the different sets of C4 tokens (besides examples from the papyri).

C4a: Luk 13:7; Luk 13:16; Luk 15:29; perhaps 2Co 12:14.

C4b: Luk 11:41; Luk 13:35 (? or C5); Luk 19:8; Luk 23:15; Jhn 7:26 (ἴδε); Jhn 12:19 (ἴδε); Act 5:28; 2Co 6:9 (? or C5); Gal 1:20; Rev 21:5 (? or C5). Tokens with ἴδε are more questionable, including ones with exclamative properties (all could be instead C3 or C5): Jhn 11:36; Mrk 13:1; Mrk 15:4. Tokens with νῦν 'now' include 2Co 6:2 (2x) with ἰδού and perhaps Mat 26:65 and Jhn 16:29 with ἴδε.

οὐκ/χ ἰδού (the rhetorical question marker): Act 2:7; often in LXX (e.g., Exo 4:14); also J&A 1.9 and J&A 21.3 (Burchard).

4.5   C5 – ἰδού and ἴδε as instructions to pay mental attention

In C5, ἰδού and ἴδε function as instructions to the hearer to pay special attention to something being said. This set is large, numbering up to ninety-five tokens, of which up to eighty-six tokens use ἰδού and nine use ἴδε. To be sure, it is also a somewhat mixed set of tokens that could benefit from further categorization. (In the discussion below, different nuances are suggested here and there.) Still, a general picture can be sketched.

What is first of all clear is that, with only a very few exceptions, C5 tokens cannot be interpreted as sentence-focus thetics. They are instead usually predicate-focus constructions (where the subject is topic) or, less frequently, constituent-focus constructions. Second, C5 diverges from C1 and C3 in that the particle is never used deictically to point to an entity in the here-and-now real world. Third, the particle never forms a syntactic unit with the constituent that immediately follows it, as we found in C1, C2c-NP and C4, but rather it modifies the entire sentence.

Syntactically, the particle in C5 always takes a position early in the sentence, after the standard sentence-initial conjunctions if present (occasionally καί or a logical conjunction, etc.) and before any 'postpositive' conjunction (i.e., γάρ, and outside the NT, δέ).[117] Since there is always another predicator present (a verb or locative), I assume that the C5 particle often functions like a sentence adverb, coming in a frozen position early in the sentence (so this position mimics the position ἰδού and ἴδε take in other uses, which in turn reflects the original position their ancestors took as imperatives of 'see'). Nevertheless, there are instances where it seems likely that the C5 particle would be syntactically independent from the rest of the clause (and thus probably set off by a pause), in which case the particle would not function as a sentence adverb.[118] And as we saw with C3, it might be helpful for translation purposes to think of such instances as imperatives (e.g., *Listen!*) or 'interjections', which would be intonationally separate from what follows. But since the term 'interjection' is problematic, I would prefer to refer to this simply as the 'independent particle use'.[119]

[117] For C5 alone do we find in the NT the 'postpositive' γάρ, that is, ἰδοὺ γάρ, seven times in fact: Luk 1:44; Luk 1:48; Luk 2:10; Luk 6:23; Luk 17:21d; Act 9:11; 2Co 7:11. In the LXX, one also finds on rare occasion ἰδοὺ δέ (Deu 20:16) and ἰδοὺ δὲ νῦν (3 Maccabees 2:13), which both occur with C5, and Fiedler (1969:20) mentions a case from a papyrus.

According to Bailey (2009:376–377), for C5 as well as other uses, the conjunction καί 'and' precedes ἰδού seventy-five times, i.e., καὶ ἰδού (especially with C2c, e.g., Mat 2:9, but occasionally with C5, e.g., Mat 28:7; Luk 1:20; καὶ ἴδε only occurs once, C4b Jhn 7:26), and occasionally καὶ νῦν 'and now' precedes ἰδού (C2d Act 13:11; C5 Act 20:22; C5 Act 20:25). Not infrequently ἰδού (or ἴδε) is preceded by a vocative (e.g., ἴδε in Mrk 11:21, ἰδού in Luk 22:31), or a participle clause that functions adverbially (e.g., a temporal point of departure, Mat 2:13), or, much less frequently, some logical conjunction such as διὰ τοῦτο 'for this reason' (C5 Mat 23:34), πλήν 'nevertheless' (C5 Luk 22:21), ὅτι 'because' (e.g., C2b Luk 23:29), or ἀλλʼ 'but' (C5 Act 13:25). The rhetorical question marker, οὐκ/χ ἰδού is an instance of a frozen idiom (Act 2:7). Twice the particle follows a left-detached topic expression: in Jhn 3:26 (C5), the topic is resumed in the main clause following ἴδε by a subject pronoun ('this'); Gal 1:20 (C4) is harder to analyze, given the elliptical oath formula.

[118] See, for example, J&A 13.7 (and J&A 13.8) where C5 ἰδού is immediately followed by a vocative. Burchard's edition, which uses punctuation sparingly, reads ἰδοὺ κύριέ μου 'Behold, my Lord …' but Philonenko's (13.6) significantly includes commas: ἰδού, κύριέ μου, …

[119] Following Crystal (1994:180), **interjections** are generally taken to be grammatically 'unproductive' words that 'do not enter into syntactic

Conceptually, the resemblance with C1 and C3 is very important. C5 begins one or more sentences that report something the speaker wishes the hearer to pay special attention to. The particles can be viewed as 'processing instructions'. While C1 and C3 instruct the hearer to pay *visual* attention to a state of affairs, C5 instructs the hearer to pay *mental* attention. Thus, C5 is a metaphorical extension of the here-and-now deictic uses, whereby a speaker 'points out' something being said that the hearer should, for whatever reason, 'mentally look at' (i.e., think about).[120]

---

relationships with other classes, and whose function is purely emotive, e.g., *Yuk!, Strewth!, Blast!, Tut tut!*' As I have argued here and in the preceding sections, ἰδού and ἴδε do indeed enter into a syntactic relationship with other words, and that relationship varies from construction to construction. My proposal here is that for C5 (and probably C3 as well) it is sometimes syntactically integrated and sometimes independent.

That a particle can be sometimes integrated and sometimes not, can be illustrated by English exclamative particles (following McCready 2006). In English, when an exclamative sentence has a predicate that explicitly evokes a degree, it is possible either to intonationally integrate the exclamative particle (e.g., *man*) into its sentence, as illustrated by (i.a) below, or to intonationally separate it, as in (i.b). The integrated version is acceptable for this example since the predicate, *hot*, evokes a degree. But in the second sentence, *came to the party* does not evoke a degree, and so only (ii.b) is felicitous. Even some predicates that do not normally evoke a degree can be so coerced, as illustrated by (iii).

(i.a) *Man this water is hot!* (no pause, integrated)
(i.b) *Man, this water is hot!* (where the comma represents a pause; a vocative could also come here)
(ii.a) **Man John came to the party last night*
(ii.b) *Man, John came to the party last night.* (comma only)
(iii) *Man we drank coffee last night.* (i.e., we drank a lot of coffee)

[120] Metaphors that equate thinking or knowing with seeing are pervasive in language. Lakoff and Johnson (1980:48) mention the metaphor of 'understanding is seeing', and Lakoff (1987:437) mentions 'looking at something is taking it into consideration'. As in Greek, so in English and other languages one can say 'Look!' when one does not expect the hearer to physically look but rather to pay attention to what is being said or about to be said. These metaphors are also illustrated by: *I'll take a look at it* (meaning 'I'll consider it'; Lakoff 1987:437); *(So) You see, ...* (so you can infer; similarly the proverbial *'I see,' said the blind man); He's not focused* (his concentration is wandering); *I can't see what you're getting at* (I don't understand what you are saying); *Let me see* (Allow me to think for a moment); *in my mind's eye* (my imagination); *view* (one's opinion and thoughts on a matter); etc. There are also examples in the Greek NT besides C5. With ὁράω: Luk 21:29 'Consider/Think about the fig tree'. With ὁράω and βλέπω: Mat 13:14c 'you will look (βλέψετε) but not

My analysis of C5 fits the first definition given by BDAG for both ἰδού and ἴδε entries, where ἰδού is described as a 'prompter of attention' and ἴδε as 'point[ing] out someth[ing] to which the speaker wishes to draw attention'. BDAG, however, combines tokens that I am categorizing as varieties of C2 with C5.

Now we may ask, what kinds of situations is *mental* pointing via C5 used for? And is there any similarity between such situations and those where *physical* pointing is used (C1)?

If someone points out to you the *physical* presence of an entity or state of affairs in the real world, he or she does so for some reason, for example, because that entity may be useful or harmful, interesting or surprising. The types of situations where *mental* pointing is used in the NT seem fairly parallel.

In the NT, C5 tokens are used when something important is being said, such as a promise, warning, oath, or curse; or a set of instructions are being given that the hearer should not forget; or the utterance is a reminder. Some of these contexts overlap. In particular, many tokens (up to half of the ninety-five) involve states of affairs that would likely be considered by the audience as *surprising* or *unexpected.*[121] As noted above, C1 and C2 also fairly frequently introduce surprising states of affairs. It is also noteworthy that many C5 tokens (more than a quarter) resemble C1 and C2 in that they have thetic-like properties, where, for example, the clause object introduces a new entity into the discourse, or where in a subsequent clause a new entity is introduced. The C5 tokens differ, however, in that they are seldom thetic (i.e., they seldom have sentence-focus structure). The subject is instead usually a topical entity.

Finally, probably all C5 tokens can be portrayed as highlighting a state of affairs that involves certainty (the speaker commits himself to its certainty).[122]

---

see (ἴδητε) [=understand]'. And with just βλέπω: 1Co 1:26 'consider your calling'; Col 4:17 'pay attention to your ministry so that you are sure to fulfill it'.

See also Chafe (1994:53) who argues that 'focus of consciousness' is much like vision.

[121] Lambrecht (1999:32–33) describes one use of *voilà* where it indicates that a state of affairs with a topical subject is 'contrary to expectation', and so '*voilà* has lost its value as a perception predicate': e.g., *Figurez-vous, Monsieur, qu'ils n'étaient pas mariés un an, paf! voilà la femme qui part en Espagne avec un marchand de chocolat.* 'Can you imagine, they hadn't even been married a year and bang! the wife runs off to Spain (lit. there's the wife running off to Spain) with a guy who sells chocolate.'

[122] I still have some questions about this portrayal, but the data suggest that most uses of C5 as well as all the other uses involve statements where the speaker speaks with certainty about a state of affairs (i.e., the speaker feels certain about them). Still, as I have discussed elsewhere (Bailey 2009:375–

There are many idioms in (modern) English used to instruct a hearer to pay special attention to something being said, each with its own nuance. Appropriate renderings of C5 include at least *pay attention, take note, listen, notice* (colloquial *hey!*), *remember (don't forget)*, metaphorical uses of *look, here,* and *there;* and (on rare occasion) *hereby* or *now.* In some contexts, *certainly* (*indeed, yes*) can also be an appropriate rendering of C5.

Here follows the list of 95 possible tokens. Alternative interpretations are mentioned in parentheses. The tokens that have been most difficult to classify are ones with a lexical (non-pronominal) subject and that could be alternatively construed as some variety of C2.

→ Mat 1:23 (LXX quote); Mat 8:29 (in narrative!); Mat 8:32 (in narrative!); Mat 10:16; Mat 11:8; Mat 11:10 (LXX quote); Mat 12:2 (or C2a or C3); Mat 13:3 (begins a parable); Mat 19:27; Mat 20:18; Mat 22:4; Mat 23:34; Mat 23:38; Mat 24:25; Mat 24:26b and Mat 24:26d (see footnote 114); Mat 26:45 (or C2d); Mat 28:7c; Mat 28:7e; Mat 28:20; Mrk 1:2 (LXX quote); Mrk 2:24 (ἴδε); Mrk 4:3 (begins a parable); Mrk 10:28; Mrk 10:33; Mrk 14:41; Mrk 15:4 (ἴδε, or C4b); Mrk 15:35 (ἴδε, or ? C3); Luk 1:20; Luk 1:31; Luk 1:44; Luk 1:48; Luk 2:10; Luk 2:34; Luk 2:48; Luk 6:23; Luk 7:25; Luk 7:27 (LXX quote); Luk 10:3; Luk 10:19; Luk 13:30; Luk 13:32; Luk 13:35 (or C4b); Luk 17:21d; Luk 18:28; Luk 18:31; Luk 22:10; Luk 22:21 (or ? C2b); Luk 22:31; Luk 23:14; Luk 24:49; Jhn 3:26 (ἴδε); Jhn 4:35; Jhn 5:14 (ἴδε); Jhn 11:3 (ἴδε, or C2d); Jhn 18:21 (?, ἴδε, see § 4.4.4); Jhn 19:4 (ἴδε); Act 5:25 (or C2d);[123] Act 7:56; Act 9:11; Act 10:21 (or ? C3); Act 13:25; Act 13:46; Act 20:22; Act 20:25; Act 27:24; Rom 9:33 (LXX quote); 1Co 15:51; 2Co 5:17; 2Co 6:9 (or C4b); 2Co 7:11; Gal 5:2 (ἴδε); Heb 10:7 (‖Heb 10:9, LXX quotes; or C3); Jas 3:5; Jas 5:4; Jas 5:7; Jas 5:11; 1Pe 2:6 (LXX quote); Jud 1:14 (apocryphal quote); Rev 1:7; Rev 1:18; Rev 2:10; Rev 2:22; Rev 3:8; Rev 3:9a; Rev 3:9e; Rev 3:20; Rev 5:5; Rev 11:14; Rev 16:15; Rev 21:3 (or C3 or C2); Rev 21:5 (or C4b); Rev 22:7; Rev 22:12.

---

376), there are rare cases where the states of affairs themselves may involve **questions** (e.g., C5 Mrk 2:24, but the speakers, some Pharisees, no doubt intend this as a positive statement and rebuke) or **negation** (e.g., C4b cases like Luk 23:15 'absolutely nothing'; the C4 rhetorical question marker οὐκ/χ ἰδού in Act 2:7 and often the LXX). 2Ki 7:10, which is apparently a C5/C2c hybrid, is noteworthy because what is asserted to (certainly) exist involves the absence of certain things: Εἰσήλθομεν εἰς τὴν παρεμβολὴν Συρίας, καὶ ἰδοὺ οὐκ ἔστιν ἐκεῖ ἀνὴρ καὶ φωνὴ ἀνθρώπου, ὅτι εἰ μὴ ἵππος δεδεμένος καὶ ὄνος ... 'We went into the camp of Syria, and, behold, there is not there a man, nor voice of man, only horses tied and asses ...' (Brenton, BibleWorks).
[123] Although Björck (p. 51) thinks the constituent order speaks against Act 5:25 being periphrastic, periphrasis makes more sense to me with ἰδού (so one complex state of affairs is introduced). Aerts (p. 71) slightly prefers Regard's interpretation, who assumes periphrasis here indicates progressive aspect ('en train de').

The following sections illustrate the claims outlined above. The first three sections are organized according to the information structure category of the ἰδού/ἴδε clause: topic-comment (§ 4.5.1), constituent-focus (§ 4.5.2), thetic and thetic-like constructions (§ 4.5.3). Section § 4.5.4 deals with the translation of a few tokens where the subject is first person but no pronoun occurs. And § 4.5.5 discusses two tokens occurring in narrative and their relation to C2c. Evaluations of renderings in English, French, and Italian are offered throughout.

4.5.1 C5 with topical subjects and predicate-focus

C5 most typically occurs with **predicate-focus** constructions. In nearly half of the C5 tokens, the subject is not expressed lexically but indexed on the verb. In all of these, the subject is topical: in some it is the primary topic of a predicate-focus construction with topic-comment function; in others it is part of a topical open proposition (see § 4.5.2).

Consider **Mat 20:18** (∥Mrk 10:33 and Luk 18:31) where the subject is the primary topic.

Mat 20:18 ἰδοὺ ἀναβαίνομεν   εἰς Ἱεροσόλυμα, καὶ ὁ   υἱὸς τοῦ
     *   we.are.going.up to Jerusalem   and the Son -

     ἀνθρώπου παραδοθήσεται   τοῖς ἀρχιερεῦσιν καὶ
     of.Man 3s.will.be.handed.over to.the chief.priests and

     γραμματεῦσιν, καὶ κατακρινοῦσιν αὐτὸν θανάτῳ
     scribes   and 3p.will.condemn him to.death

     NRS: [17] While Jesus was going up to Jerusalem, he took the twelve disciples aside by themselves, and said to them on the way, [18] "See, we are going up to Jerusalem, and the Son of Man will be handed over to the chief priests and scribes, and they will condemn him to death; [19] then they will hand him over to the Gentiles to be mocked and flogged and crucified; and on the third day he will be raised."

     NJB: Look, we are going up to Jerusalem, ...

     BFC: Écoutez, nous montons à Jérusalem, où le Fils de l'homme sera livré ...

     FBJ: Voici que nous montons à Jérusalem,

     BDS: Voici, nous montons à Jérusalem.

     NRV: Ecco, noi saliamo a Gerusalemme e il Figlio ...

The clause topic 'we' is expressed alone on the verb, ἀναβαίνομεν 'we are going up'. There is nothing particularly noteworthy about Jesus' first statement, that 'we are going up to Jerusalem'. The disciples presumably know this since they have already set out on the road for Jerusalem (v 17; this is also implied in ∥Mrk 10:32 and Luk 17:11). What is noteworthy and indeed surprising for the disciples is what follows this clause, Jesus' prediction of his trial, execution and resurrection. Thus, ἰδού is used at the **beginning** of a monologue—modifying several clauses—to instruct the audience to 'pay attention'.[124] Good translations of ἰδού in this context include *(Now) pay attention*, and *Listen*, (GNB, or *Écoutez*, BFC). Although NJB's *Look*, and NRS's *See*, can be understood metaphorically, they are more problematic because they may suggest that Jesus and his disciples are walking at that very moment, and that Jesus could be pointing at their movement as evidence—which would be entirely irrelevant. Paul Solomiac (p.c.) informs me that FBJ's *voici que* and, even more, BDS *voici* sound old fashioned or exotic and may give the impression that Jesus is referring primarily to their journey. (See below on the oddness of *ecco*.)

Similarly, the subject 'I' (expressed on the verb) in **Mat 24:25** is the clause topic. This clause **concludes** a section where Jesus has predicted many things about his second coming, not least that there will be imposters who will try to deceive God's people, claiming to be the Messiah. So the clause serves as a warning, highlighting what Jesus just told them, the implication being that the disciples should not forget the prediction. Appropriate translations of ἰδού include JBP's *Listen!* (also GNB, and BFC's *Écoutez* !), CAS's *Mark my words*, and NRS's *Take note*. (See also Mat 28:7e where the angel ends his speech with ἰδοὺ εἶπον ὑμῖν. ' ... I have told you'; but translations vary considerably in their renderings of ἰδού.)

Mat 24:25 ἰδοὺ προείρηκα   ὑμῖν.
   *   I.have.forewarned you

JBP: <u>Listen</u>, I am warning you."
CAS: <u>Mark my words:</u> I have given you warning.
NRS: <u>Take note,</u> I have told you beforehand.

---

[124] See also Luk 23:14 where the first clause following ἰδού (which is participial) is introductory, and what ἰδού actually highlights is the following indicative clause: καὶ ἰδοὺ ἐγὼ ἐνώπιον ὑμῶν ἀνακρίνας οὐθὲν εὗρον ἐν τῷ ἀνθρώπῳ τούτῳ ... [and * I before you.G having.examined.Aor nothing I.found in the.D man.D this.D ...] 'and here, having examined him in your presence, I found this man guilty of none of your charges against him' (see also Luk 1:44 for a subordinate temporal clause followed by an indicative clause). Similarly, although not subordinate, the first clause following ἰδού in Mat 28:7 is ancillary to the second clause, in which ἐκεῖ is an instance of constituent-focus: καὶ ἰδοὺ προάγει ὑμᾶς εἰς τὴν Γαλιλαίαν, ἐκεῖ αὐτὸν ὄψεσθε· [and * 3S.is.going.ahead you.A to the.A Galilee.A there him 2P.will.see] 'Now pay attention! He is going ahead of you to Galilee and it is there that you will see him!' (Act 9:11 may also fit here). In some passages, the first clause following ἰδού is probably equally significant to one or more that follow (e.g., Mat 10:16 with two clauses; Luk 1:31 with several clauses).

There are also many tokens where, even though the subject is expressed lexically, it is still topical, and the clause is not thetic. This is especially clear in tokens where the subject belongs to a greater topical open proposition (see e.g., Luk 7:25 and Luk 17:21d in § 4.5.2). There are also a few instances where the subject is the primary topic of a topic-comment construction. This applies to 'your father and I' in **Luk 2:48** where these entities are already fully activated. It is the descriptive predicate that is informative. Good models include *Think* (KNX) and *Don't you see,* (Tony Pope, p.c.). Metaphorical *Look,* (NRS) also works, though sounds weak in this emotional context. In contrast, the GNB has ignored ἰδού, and the use of *behold* in the ESV (which is supposed to be a translation in contemporary English) is especially jarring since no mother would speak to her child today in this way.

Luk 2:48 ἰδοὺ ὁ πατήρ σου κἀγὼ ὀδυνώμενοι
* the father of.you and.I being.anxious

ἐζητοῦμέν σε.
we.were.looking.for you

NRS: When his parents saw him they were astonished; and his
mother said to him, "Child, why have you treated us like
this? Look, your father and I have been searching for you in
great anxiety."

KNX: Think, what anguish of mind thy father and I have
endured, searching for thee.

GNB: Your father and I have been terribly worried trying to
find you.

ESV: Behold, your father and I have been searching for you in
great distress.

Similarly, in **Mat 10:16** the subject pronoun ἐγώ 'I' is the primary sentence topic.

Mat 10:16 Ἰδοὺ ἐγὼ ἀποστέλλω ὑμᾶς ὡς πρόβατα ἐν μέσῳ
* I I.send you as sheep in midst

λύκων· γίνεσθε οὖν φρόνιμοι ὡς οἱ ὄφεις
of.wolves be! therefore wise as the serpents

καὶ ἀκέραιοι ὡς αἱ περιστεραί.
and innocent as the doves

GNB: [16] Listen! I am sending you out just like sheep to a pack
of wolves. You must be as cautious as snakes and as gentle
as doves. [17] Watch out [προσέχετε], for there will be those
who will arrest you ...

NRV: Ecco, io vi mando come pecore in mezzo ai lupi; siate
dunque prudenti come i serpenti e semplici come le colombe.

This token comes in the middle of a long set of instructions to the disciples (Mat 10:5–42) where Jesus then highlights a set of warnings and commands, beginning them with ἰδού. The GNB appropriately renders ἰδού as *Listen!* The informative part of the clause is expressed by the predicate 'sending you as sheep among wolves', which is the comment about the topic 'I' (as the one who is already speaking, the entity 'I' is completely activated). ‖Luk 10:3 in fact lacks ἐγώ. That ἐγώ is used at all for a topical entity[125] can be explained on the grounds that Jesus is beginning a new paragraph (topical pronouns typically occur at the beginning of a discourse and a new section/paragraph within a discourse).[126] Assuming ἐγώ is a topic expression, it is impossible that ἰδοὺ ἐγώ forms a syntactic unit by itself or that it functions in the way we found with C4.

Concerning the cited Italian translations in the above passages, note that, even though many use *ecco* in these examples (e.g., in Mat 10:16 and Mat 20:18), its use is not idiomatic (Marco Librè, p.c.). Although *ecco* is readily comprehensible as a mental pointer in these, something like 'listen carefully' or 'pay attention' would still be more natural (the same seems true of *behold*). Furthermore, *ecco* tends to be taken as pointing to the first sentence that follows it (when not subordinate). Thus, a reader might think that in Mat 10:16 Jesus is primarily highlighting 'I am sending you out just like sheep to a pack of wolves' and not what follows it (both statements are important); and in Mat 20:18 'we are going up to Jerusalem' (which is clearly secondary) rather than 'the Son of Man will be betrayed … condemned … and crucified'. If one insists on using *ecco*, then it would be clearer to move it after the first clause (e.g., *Noi saliamo a Gerusalemme, ed ecco, il Figlio dell'uomo … Marco Librè, p.c.*).

In *Joseph and Aseneth*, there are several C5 tokens with topical subjects, both with and without lexical subjects. The ἰδού clauses occur as individual tokens (e.g., J&A 23.3 with ἐγώ; J&A 24.2 with lexical subject 'the sons of Bilhah and Zilpah …') and, what is more impressive, as whole lists! For example, in J&A 13.1–11, having fasted for seven days and repented from her idolatry and arrogance, Aseneth then lists for God the many proofs of her repentance, beginning each item with ἰδού. Each item highlights something she has already done, or, in two cases (verses 6 and 7), the results of her actions. Although Burchard translates each ἰδού

---

[125] Ἰδοὺ ἐγὼ ἀποστέλλω occurs in the LXX a handful of times for הִנְנִי שֹׁלֵחַ (Jer 16:16; Jer 25:9; Jer 43:10=LXX 50:10) and הִנֵּה אָנֹכִי שֹׁלֵחַ (Exo 23:20; Mal 3:22). While the Greek obviously echoes the Hebrew structure (compare BDF § 277.2; Fiedler 1969:24 note 88), this does not mean that ἐγώ here is unnatural NT Koine (for the reasons I mention).

[126] See Bailey (2011:312–317) on the various functions of topical subject pronouns, including how they can also be used to 'highlight' (or add emotive emphasis to) an utterance.

mechanically by 'behold', a more idiomatic rendering could be something like *Take notice!* or *Don't forget!* (The passage is somewhat reminiscent of Mat 19:27, also C5, where Peter points out what he and the disciples have given up for Jesus.) In eight out of ten tokens, the topic is Aseneth referring to herself in the first person; the subject pronoun ἐγώ occurs only in verses 1 and 9.[127] The topic of verse 6 is the floor of her chamber, and in 7, the clause is thetic (see § 4.5.3). See also the parallel list of C5 tokens in J&A chapter 15 (verses 2, 3a, 3b, 4, 5, 6, etc.) where the angel lists and highlights the results or rewards of Aseneth's prayer and repentance.

There is one rendering that I have not come across in English NT translations for C5 (or any other use), and that is *hereby*. This lack is somewhat puzzling since ἰδού in particular often occurs with promises and other more or less official-sounding statements, and these in turn sometimes have properties of (explicit) 'performative' speech acts.[128] In contrast, OT translators do occasionally use *hereby* for הִנֵּה 'behold', including where ἰδού occurs in the LXX. For example, the NJPS and NRS both use *hereby* in **Exo 34:10** (the subject ἐγώ is clearly topical).[129]

Exo 34:10 Ἰδοὺ ἐγὼ τίθημί   σοι   διαθήκην·
       *   I   I.establish with.you covenant

hinnēh ʾānōkî kōrēt   bərît   הִנֵּה אָנֹכִי כֹּרֵת בְּרִית
behold I   cutting.Prt covenant

NJPS: [And God] said [to Moses]: I hereby make a covenant.

Therefore, I reason that, given the right mix of contextual ingredients,[130] English NT translators could also occasionally make use of

---

[127] In contrast to Burchard's edition, which contains ten ἰδού sentences, in Philonenko's there are only seven, and ἐγώ occurs only in the seventh (13.8 in Philonenko), which is, incidentally, about Aseneth fasting for seven days and seven nights: Καὶ ἰδοὺ ἐγὼ ἑπτὰ ἡμέρας καὶ ἑπτὰ νύκτας οὔτε ἄρτον ἔφαγον οὔτε ὕδωρ ἔπιον [and * I seven days.A.p.f and seven nights.A.p.f neither bread.A.s.m 3S.ate nor water.A.s.n 3S.drank] 'and behold for seven days and seven nights I ate neither bread nor drank water'.

In neither Burchard's edition nor in Philonenko's edition is the time duration (seven days and seven nights) an instance of C4a since the time phrase does not immediately follow ἰδού nor is it in the nominative.

[128] According to Levinson (1983:232, 234), only explicit performatives, i.e., ones with 'performative verbs', are compatible with *hereby* in English.

[129] See also Num 3:12 (NJPS and NRS: *I hereby accept the Levites ...*); Jdg 1:2 (NRS: *I hereby give the land into his hand*); Num 18:21 (NJPS, NAB); the NJPS of Gen 17:20, Num 18:8, and Isa 38:5; Num 25:12 (NRS, NAB). For הֲלֹא ('is it not!') and LXX ἰδού, see Jos 1:9 (NRS *hereby*) and Jdg 6:14 (NRS *hereby*, NJPS *herewith*).

[130] Andersen (2003:50) notes about the so-called performative use of הִנֵּה that 'this nuance is constrained by pragmatics, and can be subsumed under the

hereby (the appropriateness of this translation depends on context; it is not because ἰδού literally means *hereby* or renders the clause an explicit performative). One C5 token where this rendering seems appropriate to me is **Act 13:46** (the subject, indexed only on the verb, is topic).

Act 13:46 ἐπειδὴ ἀπωθεῖσθε αὐτὸν καὶ οὐκ ἀξίους κρίνετε
        since   you.reject it   and not worthy you.judge

        ἑαυτοὺς   τῆς   αἰωνίου   ζωῆς, ἰδοὺ στρεφόμεθα εἰς
        yourselves of.the of.eternal life   *   we.turn.Pres to

        τὰ   ἔθνη.
        the Gentiles

> GNB: [45] When the Jews saw the crowds, they were filled with jealousy; they disputed what Paul was saying and insulted him. [46] But Paul and Barnabas spoke out even more boldly: "It was necessary that the word of God should be spoken first to you. But since you reject it and do not consider yourselves worthy of eternal life, <u>we will leave you and go to the Gentiles</u>. ..."

> NLT: and judged yourselves unworthy of eternal life—<u>well</u>, we will offer it to Gentiles

> REB & NIV: we <u>now</u> turn to the Gentiles.

> NRS: we are <u>now</u> turning to the Gentiles.

As can be seen by the illustrated translations, most translators seem at a loss about what to do with ἰδού here. *Now* in the REB, NIV,[131] and NRS are weak, but still better than NLT's *well*, or just the future in the GNB. I suggest instead: *We hereby turn to the Gentiles.* This passage is in fact the first of three such public statements that Paul makes to this effect (Act 18:6; Act 28:28). Other C5 tokens where *hereby* could be considered include Gal 5:2 (with ἴδε); Rev 21:5 (but see also § 4.4.3 on C4b) and maybe Luk 2:10. (For non-C5 tokens that may function as performatives, see § 4.2.3 on Act 13:11 and Rev 21:3, and see footnotes 14 and 103.)

4.5.2 C5 with constituent-focus

Considerably less frequently, we find C5 occurring with **constituent-focus**. A clear example occurs in **Luk 7:25**. The context evokes the open proposition 'people in fancy clothes and living in luxury are [in location

presentative function of *hnh*.' Miller-Naudé and van der Merwe (2011:66–69 including their footnote 54) also note several uses of *hinnēh* with performative function, especially with *qatal* verb forms, but also occasionally with verbless ('nominal') clauses (see 2Sa 16:4) and even participles (see Exo 34:10 cited above).

[131] One of NIV's favorite renderings of not just C5 but of several other uses of ἰδού is *now*, thereby leveling several uses.

X]'[132] (paraphrasable by the question 'Where are people in fancy clothes and living in luxury?'), and the clause serves to identify the location, ἐν τοῖς βασιλείοις 'in royal palaces' (in contrast to 'the desert'). But note that, unlike the C4, here ἰδού does not immediately precede the focused constituent. The GNB and CEV render ἰδού here as Ø, the NIV as *No* and the NRS as *Look*. BDAG appropriately lists this token in section 1.c 'as a call to closer consideration and contemplation *remember, consider, etc.*' (italics are BDAG's). Jesus' statement is not at all surprising. He is making use of a rhetorical device, reminding his audience of the obvious, that is, telling them to 'pay mental attention' to something they *already know*.

Luk 7:25 ἰδοὺ οἱ   ἐν   ἱματισμῷ ἐνδόξῳ καὶ τρυφῇ
        *   those with clothes   glorious and in.luxury

ὑπάρχοντες ἐν τοῖς βασιλείοις εἰσίν.
living   in the palaces   3p.are

> GNB: [24] ... "When you went out to John in the desert, what did you expect to see? A blade of grass bending in the wind? [25] What did you go out to see? A man dressed up in fancy clothes? People who dress like that and live in luxury are found in palaces! ..."

A similar εἰμί construction occurs in **Luk 17:21**. It serves to answer the implicit question 'Where is the Kingdom of God?' (i.e., the open proposition is 'the Kingdom of God is [in location X]'). The constituent ἐντὸς ὑμῶν[133] answers that question. Such a surprising answer, however, does not have a reminding function (in contrast to Luk 7:25 above) since the answer contradicts the audience's beliefs. Given the novelty of Jesus' statement, the BFC translates it as *sachez-le* ('know/realize [it]!'), that is, pay mental attention *to a new idea*. Except for the most literal English translations, most render ἰδού as Ø, probably because of the presence of γάρ 'because'.

---

[132] Since the open proposition was not fully activated prior to the utterance, the point of departure serves to activate the key component of it, which is the clause subject, 'people in fancy clothes and living in luxury'. It is 'inferentially accessible' (i.e., 'semi-active') given its inferential relationship to the previous utterance, 'A man dressed up in fancy clothes'. See footnote 19 in ch. 2.

[133] There is much debate about the precise meaning of ἐντὸς ὑμῶν.

Luk 17:21 οὐδὲ ἐροῦσιν,   ἰδοὺ ὧδε ἤ· ἐκεῖ, ἰδοὺ γὰρ ἡ
nor 3p.will.say *   here or there *   for the

βασιλεία   τοῦ   θεοῦ ἐντὸς   ὑμῶν
Kingdom   of.the God inside/among/within.reach? of.you

ἐστιν.
3s.is

> GNB: [20] Some Pharisees asked Jesus when the Kingdom of
> God would come. His answer was, "The Kingdom of God
> does not come in such a way as to be seen. [21] No one will
> say, 'Look, here it is!' or, 'There it is!'; because the Kingdom
> of God is within you."
>
> BFC: " ... Car, sachez-le, le Royaume de Dieu est au milieu de
> vous." [= 'among you']

To complement the discussion of constituent-focus in relation to C4
(sections under § 4.4), here are two lists of the likely C5 tokens with
constituent-focus:

→ **C5, focused constituent comes late in sentence**: Mat 11:8 and
‖Luk 7:25 (illustrated above); Luk 17:21d (illustrated above); Act
27:24 ('all the ones sailing with you'); Rev 5:5 ('the Lion of the
tribe of Judah'). In three other passages, it may be that a
constituent occurs clause-finally in order to emphasize *that* part
of a larger focus domain (i.e., the entire predicate is in the focus
domain, but part of it is emphasized): Mat 23:38 ('desolate'); Mat
28:20 ('all days'); Mrk 14:41 ('into the hands of sinners' is in any
case in its default postverbal position as a focal object).

→ **C5 (not C4), focused constituent immediately follows
particle**: Mat 19:27, ‖Mrk 10:28, and ‖Luk 18:28.

4.5.3   C5 preceding thetic and thetic-like constructions

Only rarely does C5 coincide with a real thetic clause, but fairly
frequently it precedes something that has 'thetic-like' properties: either
(i) it immediately precedes a clause that is thetic-like (e.g., the object
introduces something new into the discourse), or (ii) something further
off in a subsequent sentence is thetic-like or a true thetic.

I mention here first two clauses in **Luk 13:30** that could be mistakenly
taken as typical thetics. They are however not true thetics, because the
subjects are implicitly 'partitive' (meaning 'some' of a set) and εἰμί 'be'
functions not so much to introduce an entity into the discourse but
to assert that (contrary to what might be expected) the entity exists.
Moreover, since these are not statements about the here-and-now (as

in C1 where ἰδού would be the predicator) but about generic time,[134] εἰμί is expected. As an instance of C5, ἰδού instructs the hearers to 'pay attention', thereby underscoring the surprising statements Jesus makes (the relative clauses express the unpredictable elements in the assertions). Some translators, apparently for stylistic reasons, opt not to translate the highlighter (CEV, GNB).[135] *And note this* in the NLT is appropriate. *Indeed* in the NIV (and NRS, also FBJ *Oui*) works to the extent it confirms the **certainty** of a state of affairs (which in this case was unexpected). Renderings that confirm certainty seem especially appropriate when the C5 statement is anaphoric (i.e., it refers to something just suggested in the discourse).[136]

Luk 13:30 καὶ ἰδοὺ εἰσὶν ἔσχατοι οἳ ἔσονται πρῶτοι καὶ
and * 3p.are last.ones who 3p.will.be first and

εἰσὶν πρῶτοι οἳ ἔσονται ἔσχατοι.
3p.are first.ones who 3p.will.be last

NIV: [28] There will be weeping there ... when you see Abraham, Isaac and Jacob and all the prophets in the kingdom of God, but you yourselves thrown out. [29] People will come from east and west ... and will take their places at the feast in the kingdom of God. [30] Indeed there are those who are last who will be first, and first who will be last.

---

[134] As Marshall (1978) notes, 'The closing saying is proverbial in form ... [and] of general application' (compare Mat 19:30, 'many that are first will be last, and the last first'). Given the proverbial use, the subjects refer firstly to generic classes of entities (e.g., 'ones who are last').

[135] The GNB, which strives to be a very idiomatic translation, reads: *Then those who are now last will be first, and those who are now first will be last*. This is a paraphrase that makes the generic (timeless) statement more specific. One should not conclude that ἰδού can mean either 'now' or logical 'then'!

[136] There are at least two uses of Hebrew *hinnēh* that Miller-Naudé and van der Merwe (2011) sometimes render by *indeed* (or similar phrase that confirms). One use (pp. 73–74) occurs when a speaker (often in narrative, including first person) confirms an expectation (e.g., Deu 9:16 'I looked and indeed you had sinned against the LORD your God'; Gen 6:12 'God observed the earth, and *indeed*, it was corrupt'). The other use (pp. 77–8) is when *hinnēh*, as one of several possible sub-functions, points to one or more propositions in order to confirm something else in the preceding context (e.g., 1Sa 26:21: 'Then Saul said, "I have sinned. Come back my son, David. I will not harm you again, because my life was precious today for you. *Indeed*, I acted foolishly and have erred so very much"'; Isa 12:1–2: 'I praise you LORD, for though you were angry with me, your anger turned away and you comforted me. *Yes*, God is my deliverer. I will trust and not be afraid').

Under one interpretation, the ἰδού clause in **2Co 5:17** is a (typical) non-deictic thetic,[137] introducing a state of affairs (*the NEW has come!*) into an abstract mental world (it concerns the spiritual condition of every Christian).[138] I take ἰδού to be an instance of C5, 'take note!' Many translators ignore ἰδού (GNB, CEV, NLT, NJB) or at most add an exclamation mark (NLT). Perhaps *indeed* (confirming the certainty) would also be appropriate. Although the GNB and NIV lack an explicit attention pointer, the final two clauses are compatible with thetic readings (e.g., NIV: *The OLD has gone, the NEW is here*).

2Co 5:17 ὥστε εἴ τις　 ἐν Χριστῷ, καινὴ κτίσις· τὰ
　　　　 so.that if anyone in Christ   new   creation the

ἀρχαῖα　　　　παρῆλθεν,　 ἰδοὺ γέγονεν
old.things.N.p.n 3s.passed.away *   3s.have.happened

καινά·
new.things.N.p.n

GNB: Anyone who is joined to Christ is a new being; the old is gone, <u>the new has come</u>.

NIV: Therefore, if anyone is in Christ, the new creation has come: The old has gone, <u>the new is here</u>!

NLT: What this means is that those who become Christians become new persons. They are not the same anymore, for the old life is gone. <u>A new life has begun</u>!

One token occurs in *Joseph and Aseneth*, **J&A 13.7**, which I briefly referred to above in § 4.5.1, in the passage where Aseneth lists and highlights for God her proofs of repentance. Both a vocative (κύριέ μου) and a topical locative ('from my tears ...') separate ἰδού from the thetic subject (πηλὸς ... πολύς 'much mud'), and the verb is also a perfect form of γίνομαι (γέγονε), as in 2Co 5:17 above (so Burchard's edition; Philonenko's edition is comparable but, notably, has the verb ἐστί).

J&A 13.7 ἰδοὺ κύριέ μου　 ἐκ　 τῶν δακρύων μου καὶ τῆς
　　　　 *   O.Lord of.me from the.G tears.G   my and the

τέφρας πηλὸς γέγονε　　　　　 πολὺς ἐν τῷ
ash.G mud 3s.has.happened.Prf much in the.D

θαλάμῳ　 μου ὡς ἐν ὁδῷ　 πλατείᾳ.
chamber.D of.me as in road.D broad.D

---

[137] The thetic interpretation assumes that καινά 'new things' is the subject and not a predicate adjective.

[138] Paul is speaking of all Christians everywhere. It is beside the point that his generic appraisal applies to specific people, such as his present audience or himself.

^{7} <u>Behold</u>, my Lord, from my tears and the ashes much mud has been formed in my chamber, as on a broad street. (Burchard 1985)

In **Luk 22:10**, Jesus instructs Peter and John where to prepare their Passover dinner, beginning his instructions with C5 ἰδού. The first clause, a genitive absolute, has a predicate-focus structure (with topical subject; the subject pronoun is virtually mandatory in such participial clauses). This first clause is simultaneously a temporal point of departure for what follows. What follows is a typical non-deictic thetic, introducing 'a man'.[139] The CEV, GNB, and NIV ignore ἰδού. More appropriate are the NRS's *Listen* and BFC's *Écoutez*.

Luk 22:10 ἰδοὺ εἰσελθόντων   ὑμῶν εἰς τὴν πόλιν
          *   having.entered.G.Aor you.G into the city

συναντήσει ὑμῖν ἄνθρωπος κεράμιον ὕδατος βαστάζων·
3s.will.meet you man   jar   of.water carrying

ἀκολουθήσατε αὐτῷ ...
follow!   him

NRS: ^{10} "Listen," he said to them, "when you have entered the city, <u>a man carrying a jar of water will meet you</u>; follow him into the house he enters ^{11} and say to the owner ..."

In **Mat 22:4**, the first clause is formally a predicate-focus structure (with topical subject 'I'), but the object is thetic-like, introducing 'dinner'. The second clause is presumably thetic, introducing 'my bulls and fattened cattle have been slaughtered'.[140]

Mat 22:4 ἰδοὺ τὸ ἄριστόν μου   ἡτοίμακα,   οἱ ταῦροί μου
          *   the dinner of.me I.have.prepared the bulls of.me

καὶ τὰ σιτιστὰ   τεθυμένα   καὶ
and the fattened.cattle having.been.slaughtered.Prf.ps and

πάντα   ἕτοιμα· δεῦτε εἰς τοὺς γάμους
all.things ready come! to the wedding.feast

NRS: Again he sent other slaves, saying, 'Tell those who have been invited: <u>Look, I have prepared my dinner</u>, my oxen and my fat calves have been slaughtered, and everything is ready; come to the wedding banquet.'

---

[139]That ἄνθρωπος 'a man' is postverbal is typical of many non-ἰδού thetics (Bailey 2009:233–242).
[140]Perhaps some languages would treat the latter as topic-comment. The subject is 'heavy' (see Bailey 2009:61–62 and 143–146 on informationally heavy clauses).

Other tokens introducing entities in the object position of the first or second clause following ἰδού or ἴδε include: Mat 1:23; Mat 23:34; Mrk 15:35 (ἴδε); Luk 1:31; Luk 2:10; Luk 24:49; Jhn 4:35; Act 9:11; Rom 9:33; 1Co 15:51; 1Pe 2:6; Rev 3:8.

In **Act 7:56**, the predicate-focus clause ('I' is topic) introduces two states of affairs as participial object complements of the perception verb θεωρῶ 'see'. While some English translations render ἰδού as *Look* (e.g., NRS, GNB, NIV), it seems doubtful that Stephen expects his murderous audience to share his heavenly vision (C3). Instead, I assume this is another instance of C5, which in this case involves an emotion of wonder. The sense of wonder is strengthened by the choice of perception verb, θεωρῶ, which is often used for viewing something remarkable or spectacular (Tony Pope, p.c.). The Message's (MSG) use of the exclamative particle *Oh!* seems appropriate to the extent that it indicates wonder and surprise, but since *Oh!* is not really an instruction to the hearer to 'pay mental attention' but rather functions to express a speaker's spontaneous realization, it is probably less appropriate than *Listen!* (BFC: *Écoutez*). Another C5 passage where *Oh!* (or a similar particle indicating the speakers spontaneous surprise) might seem natural would be Luk 1:44, but my same reservations would apply there (see also KNX's use of *Why* there).

Act 7:56 καὶ εἶπεν· ἰδοὺ θεωρῶ τοὺς οὐρανοὺς διηνοιγμένους
and 3s.said *   I.see   the heavens   having.been.opened

καὶ τὸν υἱὸν τοῦ   ἀνθρώπου ἐκ δεξιῶν ἑστῶτα
and the Son of.the Man   at right standing.Prf

τοῦ   θεοῦ.
of.the God

NRS: "<u>Look</u>," he said, "I see the heavens opened and the Son of Man standing at the right hand of God!"

MSG: "<u>Oh</u>! I see heaven wide open and the Son of Man standing at God's side!"

BFC: Il dit: <u>Écoutez</u>, je vois les cieux ouverts et le Fils de l'homme debout à la droite de Dieu.

4.5.4 When the subject is first person and no pronoun occurs

Tokens with a first person subject indexed only on the verb deserve special comment. There are some tokens that English translators render as (hybrid) deictic thetics (on 'hybrid', see footnote 143). This is

illustrated by the NLT and NIV's renderings of **Rev 3:20** and by the GNB
and NIV's renderings (also REB, NJB) of **Heb 10:7** (and ‖Heb 10:9).[141]

Rev 3:20 Ἰδοὺ ἔστηκα   ἐπὶ τὴν θύραν καὶ κρούω·
  *   I.stand.Prf at   the door   and knock

> GNB: Listen! I stand at the door and knock, ...
> NLT: Look! Here I stand at the door and knock.
> NIV: Here I am! I stand at the door and knock.

Heb 10:7 ἰδοὺ ἥκω,   ἐν κεφαλίδι βιβλίου γέγραπται
  *   I.have.come in roll   of.book 3s.has.been.written

περὶ ἐμοῦ, τοῦ ποιῆσαι ὁ θεὸς τὸ θέλημά σου.
about me -   to.do   the God the will   of.you

> NRS: [5] ... when Christ came into the world, he said, "Sacrifices
> and offerings you have not desired, but a body you have
> prepared for me ... [7] Then I [Christ] said, 'See, God, I have
> come to do your will, O God' (in the scroll of the book it is
> written of me)."
> CEV: And so, my God, I have come to do what you want, as the
> Scriptures say.
> GNB: Here I am, to do your will, O God, ...
> NIV: Here I am–it is written about me in the scroll–I have
> come to do your will, O God.

But such English renderings are inaccurate. The clearest pattern of
deictic thetics in Greek (i.e., C1 and C2) with 'I' as the subject have an
independent pronoun as the subject (e.g., ἰδοὺ ἐγώ, 'Here I am' in Act
9:10 and Heb 2:13),[142] while the absence of a pronoun and noun phrase
in Rev 3:20 and Heb 10:7 necessarily indicates that the subject is topical.
Therefore, in these passages, (i) the subject referents ('I') are topical
and (ii) the constructions are not thetic.[143] Other translations in fact

---

[141] Heb 10:7 is a quotation of LXX Psa 39:8; this translates Psa 40:8, which is
not ... הִנֵּנִי but בָאתִי־הִנֵּה, which notably lacks the so-called 'object' suffix 'I'
on הִנֵּה. The Hebrew cannot mean *Here's ME*, and it is also doubtful that *Here
I am ...* is an ideal translation, as in NRS and GNB. More likely it means *Look/
See, I have COME* (... v 9 *to do what pleases you ...*), where the subject entity
is topical and not being introduced (see NLT and CEV). For similar Hebrew
constructions, see Num 22:38 and 2Sa 19:21.
[142] As noted earlier, even if a first person pronoun does follow ἰδού, the
pronoun can express either the sentence topic (e.g., ἐγώ in Mat 10:16, see
§ 4.5.1) or constituent-focus (ἡμεῖς 'we' in Mat 19:27).
[143] Lambrecht calls a topic with the highest degree of presupposition—which
would also be completely 'activated' in the mind of the hearer—a 'ratified
topic'; and its form is generally indicative of this high degree: 'Ratified
topics are expressed in unaccented (or phonologically null) constituents'

take ἰδού as C5 or C3: in Rev 3:20, ἰδού is rendered as *Listen* (CEV, GNB, NRS, BFC *Écoute*) or *Look* (NJB), as C5; and in Heb 10:7, as Ø (CEV), *Look* (NLT), and *See*, (NRS), which can also be viewed as C3. Thus, I assume that the net effect of these Greek constructions here is to emphasize the predicates: e.g., *Listen, I am RIGHT at your door, KNOCKING, and I have COME (indeed) to do your will.*

4.5.5   C5 tokens in narrative and parables

Only occasionally do we find C5 tokens at the beginning or in the middle of a narrative, modifying events on the story line. Thus, this use combines features of (i) C2c with features of (ii) C5, that is, (i) they occur in narrative and add vividness but (ii) have the syntactic form of typical C5 tokens (i.e., they are not thetic).

There are two C5 tokens occurring midstream in narrative: **Mat 8:29** and, three verses later, **Mat 8:32**. These resemble C2c, since they come in narrative and ἰδού functions to make the narration more immediate and vivid (there is also a providential/miraculous element in these). But since the subject entities were already introduced, they are topical, and the sentences are not thetic (i.e., not sentence-focus); one subject is expressed only on the verb and the other by a lexical NP. (Compare

---

(2000:614). To be sure, languages have hybrid constructions that are presentational (thetic) while also involving a subject that is a 'ratified topic'. In English, where pronouns cannot be omitted as easily as in Greek, we can say *Here comes the cat* (pure thetic) and *Here he comes* (with a ratified topic). *He* is appropriate if the speakers were already talking about a certain cat that had until that moment not been present (Lambrecht [1994:39–40] describes the latter as 'both presentational and predicating [i.e., topic-comment]'; in the text-internal world *he* is a topic expression, but in the text-*external* world the referent of *he* is unexpected and so the clause simultaneously has presentational function). First person is different since the speaker, who is always present, never needs full activation. But English has two common patterns (Lambrecht 1999:8): *Here I AM* (where 'I' is unaccented) assumes 'I' is already being talked about, but *(Look!) Here's ME* is appropriate if, for example, one is pointing oneself out in a picture and unexpected.

Similarly, I assume that the common Hebrew idiom, הִנֵּנִי 'Here I am', when used by a speaker to present himself as ready to listen or serve, is a hybrid construction, given that the referent 'I' is already expected to be present nearby. For example, in 1Sa 3:5, when Samuel believes that Eli is calling him, Samuel runs to Eli and says הִנֵּנִי; 'Here I am', thereby presenting himself as ready and attentive. Since the referent 'Samuel', as one just summoned, was just introduced into the text-internal world, it is topical in the response (in the text-internal world), while also being presentational (as the referent Samuel is being presented to Eli and so 'new' in the text-*external* world for Eli).

the rare construction C2c-∅-subject with thetic-like objects in § 4.2.4.4.) Some translations attempt to add vividness by means of *suddenly*. Another (more colloquial) way could be to use the sentence-initial connective *And then* together with the particle *just* and more dramatic verbs *shouted out* and *stampeded* (Tony Pope, p.c.).

Mat 8:29 καὶ ἰδοὺ ἔκραξαν   λέγοντες· τί   ἡμῖν καὶ σοί, υἱὲ
          and *   3p.cried.out saying   what to.us and to.you Son

          τοῦ θεοῦ;   ...
          -   of.God?

Mat 8:32 καὶ ἰδοὺ ὥρμησεν πᾶσα ἡ   ἀγέλη κατὰ τοῦ κρημνοῦ
          and *   rushed   all   the herd down the bank

          εἰς τὴν θάλασσαν καὶ ἀπέθανον ἐν τοῖς ὕδασιν.
          into the lake   and 3p.died in the waters

> NRS: [28] When he came to the other side, ... two demoniacs coming out of the tombs met him. They were so fierce that no one could pass that way. [29] Suddenly they shouted, "What have you to do with us, Son of God? Have you come here to torment us before the time?" [30] Now a large herd of swine was feeding at some distance from them. [31] The demons begged him, "If you cast us out, send us into the herd of swine." [32] And he said to them, "Go!" So they came out and entered the swine; and suddenly, the whole herd rushed down the steep bank into the sea and perished in the water.

> Tony Pope (p.c.): [29] And then they just shouted out ... [32] And then the whole herd of pigs just stampeded down the steep bank into the lake and perished in the water!

Mrk 4:3 deserves extended discussion as it involves some complex issues. This token occurs at the beginning of a story, the parable of the sower, as is also the case in ‖Mat 13:3. Both Fiedler (1969:22) and Pryke (1968) assume that Mark never used ἰδού in his narrative but only in reported speech. For Pryke (p. 421), this seems to mean that ἀκούετε ἰδού is separate from Jesus' parable, and that ἰδού, as a near synonym, reinforces ἀκούετε, and that, together, the two words can be translated as *Listen! Pay attention!*

Translating C5 ἰδού by *Pay attention!* is of course appropriate in many contexts, as I have already argued, but the conclusion that ἰδού is not the first word of the parable is not shared by all, and so this translation may be challenged. Fiedler in fact assumes that ἰδού does go with the parable (i.e., it is separate from ἀκούετε). But, although he has already noted for Luke that ἰδού can be used in narrative embedded in reported speech, he feels compelled to count this instance of ἰδού in Mark as not being true narrative.[144] He, like Pryke, is committed to the position that Mark never uses ἰδού in narrative since the evidence beyond this token is minimal.[145] Nevertheless, there are good reasons, to be mentioned shortly, for viewing ἰδού as part of the first clause of Jesus' parable. Part of the problem for Fiedler and Pryke may have been that they assumed there is only one use of ἰδού in narrative, the use so common in Matthew that I have described as thetic (C2c). However, if one recognizes that a vivid element can be added by means of C5 to the beginning of a narrative or parable, even in Mark, the problem vanishes.

Mrk 4:3 Ἀκούετε. ἰδοὺ ἐξῆλθεν   ὁ   σπείρων σπεῖραι.
       listen!   *   3s.went.out the sower   to.sow

> NRS: [2] [Jesus] began to teach them many things in parables, and in his teaching he said to them: [3] "Listen! A sower went out to sow. [4] And as he sowed, some seed fell on the path, and the birds came and ate it up.
>
> GNB: [3] "Listen! Once there was a man who went out to sow grain.
>
> Pryke: "Listen! Pay attention!"
>
> NJB: [3] 'Listen! Imagine a sower going out to sow.
>
> nab: Listen carefully! Picture in your mind that the sower went out to sow.

Although at first glance Mrk 4:3 and ||Mat 13:3 may appear to be thetic (C2c), nevertheless, since the subject ὁ σπείρων 'the sower' is grammatically definite (i.e., arthrous, articular), and since the predicate is not clearly one of appearance but involves a (focal) goal, the subject is better taken as a topic expression.[146] Such a first mention of a human

---

[144] Fiedler (1969:14) makes a distinction between Erzählung 'narrative' and Erzählungsstil 'narrative-style' where the latter refers to narrative embedded in reported speech. But since Luke often uses ἰδού in his own narrative, it seems Fiedler does not consider ἰδού in Luke's embedded narratives to be strange (Luk 9:39, Act 10:30, and Act 11:11). In the end, Fiedler's distinction seems artificial.

[145] One possible exception in Mark's narration is the variant reading in Mrk 5:22 (καὶ ἰδοὺ ἔρχεται with historical present), which is widely supported, including by one of the oldest manuscripts, Papyrus 45. Nevertheless, both Fiedler (1969:13) and Pryke (1968:424) dismiss this, as it is assumed that scribes inserted ἰδού to assimilate Mark to Mat 9:18 and Luk 8:41.

[146] There are also certain facts about the constituent order that would make it unusual for Mrk 4:3 and ||Mat 13:3 to be thetic. The order ἰδού–*verb–subject* is possible with C2c but rare (see footnote 61). Similarly, in thetic clauses lacking ἰδού, the order *verb-subject* at the beginning of a story is exceptional, and the inverse, *subject-verb*, is pragmatically unmarked (so neither

participant in a gospel parable by means of a definite noun phrase in fact stands out because more typically they are introduced by indefinite noun phrases.[147] That translations render ὁ σπείρων as an indefinite in a thetic construction, as illustrated by GNB's *Once there was a man who ...*, is clearly a distortion of the Greek. Although this may be a natural way to begin a story, the Greek here instead requires that we take for granted the existence of the sower, either as (i) a generic instance of a class of individuals,[148] or as (ii) a specific, identifiable individual. Most commentaries I have consulted assume it is (i) to be taken as a reference to the typical sower (alias 'preacher'), in which case this parable would be intended to portray not (just) a specific, one-time, account but a generic truth. If so, the English indefinite *a sower* as a generic designation (of a definite, known class) would be possible. But the matter is not that simple, since many also see here a veiled reference to a specific individual, the speaker himself (e.g., Gundry 2000).[149] Finally, it should be noticed that the focus of the parable is on the different types of ground that the seed falls on, and not on the sower, who is not mentioned again at all in Mark's version of the parable.

Given that Mrk 4:3 is prefaced by the command to listen (ἀκούετε), it would seem that ἰδού should not be viewed as a mere synonym, as if Jesus were merely repeating the command to pay attention. Moreover,

---

does ‖Luk 8:5 appear to be thetic; see Bailey 2009:243–249, § 4.10.3.3). In contrast, the order *verb-subject* (with or without ἰδού) is common when the subject is an established topic in the discourse.

[147] In Mark alone, introductory sentences in parables that introduce human participants by indefinite noun phrases include Mrk 12:1 ('A man planted a vineyard, ... then leased it to tenants'); Mrk 13:34 ('It is like a man going on a journey') and Mrk 4:26 (' ... is like a person [who] scattered the seed'). Thus, the occurrence of definite 'the sower' here in Mrk 4:3 stands out. Another instance of a definite noun for a first mention of a participant in a parable is 'the strong one' in Mrk 3:27, which most commentators take to refer to Satan.

[148] In Greek, nominals referring to entities that have 'generic' reference (Smyth § 1118, i.e., are non-specific or, for BDF, non-'particular') often take the article (e.g., αἱ ἀλώπεκες φωλεοὺς ἔχουσιν 'The-foxes have dens', Mat 8:20; ἄξιος γὰρ ὁ ἐργάτης τοῦ μισθοῦ αὐτου 'The-laborer is worthy of the-his-wages', Luk 10:7; Robertson 1934:757; Wallace 1996:227, 253). Since a generic subject refers to either an entire class or a typical instance of a known ('identifiable') class, it is normally interpreted as a topic expression; see Lambrecht (1994:88) and Bailey (2009:22, 44–45); see also Bailey (2004:268–269, including footnote 30) on why the subject constituent in proverbs most typically, but not always, functions as clause topic.

[149] If the next parable in Matthew is taken into consideration, 'the sower' can certainly be identified as Jesus ('the Son of Man' in Mat 13:37).

there is evidence that ancient readers considered ἀκούετε to be outside of the parable and ἰδού to be part of it. This is suggested by Williams (2017), who shows how in several important manuscripts (Vaticanus, Sinaiticus, Alexandrinus, and Bezae) the scribes graphically separated ἀκούετε from ἰδού, which is followed immediately by ἐξῆλθεν. For example, as illustrated in Codex Sinaiticus (see the top right column in Figure 3), ἰδού hangs out over the margin (i.e., it is with an *ekthesis*) and begins a separate line even though there was ample room for the scribe to write it after ἀκούετε. Williams suggests that while ἀκούετε is a 'command to use one's hearing', ἰδού is a 'command to use one's imagination [...] "Now imagine you can see ..."' (compare NJB's *Listen! Imagine a sower going out to sow*). Such an interpretation blends the metaphorical-*look!* function of C5 with the vividness function of C2c. So, assuming Jesus is telling a parable where he is a veiled participant, we could render this verse as follows: *Listen carefully! Picture in your mind (that) the sower went out to sow.*[150] In contrast to the graphic break at 4:3, there is an absence of such breaks in the left column of Figure 3 at Mrk 3:32 (C2b, ἰδοὺ ἡ μήτηρ σου, where ἰδού is broken across two lines) and Mrk 3:34 (C1, ἴδε ἡ μήτηρ μου,[151] where ἴδε is spelled ΕΙΔΕ):

---

[150] ||Mat 13:3 can presumably be translated similarly (but it lacks introductory ἀκούετε). Although the previous line in Codex Sinaiticus is flush right, ἰδού is still set off with *ekthesis* (i.e., it hangs over the margin a bit).

[151] To avoid any uncertainty, note that the standard abbreviation MHP (together with an 'overline' that spans the letters) has been used by this scribe throughout this passage for the nominative form of 'mother' (μήτηρ).

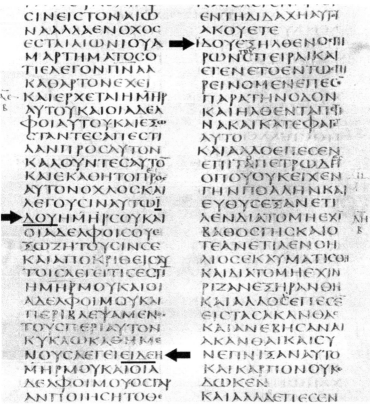

Figure 3. Codex Sinaiticus, Mrk 3:32, Mrk 3:34, and Mrk 4:3
© British Library Board, Add. 43725 f219.

4.5.6 Final comments on C5 and a summary of English renderings

To sum up, in C5, ἰδού and ἴδε have a generalized function. Syntactically, they do not function as predicators (as in C1, etc.) but occur in a clause where a more typical predicator is present (a verb or locative) and function to modify one or more following sentences. Conceptually, instead of demanding visual attention as in C1, they demand mental attention.

C5 tokens tend to involve (strong and certain) statements that count as promises and predictions,[152] warnings,[153] curses and judgments,[154] and other official-sounding statements. Many, but by no means all, tokens involve **surprise**, which I consider to be a conversational implicature (i.e., it is inferred from the context and not an inherent part of the meaning of ἰδού or ἴδε in C5).

In contrast with C4 uses (where I assume that surprise or another emotion is always present), I noted that surprise was only inconsistently present with C5 and other uses (e.g., with C1, C2, and even C3). That surprise inconsistently coincides with the various uses seems to follow from the basic use of deictic thetic constructions, which is to point out things that we think are relevant to our audience, for any number of reasons, and not only because they are surprising.

The most appropriate (modern) English renderings of C5 include at least the following: *pay attention, take note, listen, notice* (colloquial *hey!*), *remember (don't forget)*, metaphorical uses of *look, here,* and *there;* and *hereby* (when on rare occasion the utterance can be construed as a performative).

In one case, at the beginning of a parable, I suggested *Picture in your mind (that)* as a possibility, which is another metaphorical extension of vision. But otherwise in narrative, C5 functions like C2c to add vividness.

But there may be other possible translations that emphasize other semantic elements of the particles. Given that the most basic function of a prototypical here-and-now deictic thetic is to intentionally (and not incidentally) point out to the hearer an entity or state of affairs that can be presently viewed and that is necessarily certain (recall the discussion of Lakoff's central construction in § 2.2), it should not be surprising if in extended uses of ἰδού and ἴδε certain elements of this 'script' are at times especially salient. This might explain, for example, why for some C5 tokens, the **certainty** of a state of affairs would be especially salient, or why at least in translation it could be highlighted.

Thus, I think that on occasion C5 can be appropriately translated by a phrase that confirms the certainty of a state of affairs. I have

---

[152] Promises and predictions: (36 C5 tokens, 1 C2 token): Mat 1:23; Mat 11:10; Mat 20:18; Mat 23:34; Mat 28:7; Mat 28:20; Mrk 1:2; Mrk 10:33; Mrk 14:41; Luk 1:20; Luk 1:31; Luk 1:48; Luk 2:34; Luk 6:23; Luk 7:27; Luk 13:32; Luk 18:31; Luk 22:10; Luk 24:49; Act 13:11 (C2); Act 13:25; Act 20:25; Act 27:24; Rom 9:33; 1Co 15:51; 1Pe 2:6; Rev 1:7; Rev 2:10; Rev 2:22; Rev 3:8; Rev 3:9a; Rev 3:9e; Rev 3:20; Rev 11:14; Rev 16:15; Rev 22:7; Rev 22:12.

[153] Warnings: (11 C5 tokens): Mat 10:16; Mat 24:25; Mat 28:7e; Luk 10:3; Luk 13:30; Luk 22:21; Luk 22:31; Jhn 5:14; Act 13:46 (or judgment); Rom 9:33; Gal 5:2.

[154] Curses and judgments: (C5) Mat 23:38 (‖Luk 13:35); Act 5:9; and (C2) Act 13:11.

occasionally noted cases where translators have rendered C5 as well as other uses by *surely* (C5 NIV Jhn 18:21; C2b NRS Luk 23:29) or *indeed* or *yes* (C5 NIV, NRS, FBJ Luk 13:30; C5 NRS Act 27:24; C4b NRS Luk 23:15). Although these renderings might sometimes seem weak, they may at times be relevant in that they convey an important part of the meaning of the particles—namely that which is being said is *certain*.

Some English translations (e.g., NIV) also occasionally translate C5 and other uses by *now*, which capitalizes on the 'now-element' of the here-and-now script.[155] This does seem possible in, for example, Act 13:46 (NIV: *we now turn to the Gentiles*, although *hereby* seems more appropriate). But I think there are usually better ways of translating these tokens (see the NIV of C5 Mat 28:7 and Luk 1:20; C4a Luk 13:7; and C2a hybrid Mat 12:41, discussed in footnote 116).

Finally, I briefly mentioned that although an exclamative particle like *Oh!* (see MSG's translation of Act 7:56) could be appropriate to the extent that it indicates wonder and surprise, it fails to function as a direct instruction to the hearer to 'pay mental attention', but rather functions to express a spontaneous realization of the speaker.

---

[155]There is some evidence from the LXX that ἰδού can have such a function with tense. See the periphrastic form in Jdg 8:5 in the B text in Rahlfs-Hanhart (i.e., Codex Vaticanus) καὶ ἰδοὺ ἐγώ εἰμι διώκων ὀπίσω Ζεβεε 'I am (right now) pursuing Zebee' (וְאָנֹכִי רֹדֵף אַחֲרֵי זֶבַח [and-I pursuing.Prt after Zebah]) (see also 1Ki 1:25; 2Ki 17:26). Here-and-now tenses sometimes develop from deictic constructions (Welmers [1973:315–317] is suggestive). There are other interesting parallels between the LXX and Masoretic Text in passages with thetic-like properties that seem to emphasize 'right now': Exo 4:14 (NRS: *even now he is coming to meet you* καὶ ἰδοὺ αὐτὸς ἐξελεύσεται גַּם הִנֵּה־הוּא יֹצֵא [indeed behold he coming.out.Prt]); Gen 32:7 (nab: 'and (behold) he is right now coming to meet you' καὶ ἰδοὺ αὐτὸς ἔρχεται וְגַם הֹלֵךְ [and indeed coming.Prt]); perhaps also Gen 32:21 (nab: '(behold) In fact here comes your servant Jacob right behind us!' Ἰδοὺ ὁ παῖς σου Ιακωβ παραγίνεται ὀπίσω ἡμῶν, which is verbless in Hebrew גַּם הִנֵּה עַבְדְּךָ יַעֲקֹב אַחֲרֵינוּ [indeed behold your.servant Jacob behind.us]). Whatever the case, *hinnēh* (with or without a personal suffix) followed by a participle is often used to indicate states of affairs that are happening 'now' or will soon happen ('certainly').

5

Summary—Relationships between the Five Uses

Figure 1, repeated from § 3.2, illustrates the five sets of uses, including the basic split between deictic/semi-deictic and 'non-deictic' uses.

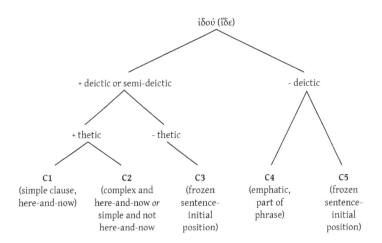

Figure 1. The five sets of uses.

In contrast to the figure above, figure 4 below attempts to outline in more detail for ἰδού the network of constructions and some of the relationships between them. Dashed lines indicate multiple relationships (i.e., 'resemblances' or 'inheritance links').

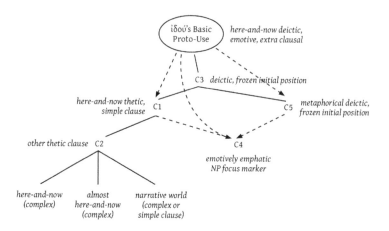

Figure 4. Relationships between the five sets of uses.

Figure 4 also suggests possible historical paths along which the different uses of ἰδού may have developed, including the direction of development, as indicated by the arrows. Such developments could have evolved organically in a relatively closed linguistic system, but it is equally possible that some innovations came about due to language contact, either with other Greek dialects or unrelated languages (e.g. Semitic languages).

All things being equal, it is reasonable to assume that, historically, something akin to C3 would be the best candidate for the original 'proto-use' of ἰδού. This is where ἰδού's journey likely began. It is here-and-now, deictic, extra-clausal, and it basically means physically 'Look!'. From it then presumably developed the different 'daughter' constructions.

C1 and C2 form the thetic branch of the network. C1 is cognitively simpler and more basic than the C2 subtypes, so C1 likely preceded C2 historically (especially the extended subtypes that involve the 'almost here-and-now' and 'narrative world').[1]

C5 is most directly related to C3. It's an easy journey from C3 to C5, since the main difference is that, while C3 points to the real world, C5 points to a mental world of the discourse. The cognitive road from physical sight to mental sight seems to be a common one cross-linguistically (see footnote 120 in ch. 4).

[1] In particular, C2c (i.e., the use of ἰδού to vividly underscore the introduction of entities into the 'narrative world') seems likely to have developed through language contact, given its apparent lack in Classical Greek and its use in the LXX and the similar use of Hebrew hinnēh.

C4 has the most dashed lines connecting to it. It resembles what must have been the proto-use as well as C1 and C5: It resembles the proto-use in having an emotive element (like the old middle voice of the verb), and it resembles C1 in being syntactically simple (that is, it forms a small phrase or even clause), and it resembles C5 in that it is only deictic in an extended sense (i.e., it points to mental space, that is, to something in the discourse, but not to something physical in the here-and-now).

Although the above suggested history is hypothetical, it sketches a reasonable set of diachronic relationships between what are in any case clearly differentiated uses of ἰδού as found in the New Testament and related literature. In this study, much attention has been given to illustrating the different uses and defining their syntax and semantics while also illustrating the range of appropriate translations. To use a visual metaphor, I have tried to illustrate the range of colors and textures that each of the different uses of ἰδού and ἴδε offer to the text. The task of the translator is therefore to correctly convey an appropriate color and texture depending on context. To ignore the differences or reduce them to a single color would be like ignoring and flattening the brilliant color and vibrant texture in a painting by Vincent van Gogh.

Glossary

This short glossary explains the way certain technical terms are used in this book. It concerns especially terms pertaining to information structure, discourse-pragmatics, perspective (point of view), and the linguistic expression of emotion. Terms and phrases in **bold** inside the following entries indicate terms and phrases defined elsewhere in this glossary.

constituent-focus (argument focus, narrow focus): A structure where a sentence constituent comprises the focus domain (e.g., subject, object, oblique phrase; Lambrecht [1994:224] excludes the predicating constituent). Constituent-focus constructions function to identify an element in an open proposition. The open proposition is 'in the presupposition' (what is taken as the common ground between the speaker and hearer). Constituent-focus constructions thus serve to answer an implicit or explicit content question: e.g., *(What broke down?)* [*My CAR*]Focus Domain [*broke down.*]Open Proposition (the open proposition is 'X broke down'; the focus domain is 'my car'). They are sometimes used to correct the hearer's mistaken beliefs: e.g., *It was my MOTORCYCLE that broke down* (not my car). See Lambrecht on 'argument-focus' (1994:222–224, 233–235; 2000:612–615) and on 'identificational sentences' (1994:122–123, 126, 260–261).

deictic thetic (deictic presentational) construction: A **thetic construction** that introduces something into the hearer's perceptual awareness of the here-and-now (**text-external**) world (and, simultaneously, into the hearer's mental representation of the **text-internal** world). They are used intentionally (and not incidentally) to point out to the hearer an entity or state of affairs that, prototypically, can be presently viewed (Waiter: *Here's your pizza!* Traveling companion: *There goes our train!*), or, less prototypically, otherwise directly perceived (Student: *There goes the bell!*). See also the various English deictic *here/there* constructions illustrated in section § 2.2 in this study, including less prototypical varieties, which involve metaphorically extended uses of the deictic adverbs *here* and *there* to refer to things that are not visually present in the here-and-now physical world.

deixis, deictic: Deictic constructions (e.g., deictic words) refer to something in (or relative to) the immediate (**text-external**) context of the utterance, such as the speaker or hearer, the time or location of speaking, or the location in the discourse. Examples include *I* and *you* (the speaker and addressee), *now, tomorrow* (which is defined relative to now), *here*, and (deictic) *there*. Deictic constructions can also be used in metaphorically extended ways.

discourse-new/discourse-old: Following Ellen Prince (1992), a *discourse-new* entity is one that has not been mentioned before in the discourse (e.g., 'Mark Twain' in this book), but a *discourse-old* one has been mentioned (e.g., 'Ellen Prince'). Although Prince's discourse-new/old distinction is not as finely tuned as the consciousness-state distinctions of 'active, accessible, and inactive' (used by Chafe and Lambrecht), the discourse-new/old distinction is easier to apply when studying written texts, especially ancient ones (Bailey 2009:25). See **hearer-new/hearer-old** and see the 'viewer-new/old' distinction under **perception report.**

emotive emphasis: As used in traditional grammars and exegetical commentaries, the term 'emphasis' tends to be an umbrella term for many different phenomena and is therefore vague. As used in this study, the phrase *emotive emphasis* refers to the expression of a heightened emotional state (e.g., surprise, fear, anger, irritation, joy, etc.) felt by the speaker, where this expression is linguistically signaled (e.g., lexically, morphologically, in constituent order, or intonationally). Emotive emphasis may coincide with focus marking, but need not do so, as topical elements of a sentence may also involve emotive emphasis (see Bailey 2009:40–43). **Exclamative constructions** are one common way of expressing emotive emphasis (especially surprise), which may also involve particles or interjections. Mirative constructions are another category, though apparently rare in languages. It is argued in this study that emotive emphasis is often involved in ἰδού constructions, especially C4 constructions.

emphatic: See **emotive emphasis.**

exclamative construction: According to Michaelis (2001), an exclamative construction expresses an emotional judgment about a state of affairs that the speaker feels is surprising. The utterance evokes an open proposition where the open variable is a degree. Against that presupposition, the utterance asserts 'a particular scalar degree' that the speaker feels emotional about (e.g., an extreme degree of temperature: *Man(,) it's hot in Dallas!* of intelligence: *What a genius!* or of deliciousness: *What delicious desserts John bakes!*).

focus (of assertion) and **focus domain:** Although there exist other approaches to information structure and other definitions of 'focus' (see e.g., the overview in Matić 2015; see also Dooley 2017), the present study assumes Lambrecht's framework, which has much to commend itself. In his framework, Lambrecht distinguishes (a) *focus (of assertion)*, which is defined in relation to the (notional) proposition evoked by an utterance, from (b) *focus domain*, which is defined as a grammatical category (Lambrecht 1994:214; 2000:615; see also § 2.3 in this study and chapter 2 in Bailey 2009, especially pp. 8–11).

More specifically, (a) *focus* (or 'focus of assertion' or 'focus of the new information') is defined by Lambrecht (2000:612; compare 1994:213 and much of Lambrecht's chapter 5) as:

> [...] that element of a pragmatically structured proposition whose occurrence makes it possible for the sentence to express a "pragmatic assertion", i.e. to convey new information to an addressee. Somewhat more technically, the focus is that element whereby the presupposition [or more generally, 'common ground', nab] and the assertion differ from each other. A focus denotatum is by definition a communicatively unpredictable element of a proposition.

(b) Languages differ in the grammatical means they use to indicate the *focus domain*. Common means include intonation (i.e., prosodic stress), particles, constituent order, as well as combinations of such means. Moreover, Lambrecht (1994:214–215; 2000:615) assumes that the focus domain is expressed in *phrasal categories* (e.g., of verb or adjective phrases, noun phrases, prepositional phrases, adverbial phrases, and sentences). According to Lambrecht (1994:222, 2000:611–612), three major types include when the focus domain is (i) the predicate (see **predicate-focus**), (ii) a single constituent (see **constituent-focus**), or (iii) the whole sentence (see **sentence-focus**). For a fourth possible type, see **polarity focus**.

grammatical construction: A grammatical construction is a conventionalized form-function unit. It has a form, which is its phonological and morphosyntactic structure; and it has a function, which consists of its meaning and use conditions (see Lakoff 1987:467). 'A construction is posited in the grammar if it can be

shown that its meaning and/or its form is not compositionally
derived from other constructions existing in the language'
(Goldberg 1995:4). Many constructions are to one degree or another
schematic, by which is meant that one or more elements, or 'slots',
can be filled by a range of expressions while any remaining
elements may involve fixed forms or fixed orders (Croft and Cruse
2004:233–234). For example, the ditransitive English clause involves
four schematic 'slots': *Subject + Verb + Object-1 + Object-2* (there are
other restrictions, e.g., verb type); an English existential
construction involves a template where, when used in its
declarative form, the fixed elements, existential *there* + 'be', precede
the Subject: *there-BE-Subject*; and the C1 construction, as described
in this study, involves a fixed order with the fixed element, ἰδού/ἴδε,
followed by a slot that is filled by a nominative case noun phrase.
See section § 2.1 in this study for more background.

hearer-new/hearer-old: Following Prince (1992), a *hearer-new entity*
(referent) is one that the hearer (audience, reader) does not know or
have previous awareness of. Thetic *there* sentences ('existential *there*
sentences') normally introduce a hearer-new entity into the
discourse: e.g., *Once there was a boy ...* In contrast, a *hearer-old* entity
is one that the hearer already has an awareness of. The *hearer-new/
old* distinction corresponds in most respects to the +/– *identifiable*
distinction used by Lambrecht (1994) and Chafe (1994).

information structure: Following Lambrecht (1994:7), the domain of
information structure is the sentence (or clause), and it is thus an
element of sentence grammar: 'It is not concerned with the
organization of discourse, but with the organization of the sentence
within a discourse'. It concerns the way sentences are 'packaged'
(Chafe 1976:28) or 'tailored' (Prince 1981:224) to fit the assumed
mental states of ideas in the mind of the hearer (Lambrecht
1994:2–3). Information structure does not so much concern the
actual content of utterances, that is, their semantic or propositional
meaning, as the way this content is 'transmitted' in a specific
communicative context (Chafe 1976:27). Such packaging enables a
hearer to process an utterance with relatively minimal effort.
Ideally, this means that the hearer can, with relative ease, access the
intended set of background assumptions (i.e., the 'common ground')
as well as the new informative proposition which the speaker
intends to communicate in relation to the background.

left-detachment: A left-detached phrase is an extra-clausal phrase
(i.e., not syntactically integrated into the main predication that
follows) that is typically set off by a pause from what follows and
accompanied by a distinct intonation; the referent of the detached

phrase may also be resumed in the main predication by a minimal form (e.g., by an unaccented pronoun in some languages). According to Lambrecht (2001b:1073), cross-linguistically, left-detached phrases are typically used to promote an 'accessible' entity (that is, a **hearer-old** or 'identifiable' entity that is currently in semi-active state of consciousness, i.e., 'to some degree expectable at the time of utterance') to 'active' state so that it may become a topic of the main predication that follows. Depending on language, there may be other uses, such as to indicate a contrastive topic or that a new theme or episode about the same entity is commencing, e.g., at a paragraph boundary (Lambrecht 1994:183–184). For more on left-detached expressions, see also Bailey (2009:32–34), and for a discussion of how some are used in the Greek New Testament with a **thetic-like** function to introduce **hearer-new/discourse-new** entities, see Bailey (2009:181–186).

omniscient perspective: See **personal perspective.**

perception report: A *perception report* (a term used by Lambrecht 2002:177, footnote 3) is a sentence used by a speaker to report what he or she or someone else saw, heard, or otherwise perceived. Perception reports are often used to introduce a new entity or state of affairs into a discourse, and in this sense they may be **thetic-like,** that is, they may function as thetic constructions: e.g., *Then suddenly I heard a bang. Yesterday, I saw a bear running down the street.* Lambrecht says 'perception report' is a translation of Kleiber's 'compte-rendu de perception'. Johannessohn (1937) used the term 'Wahrnehmungssatz' (i.e., perception clause) with the same sense in his study of such sentences in Biblical Hebrew, Biblical Greek, and other languages. Perception reports can blend different **personal perspectives:** that of the speaker (or narrator), that of the hearer (or audience), and that of a discourse internal participant who is the perceiver. On analogy with Prince's (1992) **hearer-new/old** and **discourse-new/old** parameters, the perceiver's perspective can be described in terms of being 'viewer-new/old' when perception is expressed by a vision verb (Bailey 2009:89–96 and 280–313), or, more generally, in terms of a 'perceiver-new/old' parameter.

personal perspective: The presentation of a new entity or event into a narrative can be from different perspectives. In some cases, it may involve a *personal perspective,* by which is meant that it is presented from the perspective of one or more story-internal participants. In other cases, it may involve a relatively more *omniscient perspective,* in which the audience (hearer or reader) is expected to view the introduction from a more general perspective.

polarity focus (verum focus): Lambrecht (1994:236, 336) briefly mentions the marking of the polarity of the proposition as perhaps a fourth type of focus structure. For the relevance of polarity focus to New Testament Greek exegesis, see discussion on 'polar focus' in Bailey (2009:38–39, 69–72, 162–174, etc.) and (2011:297, 317–320). For a recent critical discussion of polarity focus as a universal linguistic category, see Matić and Nikolaeva (2018).

predicate-focus: A structure where the predicate of the sentence constitutes the **focus domain**. Predicate-focus constructions most typically have a **topic-comment** function; the predicate makes a comment (says something unpredictable or newsworthy) about an entity that is expressed by the subject: e.g., *(What happened to your car?)* *[It]*$_{\text{Topic}}$ *[broke DOWN.]*$_{\text{Focus Domain}}$. See Lambrecht (1994:222–223, 226–228; 2000:612–616).

presentational, presentative: In the literature, the terms *presentative* and *presentational* are often used synonymously. These terms are also sometimes used more or less synonymously with the way **thetic** is used, but sometimes presentational and presentative are restricted to those thetic sentences that can be characterized as 'entity-central' (not 'event-central'): *Once there was a boy. (Oh, look!) Here comes Harry!* See section § 2.3 in this study.

reminder: A construction functions as a reminder if the speaker uses it to remind the hearer about something he or she might have forgotten. For example, if two people needed to fetch something from the yard of a neighbor who was away, and one remembered that the neighbor had a dog (which both had previously known about), he might say to the other: *But there's the DOG!* On the use of existential *there* clauses with definite subjects as reminders, see Lakoff (1987:561–562) and the longer discussion and references in Bailey (2009:74–76).

sentence-focus: A sentence-focus construction functions to introduce an entity or event (state of affairs) into the discourse and has a grammatical structure where both the subject and predicate comprise the focus domain. The subject constituent is necessarily marked as a non-**topic** (e.g., via intonation, particles, constituent order, or other morphosyntactic means, including a combination of such means). For example, *(Why are you late?)* *[My CAR broke down.]*$_{\text{Focus Domain}}$ See Lambrecht (2000:612–622 and 1994:145, 222–223, 228–233).

text-external and **text-internal worlds:** Following Lambrecht (1994:36–37), the *text-external world* 'comprises (i) SPEECH PARTICIPANTS, i.e. a speaker and one or several addressees, and (ii) a SPEECH SETTING, i.e. the place, time and circumstances in which a speech event takes place.' In contrast, the *text-internal world* 'comprises LINGUISTIC EXPRESSIONS (words, phrases, sentences) and their MEANINGS.' These 'worlds' are mental representations that are derived, not only from the linguistic material in the text, but also from native (culture-specific) encyclopedic knowledge (cultural patterns, scripts, semantic frames, etc.).

thetic construction: As used in this study, a thetic construction is a sentence-focus construction. It functions to introduce an entity or event (state of affairs) into the discourse, and the subject constituent is necessarily marked linguistically as a non-topic (e.g., via intonation, particles, constituent order, or other morphosyntactic means, including a combination of such means). In some languages, however, a predicate-focus construction can also be used with a thetic *function*. Contrast, for example, the Russian sentence-focus construction, *DOSHT idyot* (ДОЖДЬ идёт) [RAIN goes] with the corresponding predicate-focus construction *It's RAINING* in English. See Lambrecht (1994:141) and Bailey (2009:16–17).

thetic-like: As used in this study, a grammatical construction is functionally thetic-like if it introduces something into the discourse but does not have a sentence-focus structure. This phrase has been used in this study especially for constructions that introduce an entity or event into the discourse by means of an object constituent. In narrative, perception reports are often used to introduce something into the discourse by means of the object, e.g., *Then suddenly we heard a bang; And then I saw a man getting on the train.*

topic-comment function: A sentence has a topic-comment function if it serves primarily to increase the hearer's knowledge of (or in some way express something relevant about) a topic that is evoked by the sentence lexicogrammatically (e.g., by a full noun phrase, a minimal form like a pronoun or zero form, or only marked on the verb); that is, it 'pragmatically predicates some property of an already established discourse referent' (Lambrecht 1994:126). In languages where subject is grammaticalized (i.e., not in 'topic prominent' languages), in most sentences the grammatical subject expresses the sentence topic. According to Lambrecht, most sentences with **predicate-focus** structure have a topic-comment function. See Lambrecht (1994:126, 131–133, 141) on the fact that, in English and many other languages, grammatical 'subjects are unmarked topics', and 'topic-comment articulation' (i.e., function) 'is the unmarked pragmatic sentence articulation.'

topic, discourse topic: A *discourse topic* is distinguished from *sentence topic* (Lambrecht 1994:117; Dooley and Levinsohn 2001:69–70). For the purposes of this study, a discourse topic concerns what a coherent stretch of text (e.g., of a paragraph, episode or larger unit) 'is about', including its 'theme' or 'macrostructure'. A discourse topic can often be expressed in summary form as one or more propositions, although for some genres (e.g., argumentational) and some texts, a discourse topic can be difficult to define or discern. For a sentence to have a *sentence topic*, it must be lexicogrammatically evoked; in contrast, a *discourse topic* need not be explicitly expressed at all in a discourse but only implied.

topic, sentence topic: A sentence topic is what a sentence is 'about' in a given discourse context. A linguistic expression (most typically the grammatical subject) that expresses a sentence topic is what the sentence serves to increase the hearer's knowledge of or in some way say something relevant about (the linguistic expression may be a full noun phrase, a minimal form like a pronoun or zero form, or only marked on the verb). Since information structure concerns the underlying propositions expressed by sentences, Lambrecht & Michaelis (1998:494) define sentence topic as follows: 'A referent which a proposition is construed to be about in a given discourse situation; a proposition is about a referent if it expresses information which is relevant to, and which increases the hearer's knowledge of, this referent.' See also especially chapter 4 in Lambrecht (1994).

References

Greek grammars, Greek lexicons, and analytical keys to the New Testament that are cited by abbreviation in this book are highlighted in **bold** in (i) 'General references'. Separate reference lists are given for (ii) 'Ancient texts' and (iii) 'Translations'. The source language texts and translations that were accessed in digital forms (BART, BibleWorks, and Paratext) are indicated below.

(i) General references

Abraham, Werner, Elisabeth Leiss, and Yasuhiro Fujinawa, eds. 2020. *Thetics and categoricals*. Amsterdam: John Benjamins.

Aerts, Willem Johan. 1965. *Periphrastica: An investigation into the use of εἶναι and ἔχειν as auxiliaries or pseudo-auxiliaries in Greek from Homer up to the present day*. Amsterdam: Adolf M. Hakkert.

Allan, R. J. 2006. Sophocles' voice: Active, middle and passive in the plays of Sophocles. In I. J. F. de Jong and A. Rijksbaron (eds.), *Sophocles and the Greek language: Aspects of diction, syntax and pragmatics*, 111–126. Leiden: Brill.

Andersen, Francis I. 2003. Lo and behold! Taxonomy and translation of Biblical Hebrew הִנֵּה. In M. F. J. Baasten and W. Th. van Peursen (eds.), *Hamlet on a hill: Semitic and Greek studies presented to Professor T. Muraoka on the occasion of his sixty-fifth birthday*, 25–56. Leuven: Peeters.

Arzt-Grabner, Peter, Ruth Elisabeth Kritzer, Amphilochios Papathomas, and Franz Winter. 2006. *1. Korinther: Papyrologische Kommentare zum Neuen Testament*, Band 2. Göttingen: Vandenhoeck & Ruprecht.

Bailey, Nicholas A. 2004. A second look at double preverbal constituents. Review of *Doppelt besetztes Vorfeld: Syntaktische, pragmatische und übersetzungstechnische Studien zum althebräischen Verbalsatz*, by Walter Gross. *Hebrew Studies* 45:253–276.

Bailey, Nicholas A. 2009. Thetic constructions in Koiné Greek: With special attention to clauses with εἰμί 'be', γίνομαι 'occur', ἔρχομαι 'come', ἰδού/ἴδε 'behold', and complement clauses of ὁράω 'see'. PhD dissertation, Vrije Universiteit Amsterdam. https://research.vu.nl/ws/portalfiles/portal/42185508/complete+dissertation.pdf.

Bailey, Nicholas A. 2011. Information structure issues in copular εἶναι clauses. In Steven E. Runge (ed.), *Discourse studies and biblical interpretation: Festschrift for Stephen H. Levinsohn*, 289–333. Bellingham, WA: Lexham Press.

BART = Biblical Analysis Research Tool, version 5.2. 1998–2005. Dallas, TX: SIL International.

Bauer, Walter. 1958. *Griechisch-deutsches Wörterbuch zu den Schriften des Neuen Testaments und der übrigen unchristlichen Literatur*. Fifth edition. Berlin: Alfred Töpelmann.

BAGD = Gingrich, F. Wilbur and Frederick W. Danker, eds. 1979. *A Greek-English lexicon of the New Testament and other early Christian literature*. Second edition. A translation and adaptation by William F. Arndt and F. Wilbur Gingrich of the fourth revised and augmented edition of Walter Bauer's *Griechisch-deutsches Wörterbuch zu den Schriften des Neuen Testaments und der frühchristlichen Literatur*. Fourth edition. Chicago, IL: University of Chicago Press.

BDAG = Danker, Frederick W. 2000. *A Greek-English lexicon of the New Testament and other early Christian literature*. Third edition. Based on Walter Bauer's *Griechisch-deutsches Wörterbuch zu den Schriften des Neuen Testaments und der frühchristlichen Literatur*. Sixth edition, ed. by Kurt Aland and Barbara Aland, with Viktor Reichmann and on previous English editions by W. F. Arndt, F. W. Gingrich, and F. W. Danker. Chicago, IL: University of Chicago Press. (BibleWorks version.)

BDF = Blass, F., A. Debrunner, and Robert W. Funk. 1961. *A Greek grammar of the New Testament and other early Christian literature*. Chicago, IL: University of Chicago Press.

BibleWorks = BibleWorks for Windows, version 6.0. 2003. Norfolk, VA. http://www.bibleworks.com.

Birner, Betty J. 1994. Information status and word order: An analysis of English inversion. *Language* 70.233–259.

Björck, Gudmund. 1940. ΗΝ ΔΙΔΑΣΚΩΝ *Die periphrastischen Konstruktionen in Griechischen*. Skrifter utgivna av K. Humanistiska Vetenskaps-Samfundet i Uppsala, 32.2. Uppsala: Almqvist & Wiksells Boktryckeri.

Blyth, Carl, Karen Kelton, Lindsy Myers, Catherine Delyfer, Yvonne Munn, and Jane Lippmann, eds. 2006. *Tex's French Grammar*. The Department of French and Italian and Liberal Arts Instructional Technology Services (LAITS) of the University of Texas at Austin. Retrieved February 3, 2009 at http://www.laits.utexas.edu/tex/index.html.

Bruce, F. F. 1990. *The Acts of the Apostles: The Greek text with introduction and commentary*. Third edition. Grand Rapids, MI: Eerdmans.

Burchard, Christoph. 2005. The text of *Joseph and Aseneth* reconsidered. *Journal for the Study of the Pseudepigrapha* 14.2.83–96.

Chafe, Wallace. 1976. Givenness, contrastiveness, definiteness, subjects, topics and point of view. In Charles N. Li (ed.), *Subject and topic*, 25–55. New York: Academic Press.

Chafe, Wallace. 1987. Cognitive constraints on information flow. In Russell Tomlin (ed.), *Coherence and grounding in discourse*, 21-51. Amsterdam: John Benjamins.

Chafe, Wallace. 1994. *Discourse, consciousness, and time: The flow and displacement of conscious experience in speaking and writing*. Chicago, IL: University of Chicago.

Chomsky, Noam. 1981. *Lectures on government and binding*. Dordrecht: Foris.

Chomsky, Noam. 1993. A minimalist program for linguistic theory. In Kenneth Hale and Samuel Jay Keyser (eds.), *The view from Building 20: Essays in linguistics in honor of Sylvain Bromberger*, 1-52. Cambridge, MA: MIT Press.

Croft, William, and D. Alan Cruse. 2004. *Cognitive linguistics*. Cambridge Textbooks in Linguistics. Cambridge, UK: Cambridge University Press.

Crystal, David. 1994. *A dictionary of linguistics and phonetics*. Oxford: Blackwell. (Reprint of 1991 third edition.)

Dana, H. E., and Julius R. Mantey. 1955. *A manual grammar of the Greek New Testament*. New York: Macmillan.

Danker, Frederick W. 1970. Review of *Die Formel 'und siehe' im Neuen Testament*, by Peter Fiedler. *Journal of Biblical Literature* 89(4):511–512.

Dooley, Robert A. 2017. *Information structure: An introduction*. SIL Electronic Working Papers 2017-002. Dallas, TX: SIL International. Retrieved December 10, 2020 at https://www.sil.org/resources/publications/entry/70582.

Dooley, Robert A., and Stephen H. Levinsohn. 2001. *Analyzing discourse: A manual of basic concepts*. Dallas, TX: SIL International.

Doudna, John Charles. 1961. *The Greek of the Gospel of Mark*. SBL Monograph Series 12. Philadelphia, PA: Society of Biblical Literature.

Ellingworth, Paul. 1993. *The Epistle to the Hebrews: A commentary on the Greek text*. Grand Rapids, MI: Eerdmans.

Fauconnier, Gilles. 2007. Mental Spaces. In Dirk Geeraerts and Hubert Cuyckens (eds.), *The Oxford handbook of cognitive linguistics*. Oxford: Oxford University Press.

Fiedler, Peter. 1969. *Die Formel 'und siehe' im Neuen Testament*. München: Kösel Verlag.

Fillmore, Charles J., Paul Kay, and Mary Catherine O'Connor. 1988. Regularity and idiomaticity in grammatical constructions: The case of *let alone*. *Language* 64.501–538.

Foakes Jackson, F. J., and Kirsopp Lake. 1933. *The beginnings of Christianity, Part I: The Acts of the Apostles*. Vol. 4. London: MacMillan.

Follingstad, Carl M. 2001. *Deictic viewpoint in Biblical Hebrew text: A syntagmatic and paradigmatic analysis of the particle kî*. Dallas, TX: SIL International.

Gesenius-Kautzsch-Cowley = Kautzsch, E., ed. 1910. *Gesenius' Hebrew grammar*. Second English edition. Revised by A. E. Cowley. Oxford: Clarendon Press.

Goldberg, Adele E. 1995. *Constructions: A Construction Grammar approach to argument structure*. Chicago, IL: University of Chicago Press.

Goldberg, Adele E. 2006. *Constructions at work: The nature of generalization in language*. Oxford: Oxford University Press.

Goldberg, Adele E. 2009. The nature of generalization in language. *Cognitive Linguistics* 20.93–127.

Goldberg, Adele E., and Devin Casenhiser. 2006. English constructions. In Bas Aarts and April McMahon (eds.), *Handbook of English linguistics*, 344–355. Oxford: Blackwell.

Gundry, Robert H. 2000. *Mark: A commentary on his apology for the cross*. Grand Rapids, MI: Eerdmans.

Hall, Robert A., Jr. 1953. The classification of Italian *ecco* and its cognates. *Romance Philology* 6.278–280.

Haspelmath, Martin. 1997. *From space to time: Temporal adverbials in the world's languages*. Lincom Studies in Theoretical Linguistics 3. München and Newcastle: Lincom Europa.

Heckert, Jakob K. 1996. *Discourse function of conjoiners in the Pastoral Epistles*. Dallas, TX: Summer Institute of Linguistics.

Hf&S = Hoffmann, Ernst G., and Heinrich von Siebenthal. 1990. *Griechische Grammatik zum Neuen Testament*. Second edition. Riehen: Immanuel-Verlag.

Holmstedt, Robert D. 2014. Analyzing זֶה grammar and reading זֶה texts of Ps 68:9 and Judg 5:5. *Journal of Hebrew Scriptures* 14(8):1–26.

Humphrey, Edith M. 2000. *Joseph and Aseneth*. Guides to the Apocrypha and Pseudepigrapha. Sheffield: Sheffield Academic Press.

Johannessohn, Martin. 1937. Der Wahrnehmungssatz bei den Verben des Sehens in der hebräischen und griechischen Bibel. *Zeitschrift für vergleichende Sprachforschung auf dem Gebiete der indogermanischen Sprachen* 64:145–260.

Johannessohn, Martin. 1939. Das biblische καὶ ἰδού in der Erzählung samt seiner hebräischen Vorlage (Part I). *Zeitschrift für vergleichende Sprachforschung auf dem Gebiete der indogermanischen Sprachen* 66:145–195.

Johannessohn, Martin. 1942. Das biblische καὶ ἰδού in der Erzählung samt seiner hebräischen Vorlage (Part II). *Zeitschrift für vergleichende Sprachforschung auf dem Gebiete der indogermanischen Sprachen* 67:30–84.

Joüon & Muraoka = Joüon, Paul. 2000. *A grammar of Biblical Hebrew*. Subsidia Biblica 14. Translated and revised by Takamitsu Muraoka (reprint of first edition with corrections). Rome: Editrice Pontificio Istituto Biblico (Biblical Institute Press).

Kilpatrick, George Dunbar. 1967. Ἰδού and ἴδε in the Gospels. *The Journal of Theological Studies* 18:425–426.

Kim, SeungJung. 2017. Toward a phenomenology of time in Ancient Greek art. In Jonathan Ben-Dov and Lutz Doering (eds.), *The construction of time in antiquity*, 142–172. Cambridge, UK: Cambridge University Press.

Lakoff, George. 1987. *Women, fire, and dangerous things: What categories reveal about the mind*. Chicago, IL: University of Chicago Press.

Lakoff, George, and Mark Johnson. 1980. *Metaphors we live by*. Chicago, IL: University of Chicago Press.

Lambdin, Thomas O. 1971. *Introduction to Biblical Hebrew*. New York: Charles Scribner's Sons.

Lambrecht, Knud. 1987. Sentence focus, information structure, and the thetic-categorical distinction. *Berkeley Linguistics Society* 13.366–382.

Lambrecht, Knud. 1994. *Information structure and sentence form: Topic, focus, and the mental representations of discourse referents*. Cambridge, UK: Cambridge University Press.

Lambrecht, Knud. 1999. Internal and external contextualization in English and French presentational constructions. Prepub Ms. Forthcoming in Carlota Smith (ed.), *Proceedings of the workshop on the structure of spoken and written texts*. Austin, TX: Texas Linguistic Forum. Department of Linguistics, University of Texas at Austin.

Lambrecht, Knud. 2000. When subjects behave like objects: An analysis of the merging of S and O in sentence-focus constructions. *Studies in Language* 24:611–682.

Lambrecht, Knud. 2001a. A framework for the analysis of cleft constructions. *Linguistics* 39(3):463–516.

Lambrecht, Knud. 2001b. Dislocation. In Martin Haspelmath, Ekkehard König, Wulf Oesterreicher, and Wolfgang Raible (eds.), *Language typology and language universals: An international handbook*. Vol. 1. Handbücher zur Sprach- und Kommunikationswissenschaft 20(1):1050–1078. Berlin: Walter de Gruyter.

Lambrecht, Knud, and Laura A. Michaelis. 1998. Sentence accent in information questions: Default and projection. *Linguistics and Philosophy* 21.477–544.

Levinsohn, Stephen H. 2000. *Discourse features of New Testament Greek: A coursebook on the information structure of New Testament Greek*. Second edition. Dallas, TX: SIL International.

Levinson, Stephen C. 1983. *Pragmatics*. Cambridge Textbooks in Linguistics. Cambridge, UK: Cambridge University Press.

Louw, Johannes P., and Eugene A. Nida (eds.) 1988. *Greek-English lexicon of the New Testament: Based on semantic domains*. New York: United Bible Societies.

LSJ = Liddell, Henry George, and Robert Scott. 1940. *A Greek-English lexicon*. Revised by Sir Henry Stuart Jones and Roderick McKenzie. Oxford: Clarendon Press.

Marshall, I. Howard. 1978. *The book of Luke: A commentary on the Greek text*. Grand Rapids, MI: Eerdmans.

Matić, Dejan. 2015. Information structure in linguistics. In James D. Wright (ed.), *International Encyclopedia of the Social and Behavioral Sciences*. Second edition, 95–99. Oxford: Elsevier.

Matić, Dejan, and Irina Nikolaeva. 2018. From polarity focus to salient polarity: From things to processes. In Christine Dimroth and Stefan Sudhoff (eds.), *The grammatical realization of polarity contrast: Theoretical, empirical, and typological approaches*, 9–53. Amsterdam: John Benjamins.

Matras, Yaron, and Hans-Jürgen Sasse, eds. 1995. *Verb-subject order and theticity in European languages*. Sprachtypologie und Universalienforschung, 48–1/2. Berlin: Akademie-Verlag.

McCready, Eric. 2006. Functions of English *man*. In Christian Ebert and Cornelia Endriss (eds.), *Proceedings of Sinn und Bedeutung 10*, 211–223. Berlin (Humboldt Universität): Zentrum für allgemeine Sprachwissenschaft.

Meisterhans, Konrad, and Eduard Schwyzer. 1900. *Grammatik der Attischen Inschriften*. Third edition. Berlin: Weidmann.

Michaelis, Laura A. 2001. Exclamative constructions. In Martin Haspelmath, Ekkehard König, Wulf Oesterreicher, and Wolfgang Raible (eds.), *Language typology and language universals: An international handbook.* Vol. 1. Handbücher zur Sprach-und Kommunikationswissenschaft 20(1):1038–1050. Berlin: Walter de Gruyter.

Michaelis, Laura A. 2006. Construction Grammar. In Keith Brown (ed.), *The encyclopedia of language and linguistics.* Vol. 3. Second edition, 73–84. Oxford: Elsevier.

Miller-Naudé, Cynthia L., and C. H. J. van der Merwe. 2011. הִנֵּה [Hinnēh] and mirativity in Biblical Hebrew. *Hebrew Studies* 52.53–81.

Moule, C. F. D. 1988. *An idiom book of New Testament Greek.* (Reprint of 1959 second edition.) Cambridge, UK: Cambridge University Press.

Moulton, James Hope. 1908. *A grammar of New Testament Greek: Prolegomena.* Vol. 1. Third edition. Edinburgh: T. & T. Clark.

Moulton, James Hope, and Wilbert Francis Howard. 1929. *A grammar of New Testament Greek: Accidence and word-formation with an appendix on Semitisms in the New Testament.* Vol. 2. Edinburgh: T. & T. Clark.

Moulton, James Hope, and George Milligan. 1930. *The vocabulary of the Greek Testament illustrated from the papyri and other nonliterary sources.* Grand Rapids, MI: Eerdmans.

Paratext = Paratext (Scripture Translation and Publishing Software), versions 5 to 7.5. United Bible Societies and SIL International. http://www.paratext.org.

Pope, Tony. 1988. The use of the present indicative to signal future time in New Testament Greek, with special reference to the Gospel of John. *Occasional Papers in Translation and Textlinguistics* 2.2.27–38.

Porter, Stanley E. 1994. *Idioms of the Greek New Testament.* Second edition. Sheffield: Sheffield Academic Press.

Prince, Ellen F. 1981. Toward a taxonomy of given-new information. In Peter Cole (ed.), *Radical pragmatics*, 223–255. New York: Academic Press.

Prince, Ellen F. 1992. The ZPG letter: Subjects, definiteness, and information-status. In William C. Mann and Sandra A. Thompson (eds.), *Discourse description: Diverse linguistic analyses of a fund-raising text*, 295–325. Amsterdam: John Benjamins.

Pryke, E. J. 1968. 'ΙΔΕ and ΙΔΟΥ'. *New Testament Studies* 14.418–424.

Robar, Elizabeth. 2016. The historical present in NT Greek: An exercise in interpreting Matthew. In Steven E. Runge and Christopher J. Fresch (eds.), *The Greek verb revisited: A fresh approach for biblical exegesis*, 329-352. Bellingham, WA: Lexham Press.

Robertson, A. T. 1934. *A grammar of the Greek New Testament in the light of historical research.* Reprint of the 1923 fourth edition. Nashville, TN: Broadman Press.

Runge, Steven E. 2008. *The Lexham Discourse Greek New Testament: Introduction.* Bellingham, WA: Lexham Press.

Sag, Ivan A., Hans C. Boas, and Paul Kay. 2012. Introducing Sign-Based Construction Grammar. In Hans C. Boas and Ivan A. Sag (eds.), *Sign-Based Construction Grammar*, 1–29. Stanford, CA: CSLI Publications.

Sasse, Hans-Jürgen. 1987. The thetic/categorical distinction revisited. *Linguistics* 25.511–580.

Sasse, Hans-Jürgen. 1995a. 'Theticity' and VS order: A case study. In Matras and Sasse, 3–27.

Sasse, Hans-Jürgen. 1995b. A contrastive study of VS clauses in Modern Greek and Hungarian. In Matras and Sasse, 142–188.

Sasse, Hans-Jürgen. 1996. Theticity. *Arbeitspapier 27 (Neue Folge).* Köln: Institut für Sprachwissenschaft, Universität zu Köln.

Schwyzer, Eduard. 1950. *Syntax und syntaktische Stilistik, vervollständigt und herausgegeben von Albert Debrunner.* München: Beck'sche.

Smyth, Herbert Weir. 1956. *Greek grammar.* Revised by Gordon M. Messing. Harvard, MA: Harvard University Press.

Thackeray, Henry St. John. 1909. *A grammar of the Old Testament in Greek.* Vol. I. Cambridge, UK: Cambridge University Press.

Titrud, Kermit. 1992. The function of καί in the Greek New Testament and an application to 2 Peter. In David Alan Black, Katharine Barnwell, and Stephen Levinsohn (eds.), *Linguistics and New Testament interpretation: Essays on discourse analysis*, 240–270. Nashville, TN: Broadman.

Tov, Emanuel. 2001. *Textual criticism of the Hebrew Bible.* Second revised edition. Assen, The Netherlands: Royal Van Gorcum.

Turner, Nigel. 1963. *A grammar of New Testament Greek. Syntax.* Vol. 3. Edinburgh: T. & T. Clark.

Varner, William. 2014. A 'majority' reading for James 3.3 supported by both external and internal evidence. *Journal of Greco-Roman Christianity and Judaism* 10.132–137.

Wallace, Daniel B. 1996. *Greek grammar beyond the basics: An exegetical syntax of the New Testament.* Grand Rapids, MI: Zondervan. (BibleWorks version).

Waltke, Bruce K., and M. O'Connor. 1990. *An introduction to Biblical Hebrew syntax.* Winona Lake, IN: Eisenbrauns.

Welmers, William. E. 1973. *African language structures.* Berkeley: University of California Press.

Williams, Peter. 2017. Where does the Parable of the Sower begin? (Mark 4:3). Retrieved November 25, 2017 at http://evangelicaltextualcriticism.blogspot.ch/2017/11/where-does-parable-of-sower-begin-mark.html.

Z&G (New Testament analytical key) = Zerwick, Max, and Mary Grosvenor. 1993. *A grammatical analysis of the Greek New Testament.* Rome: Editrice Pontificio Istituto Biblico (Biblical Institute Press).

Zerwick, Maximillian. 1963. *Biblical Greek illustrated by examples.* English edition adapted from the fourth Latin edition by Joseph Smith. Rome: Scripta Pontificii Instituti Biblici.

Zilliacus, Henrik. 1943. Zur Sprache griechischer Familienbriefe des III Jahrhunderts n. Chr. (P. Michigan 214–221). *Commentationes Humanarum Litterarum* 13.3.1–51. Helsingfors (Helsinki): Societas Scientiarum Fennica.

(ii)   Ancient texts and their translations

Burchard, Christoph. 1985. Joseph and Aseneth: A new translation and introduction. In James H. Charlesworth (ed.), *The Old Testament Pseudepigrapha.* Vol. 2, 177–247. New York: Doubleday.

Burchard, Christoph, ed. 2003. *Joseph und Aseneth.* Pseudepigrapha Veteris Testamenti Graece 5. With support from Carsten Burfeind and Uta Barbara Fink. Leiden: Brill.

Cook, David, trans. 1984. Joseph and Aseneth. In H. F. D. Sparks (ed.), *The Apocryphal Old Testament,* 465–503. Oxford: Oxford University Press. Also available at http://www.markgoodacre.org/aseneth/translat.htm.

Goold, G. P., ed. and trans. 1995. *Chariton: Callirhoe.* Cambridge, MA: Harvard University Press.

LXX = Rahlfs, Alfred, and Robert Hanhart, eds. 2006. *Septuaginta.* 2nd edition. Stuttgart: *Deutsche Bibelgesellschaft.*

Masoretic Text = *Biblia Hebraica Stuttgartensia* (Leningrad Codex). Stuttgart: Die Deutsche Bibelgesellschaft. (BART).

Nestle-Aland = *Novum Testamentum Graece.* 2012. Twenty-eighth edition. Stuttgart: Die Deutsche Bibelgesellschaft.

Perseus = Unless noted otherwise, Classical and Koine Greek texts are cited from the *Perseus Digital Library Project.* http://www.perseus.tufts.edu. Authors cited include Aristophanes, Epictetus, and Chariton.

Philonenko, Marc, ed. and trans. 1968. *Joseph et Aséneth: Introduction, texte critique, traduction et notes.* Studia Post-Biblica 13. Leiden: Brill.

Reardon, B. P., ed. 1989. *Collected Ancient Greek novels.* Berkeley: University of California Press.

Robinson & Pierpont = Robinson, Maurice A., and William G. Pierpont, eds. 2005. *The New Testament in the original Greek: Byzantine textform.* Southborough, MA: Chilton Book Publishing.

Swete, Henry Barclay, ed. 1901. *The Old Testament in Greek according to the Septuagint.* Third edition. Vol. 1, Genesis – IV Kings. Cambridge, UK: Cambridge University Press. https://archive.org/details/oldtestamentingr01swetuoft/page/n5/mode/2up.

Trzaskoma, Stephen M., trans. 2010. *Two novels from Ancient Greece: Chariton's Callirhoe and Xenophon of Ephesos' An Ephesian Story: Anthia and Habrocomes.* Indianapolis, IN: Hackett.

UBS (Greek) NT = *The Greek New Testament.* 2014. Fifth edition. Edited by Barbara Aland, Kurt Aland, Johannes Karavidopoulos, Carlo M. Martini, and Bruce M. Metzger in cooperation with the Institute for New Testament Textual Research, Münster/Westphalia. Stuttgart: Die Deutsche Bibelgesellschaft. (New York: United Bible Societies). (BART and BibleWorks).

(iii)   Bible translations

English Bible translations

CAS = Cassirer, Heinz W. 1989. *God's New Covenant: A New Testament Translation.* Grand Rapids, MI: Eerdmans.

CEV = *Contemporary English Version.* Second edition (CEV®). 2006. Philadelphia, PA: American Bible Society. (Paratext).

ESV = *ESV® Bible (The Holy Bible, English Standard Version®).* 2001. Wheaton, IL: Crossway Bibles.

GNB = *Good News Bible.* 1994. Glasgow: Bible Societies/HarperCollins Publishers Ltd UK, *Good News Bible.* 1992. Philadelphia, PA: American Bible Society. (Paratext).

JBP = Phillips, J. B. 1960. *The New Testament in Modern English.* London: The Archbishops' Council of the Church of England. (Translator's Workplace 4).

KNX = Knox, Ronald. (1955) 2013. *The Holy Bible translated from the Latin Vulgate* by Msgr. Ronald Knox and published by Baronius Press. London: Westminster Diocese. Retrieved December 4, 2015 at http://www.newadvent.org/bible/gen001.htm.

MSG = Peterson, Eugene H. 2002. *The Message: The Bible in contemporary language.* 2002. Colorado Springs, CO: NavPress. Represented by Tyndale House Publishers, a Division of Tyndale House Ministries. Retrieved December 4, 2015 at https://www.biblegateway.com/passage/?search=Act+7%3A56&version=MSG.

nab = The author's own translation or paraphrase (N. A. Bailey).

NAB = *New American Bible.* 1991. The New American Bible with Revised
New Testament and Revised Psalms, and with Roman Catholic
Deuterocanon. (BibleWorks).
NAS = *New American Standard Bible®* (*NASB*). 1995. La Habra, CA: The
Lockman Foundation. https://www.Lockman.org. (BART).
NET = *A New English Translation* (*Net Bible®*). 2019. Richardson, TX:
Biblical Studies Press. http://www.netbible.org. (BibleWorks).
NETS = *New English Translation of the Septuagint.* 2007. Oxford: Oxford
University Press. Retrieved December 3, 2015 at
http://ccat.sas.upenn.edu/nets/edition/.
NIV = *Holy Bible, New International Version.* 2011. Colorado Springs, CO:
Biblica.
NJB = *The New Jerusalem Bible.* 1985. London: Darton, Longman and Todd.
(BibleWorks).
NJPS = *The New JPS Translation* (*TANAKH*). 1985. Philadelphia, PA: The
Jewish Publication Society. (Paratext).
NLT = *Holy Bible, New Living Translation.* 2015. Carol Stream, IL: Tyndale
House Foundation. (Paratext).
NRS = *New Revised Standard Version.* 1989. Washington, DC: National
Council of the Churches of Christ in the U.S.A. (Paratext).
REB = *The Revised English Bible.* 1989. Cambridge, UK: Cambridge
University Press and Oxford University Press. (Paratext).
RSV = *Revised Standard Version.* 1952. Washington, DC: National Council
of the Churches of Christ in the United States of America. (Paratext).
The New Greek-English Interlinear New Testament. 1990. Electronic version,
2003. Carol Stream, IL: Tyndale House Publishers. (BART).
WMS = Williams, Charles B. 1937. *The New Testament: A translation in the
language of the people.* Currently copyrighted by Charlotte Williams
Sprawls, DBA Sprawls Educational Publishing, Montreat, NC.

French Bible translations

BDS = *La Bible du Semeur.* 1999. International Bible Society. Retrieved
December 2008 at http://www.ibs.org/bible/books/?q=bds.
BFC = *La Bible en français courant* [French Common Language Version].
1997. Paris: Société biblique française – Bibli'O. (Paratext).
FBJ = *Bible de Jérusalem, Les Éditions du Cerf.* 1973. (BibleWorks).
NVS78 = *Nouvelle Version Segond Révisée* (Colombe). 1978. (Paratext).
PDV = *Parole de Vie.* 2000. (Paratext).
TOB = *Traduction Oecuménique de la Bible.* 1988. (BibleWorks and
Paratext).

German Bible translations

EIN = *Einheitsübersetzung der Heiligen Schrift, vollständig durchgesehene und überarbeitete Ausgabe*. 2016. Stuttgart: Katholische Bibelanstalt GmbH. (BibleWorks).

ELB = *Elberfelder Bible*. 2006. Holzgerlingen: SCM R.Brockhaus in the SCM Verlagsgruppe GmbH, Witten. (BibleWorks).

GND = *Gute Nachricht Bibel*, revidierte Fassung [Good News Bible Revised]. 1997. Stuttgart: Deutsche Bibelgesellschaft. (Paratext).

LUT = *Lutherbibel*, revidiert 1984, durchgesehene Ausgabe [Luther Bible, revised 1984, revised edition]. 1999. Stuttgart: Deutsche Bibelgesellschaft. (Paratext and BibleWorks).

Italian Bible translations

NVBTO = *Nuovissima Versione della Bibbia dai Testi Originali*. 1995. Milan, Italy: San Paolo Edizioni. (BibleWorks).

LND = *La Nuova Diodati*. 1991. Trepuzzi, Italy: La Buona Novella Inc. (BibleWorks).

NRV = *La Sacra Bibbia - Nuova Riveduta*. 1994. Turin, Italy: Società Biblica di Ginevra. (BibleWorks).

Russian Bible translations

NRT = Новый Перевод на Русский Язык [Holy Bible, New Russian Translation]. 2014. Colorado Springs, CO: Biblica. (Paratext 8).

CRV = Библия, Современный русский перевод [Contemporary Russian Version Bible]. 2011. Moscow: Bible Society of Russia. (Paratext 8).

Index of Passages

Old Testament

New Testament

Other

Non-Biblical Sources

Nicholas A. Bailey has been involved in translation and linguistic research with SIL International since 1984. He has worked as an advisor and as a translation consultant in various translation projects in Eurasia. He has had an ongoing interest in discourse grammar, information structure, and the linguistic expression of emotion. He completed his PhD in linguistics at the Vrije Universiteit, Amsterdam, in 2009 (dissertation title: "Thetic constructions in Koine Greek: With special attention to clauses with εἰμί 'be', γίνομαι 'occur', ἔρχομαι 'come', ἰδού/ἴδε 'behold', and complement clauses of ὁράω 'see'").

Selected publications and unpublished papers

2021. Poetic packagings of the Psalms: Insights from the 1500s and 1600s on their translation. Paper presented online at the Bible Translation Conference, Dallas, TX, October 4, 2021.

2021. Understanding, tracking, and translating emotion in the Gospel of Luke. Paper presented at the SIL Eurasia Area Consultant Training Event, June 18, 2021.

2011. Information structure issues in copular εἶναι clauses. In Steven E. Runge (ed.), *Discourse studies and biblical interpretation: Festschrift for Stephen H. Levinsohn*, 289–333. Bellingham, WA: Lexham Press.

2009. Thetic constructions in Koine Greek: With special attention to clauses with εἰμί 'be', γίνομαι 'occur', ἔρχομαι 'come', ἰδού/ἴδε 'behold', and complement clauses of ὁράω 'see'. PhD dissertation. Vrije Universiteit, Amsterdam. Accessed 26 October 2020. https://research.vu.nl/ws/portalfiles/portal/42185508/complete+dissertation.pdf.

2007. Proper names in the Bible: Translation and transliteration issues. *Word&Deed* 6(1):1-26. Dallas, TX: SIL International.

2004. A second look at double preverbal constituents. Review of *Doppelt besetztes Vorfeld: Syntaktische, pragmatische und übersetzungstechnische Studien zum althebräischen Verbalsatz*, by Walter Gross. *Hebrew Studies* 45:253–276. https://muse.jhu.edu/article/439079.

1998. What's wrong with my word order? *Journal of Translation and Textlinguistics* 10:1–29.

1994. Some literary and grammatical aspects of genealogies in Genesis. In Robert D. Bergen (ed.), *Biblical Hebrew and discourse linguistics*, 267–282. Dallas, TX: Summer Institute of Linguistics.

1992. (with Stephen H. Levinsohn). The function of preverbal elements in independent clauses in the Hebrew narrative of Genesis. *Journal of Translation and Textlinguistics* 5:179-207.

1990. Nehemiah 3:1–32: An intersection of the text and the topography. *Palestine Exploration Quarterly*, January-June 1990, 34–40. (Also published 1992, *Journal of Translation and Textlinguistics* 5(1):1–12.)

1983. A tense-aspect-discourse study of the Hebrew perfect verb in Genesis narrative. MA thesis. University of Texas at Arlington.

SIL International® Publications

Publications in Translation and Textlinguistics Series

ISSN 1550-588X

10. **The article in Post-Classical Greek**, Edited by Daniel King, 2019, 216 pp., ISBN: 978-1-55671-413-9.
9. **Paul's anthropological terms in the light of discourse analysis**, by Sunny Chen, 2019, 286 pp., ISBN 978-1-55671-421-4.
8. **Studies in the Psalms: Literary-structural analysis with application to translation**, by Ernst R. Wendland, 2017, 538 pp., ISBN 978-1-55671-401-6.
7. **Prophetic rhetoric: Case studies in text analysis and translation.** Second edition, by Ernst R. Wendland, 2014, 719 pp., ISBN: 978-1-55671-345-3.
6. **Orality and the Scriptures: Composition, translation, and transmission**, by Ernst R. Wendland, 2013, 405 pp., ISBN 978-1-55671-298-2.
5. **Lovely, lively lyrics: Selected studies in Biblical Hebrew verse**, by Ernst R. Wendland, 2013, 461 pp., ISBN 978-1-55671-327-9.
4. **LiFE-style translating: A workbook for Bible translators.** Second edition, by Ernst R. Wendland, 2011, 509 pp., ISBN 978-155671-243-2.
3. **The development of textlinguistics in the writings of Robert Longacre**, by Shin Ja Hwang, 2010, 423 pp., ISBN 978-1-55671-246-3.
2. **Artistic and rhetorical patterns in Quechua legendary texts**, by Ågot Bergli, 2010, 304 pp., ISBN 978-1-55671-244-9.
1. **Translating the literature of Scripture: A literary-rhetorical approach to Bible translation**, by Ernst R. Wendland, 2004, 509 pp., ISBN 978-1-55671-152-7.

SIL International Publications
7500 W. Camp Wisdom Road
Dallas, TX 75236-5629 USA

General inquiry: publications_intl@sil.org
Pending order inquiry: sales@sil.org
publications.sil.org

Milton Keynes UK
Ingram Content Group UK Ltd.
UKHW031822140224
437823UK00014B/309